JOSEPH F. SMITH
Portrait of a Prophet

JOSEPH F. SMITH, CA. 1889–90
C. R. SAVAGE, MLUU (P0036 #128). JOSEPH F. SMITH WROTE BELOW THE IMAGE: "YOURS TRULY JOS. F. SMITH. AGED 51," INDICATING IT WAS TAKEN BETWEEN 13 NOVEMBER 1889 AND 13 NOVEMBER 1890.

JOSEPH F. SMITH
Portrait of a Prophet

Richard Neitzel Holzapfel & R. Q. Shupe

DESERET BOOK COMPANY
SALT LAKE CITY, UTAH

FOR MY BROTHERS-IN-LAW:

*Ronald C. Lindsey, Ronald W. Meacham,
D. Gene Taylor, and Baron J. Truesdell*

—RICHARD NEITZEL HOLZAPFEL

FOR MY CHILDREN:

*Alyssa, Sarah, Garrick, Meiken,
Taylor, Meleah, and Kamryn*

—R. Q. SHUPE

© 2000 Richard Neitzel Holzapfel and R. Q. Shupe

All rights reserved. No part of this book may be reproduced in any form or by any means without permission in writing from the publisher, Deseret Book Company, P. O. Box 30178, Salt Lake City, Utah 84130. This work is not an official publication of The Church of Jesus Christ of Latter-day Saints. The views expressed herein are the responsibility of the author and do not necessarily represent the position of the Church or of Deseret Book Company.

Deseret Book is a registered trademark of Deseret Book Company.

Visit us at www.deseretbook.com

Library of Congress Cataloging-in-Publication Data

Holzapfel, Richard Neitzel.
   Joseph F. Smith: a portrait of a prophet / Richard Neitzel Holzapfel and R. Q. Shupe.
     p. cm.
   Includes bibliographical references and index.
   ISBN 1-57008-683-4
   1. Smith, Joseph F., 1838–1918. 2. Smith, Joseph F., 1838–1918—Portraits.
   3. Mormon Church—Presidents—Biography. 4. Church of Jesus Christ of
     Latter-day Saints—Presidents—Biography. I. Shupe, R. Q. II. Title.
BX8695.S63 H65 2000
289.3'092—dc21
[B]
                                                                                                 00-034604
                                                                                                  CIP

Printed in the United States of America   42316-6585
10 9 8 7 6 5 4 3 2 1

Contents

LIST OF PHOTOGRAPHS AND ILLUSTRATIONS vi

ACKNOWLEDGMENTS vii

KEY TO ABBREVIATIONS OF FREQUENTLY QUOTED SOURCES viii

INTRODUCTION
JOSEPH F. SMITH: SOME THOUGHTS AND REFLECTIONS ix

CHAPTER ONE
THE LEGACY OF A NAME 1

CHAPTER TWO
FROM BIRTH TO THE APOSTLESHIP, 1838–1867 11

CHAPTER THREE
THE QUORUM OF THE TWELVE AND THE
FIRST PRESIDENCY, 1867–1901 43

CHAPTER FOUR
THE TWENTIETH-CENTURY PROPHET, 1901–1918 121

CHAPTER FIVE
A DOCTRINAL LEGACY 245

CONCLUSION
A TRIBUTE TO PRESIDENT JOSEPH F. SMITH, JUNE 1919 267

INDEX OF PHOTOGRAPHS AND ILLUSTRATIONS 363

SUBJECT INDEX 367

LIST OF PHOTOGRAPHS AND ILLUSTRATIONS

All photographs from the following institutions are used by permission, all rights reserved.

Institutional Collections

BYU: Special Collections and Manuscripts or Photographic Archives, Harold B. Lee Library, Brigham Young University, Provo, Utah.

LDSCA: Archive Division, Church Historical Department, The Church of Jesus Christ of Latter-day Saints, Salt Lake City, Utah.

MCHA: Museum of Church History and Art, The Church of Jesus Christ of Latter-day Saints, Salt Lake City, Utah.

MLUU: Manuscripts Division, J. Marriott Library, University of Utah, Salt Lake City, Utah.

RLUA: Alaska and Polar Regions Archives, Rasmuson Library, University of Alaska, Fairbanks, Alaska.

USA: Department of Administrative Services, Utah State Archives and Records Service, State of Utah, Salt Lake City, Utah.

USHS: Utah State Historical Society, Salt Lake City, Utah.

Private Collections

Ashworth Collection: Brent F. Ashworth, Provo, Utah.
Balls Collection: Pat Balls, Hyde Park, Utah.
Bunker Collection: Gary L. and Carol B. Bunker, Orem, Utah.
Jackson Collection: Scott T. Jackson, Provo, Utah.
King Collection: Carole Call King, Mountain Green, Utah.
A. S. McConkie Collection: Amelia Smith McConkie, Salt Lake City, Utah.
J. F. McConkie Collection: Joseph Fielding McConkie, Orem, Utah.
Nebeker Collection: Ann Alice Smith Nebeker, Salt Lake City, Utah.
Nichols Collection: Elaine Cannon Nichols, Salt Lake City, Utah.
Shupe Collection: R. Q. and Susan Shupe, San Juan Capistrano, California.
Wadsworth Collection: Nelson B. Wadsworth, Salt Lake City, Utah.
Walker Collection: Mary Lou Walker, Salt Lake City, Utah.

ACKNOWLEDGMENTS

We are grateful for the assistance of many individuals who have brought this work to completion. Particularly, we appreciate Jeni Broberg Holzapfel and Ted D. Stoddard for reviewing, critiquing, and editing draft versions of the manuscript.

Vivian M. Adams, Brent F. Ashworth, John N. Cannon, Mary M. Donoho, Scott T. Jackson, Carole Call King, Amelia Smith McConkie, Mark L. McConkie, Joseph Fielding McConkie, Rebecca M. Pinegar, Marjorie Virginia Porter, Ann Alice Smith Nebeker, Elaine Cannon Nichols, and Mary Lou Walker graciously provided artifacts, documents, and photographs included herein.

BYU student assistants Wendy Agle, Matthew J. Grey, Lisa Moorehead, and Melissa Whitchurch furnished valuable source checking help along the way.

The staff of the LDS Church Archives; LDS Church Historical Library; LDS Museum of Church History and Art; Special Collections and Manuscripts, Harold B. Lee Library, Brigham Young University; Photographic Archives, Harold B. Lee Library, Brigham Young University; Manuscripts Division, J. Willard Marriott Library, University of Utah; Department of Administrative Services, Utah State Archives and Records Service, State of Utah; and the Information Center, Utah State Historical Society, provided considerable assistance.

Of particular note, we acknowledge Alan Barnett, Janell Brimhall, Michelle Call, Wendy Checketts, Lorraine Crouse, D. Randall Dixon, Linda Haslam, Jeffery O. Johnson, Stan Larson, Steven R. Sorensen, April Williamsen, Veneese Nelson, Ronald W. Read, William W. Slaughter, Russell C. Taylor, Ronald G. Watt, Thomas R. Wells, and P. Bradford Westwood. We also acknowledge the valuable support of colleagues at Brigham Young University: Alexander L Baugh, Donald Q. Cannon, Richard O. Cowan, Alan K. Parrish, Robert L. Millet, Paul H. Peterson, and Larry C. Porter.

The owners and staff of Allen Camera, Borge B. Anderson & Associates, and Panorama photographic companies provided help in reproducing images for inclusion in this book. Specifically, we thank Rex K. Allen, Kris Brunson, Charlotte Stewart, Kim Thompson, and Russell P. Winger.

Finally, we appreciate our publisher, Deseret Book, especially the efforts of our longtime friends Cory H. Maxwell, Jana Erickson, Thomas E. Hewitson, and Jennifer Adams.

KEY TO ABBREVIATIONS OF FREQUENTLY QUOTED SOURCES

CR	Conference Reports of The Church of Jesus Christ of Latter-day Saints.
FPS	Hyrum M. Smith III and Scott G. Kenney, *From Prophet to Son: Advice of Joseph F. Smith to His Missionary Sons*. Salt Lake City: Deseret Book, 1981.
GD	Joseph F. Smith, *Gospel Doctrine: Selections from the Sermons and Writings of Joseph F. Smith, Sixth President of The Church of Jesus Christ of Latter-day Saints*. Salt Lake City: Deseret Book, 1966.
JH	The Journal History of The Church of Jesus Christ of Latter-day Saints, Historical Department Archives. The Church of Jesus Christ of Latter-day Saints. Salt Lake City, Utah.
JD	*Journal of Discourses*, 26 vols. London: Latter-day Saints' Book Depot, 1854–86.
LJFS	Joseph Fielding Smith, comp., *Life of Joseph F. Smith: Sixth President of The Church of Jesus Christ of Latter-day Saints*. Salt Lake City: Deseret Book, 1938.
MFP	James R. Clark, comp., *Messages of the First Presidency of The Church of Jesus Christ of Latter-day Saints*, 6 vols. Salt Lake City: Bookcraft, 1965–75.
TC	Joseph Fielding McConkie, ed., *Truth and Courage: Joseph F. Smith Letters*. N. p., 1998.

INTRODUCTION
JOSEPH F. SMITH
SOME THOUGHTS AND REFLECTIONS

This work is primarily an effort to produce a "Joseph F. Smith photographic scrapbook," highlighting some of the wonderful images from an impressive visual record of his life. It is not an effort to supplant the existing historical efforts of previous authors who provide details, insights, and interpretations of his labors and ministry.[1] In the introduction to the first full-length biography of his life, his son and biographer, Joseph Fielding Smith, wrote, "It is impossible in one brief volume to portray all that is of historical value and family interest from a life so filled with vital events as that of President Joseph F. Smith."[2]

If the above is true regarding a full-length biography, it is even more true of this small volume. There are many important historical incidents in Joseph F.'s life that are not discussed in detail or even noted in this work. For example, there is no attention given to the incorporation of the Church's first successful life insurance business, Beneficial Life Insurance Company, in 1905; to the painful resignation of John W. Taylor and Matthias F. Cowley from the Council of the Twelve in 1906; to the beginning of weekly priesthood meetings and the introduction of standardized priesthood manuals in 1908; to the beginning of Church involvement and sponsorship of the Boy Scout program starting in 1911; or to the exodus of the Latter-day Saints from the Mormon colonies in Mexico in 1912.[3]

PLATE 3
Personal Belongings of Joseph F. Smith
MCHA. COUNTERCLOCKWISE FROM UPPER LEFT: A SYMBOL OF HAWAIIAN ROYALTY, A GIFT FROM HAWAIIAN SAINTS; FIRST HAWAIIAN EDITION OF THE BOOK OF MORMON (1905); HAWAIIAN EDITION OF THE DOCTRINE AND COVENANTS AND PEARL OF GREAT PRICE RECEIVED AT THE TIME OF THE TEMPLE-SITE DEDICATION IN 1915; CUT PAPER LEI RECEIVED AT THE TIME OF THE TEMPLE-SITE DEDICATION IN 1915; BOOTS AND COIN PURSE.

A Man Like Us

Though he became a mighty prophet in Israel, Joseph F. knew better than anyone else that he was susceptible to the foibles common to other men and women—a man like us. He told the Saints assembled in the Tabernacle shortly after his call to the Twelve in 1868: "We are all fallible and all liable to err, susceptible of prejudices and assailed by good and bad influences. In every condition of life we are more or less liable to be influenced and controlled in our thoughts and actions by the circumstances by which we are surrounded; the result is we are sometimes alive to the truth and faithful before the Lord, full of kindness, of friendship and love towards our brethren—the servants of God—and towards the work in which we are engaged; and sometimes we are luke-warm and indifferent about these things."[4]

On numerous occasions, Joseph F. talked about real challenges, struggles, and setbacks he encountered during his life. While some people focus on the weaknesses of great men and women in an effort to make them more human, we miss the point of Joseph F.'s greatness when we do not acknowledge his efforts to follow the advice of the great Book of Mormon prophet King Benjamin, who taught that men and women must "yield to the enticings of the Holy Spirit, and putteth off the natural man and becometh a saint through the atonement of Christ the Lord, and becometh as a child, submissive, meek, humble, patient, full of love, willing to submit to all things which the Lord seeth fit to inflict upon him, even as a child doth submit to his father" (Mosiah 3:19). In this way, Joseph F. provided the Saints an example of one who washed his robes "and made them white in the blood of the Lamb" (Revelation 7:14).

When visiting the Saints, he was not an aloof counselor and advisor. He sympathized and empathized with them and often shared with them the difficult challenges he faced earlier in life. Having overcome such challenges, he often planted in them a desire to face their own problems with renewed determination to overcome challenges.

Most likely, if Joseph F. were born today, modern society would have targeted him for every social, educational, and occupational assistance program possible because of the challenges he faced during the first years of his life: his father was murdered when he was only five years of age; his single mother was forced to move several times, barely keeping food on the table for her family for the next eight years; and he was orphaned at fourteen years of age and left alone to take care of a younger sister. He struggled in school and was eventually expelled as a young teenager for fighting with a teacher. In the end, he lacked the social and educational opportunities often considered necessary to make someone a responsible adult.

Yet Joseph F. rarely let these truly difficult challenges and personal tragedies prevent him from becoming a Latter-day Saint in word and deed. Nor did he allow the bitterness and anguish he experienced during his youth to relieve him of responsibility for his own actions. By his own righteous desire and the Lord's help, he overcame what many today believe to be impossible odds for a young person and became one of the greatest leaders of the twentieth century. One associate, most likely Andrew Jenson, noted: "Your hair is like a beautiful silver cloud that rests upon your pretty head: In my opinion you don't need a halo."[5]

By the time he passed from this life, Joseph F. had become "a tender father figure for a whole generation of Western Latter-day Saints who grew up in the first two decades of the twentieth century."[6] For them, he did not "need a halo."

Extended Family Relations

One of the unique challenges Joseph F. faced was the division between his father's family (Hyrum Smith) and his uncle's family (Joseph Smith) following the rise of the Reorganized Church of Jesus Christ of Latter Day Saints in 1860. It was during this same period that the claims of truth held by the sons of the martyrs came into conflict, heightening the tension, mistrust, and missed opportunities that occurred between these two families. However, despite the separation

INTRODUCTION

between Jospeh F. and his cousin Joseph III, presidents of two churches, there were moments of warmth and concern, suggesting Joseph F.'s efforts to reach beyond the theological barrier separating them.

In 1896, Joseph Smith III lost his wife, Bertha Madison Smith. Joseph F. wrote his cousin shortly after her death on 19 October: "Altho far removed from each other by almost every interest and hope in life, and unalterably fixed in our opposite views on many points, still I am not unmindful of the kindred tie."[7] He attempted to provide comfort and encouragement during this difficult time for his cousin who had lost a "faithful and devoted wife."[8] The letter is one of the examples that demonstrate his efforts to practice what he preached during his entire ministry.

Punctual Person

There are many sterling qualities for which Joseph F. is still known today, and among them was his punctuality. On very few occasions, and always to his embarrassment, he failed to keep an appointment as planned. In October 1896, President Wilford Woodruff invited him to attend the annual "Founders' Day" at Brigham Young Academy in Provo. Apparently, his watch failed him, and he wrote President Cannon to explain his failure to arrive at the train station on time: "My watch deceived and delayed me this morning just seven minutes, at the [Union Pacific Railway], leaving only three minutes to reach the [Rio Grande Railway]. So I gave up the chase. I felt like smashing my watch, for it had just been regulated, and I depended upon it. When Sterling pays a dividend I will get a new watch. Express my regrets to Pres. Woodruff and our Friends."[9]

INTRODUCTION

A Grateful Person

Joseph F. was a thankful person who helped others appreciate what they received from the Lord. President Ezra Taft Benson related a story he heard from his own grandfather, regarding an incident at the Benson home when Joseph F. visited Whitney, Idaho, during a Church conference. President Benson recalled: "Grandfather said that they were seated in the living room/dining room combination of the farm home. The table was laden with good things to eat. The family was gathered around—I don't know how many (there were 13 children in that wonderful family and I presume some of them were away on missions as they usually were). Just before they were ready to start the meal, President Smith stretched his long arms over the table and turned to my grandfather and said, 'Brother Benson, all this and the gospel too?'"[10]

The Visual Record

In addition to the vast written record of Joseph F.'s life, there is a remarkably full photographic record that covers his life from the time he was a teenager until just months before his death in 1918. It is true, as Davis Bitton so astutely argues in his work on the visual images of Joseph Smith, that "no painting, no photograph, does *justice* to its subject. . . . We don't hear the sound of his voice, feel his human warmth, see the way he moved and held himself, sense his ability to relate—none of this is captured."[11]

Yet, because Joseph F. lived into the twentieth century, he was the first President of the Church to be captured in motion pictures. And

INTRODUCTION

while these movie clips are in black and white and without sound, they capture his movement instead of the still, formal portraits we generally see of him. Produced by Shirley Y. and Chester Clawson (brothers who did commercial and Church work), these motion-picture clips show President Smith, beginning in 1911, walking with the General Authorities from the Salt Lake Temple, riding in an automobile, greeting Church leaders, visiting with his family on the lawn of his home in southern California, talking in close-up images (no sound in the film), taking his hat off, and removing his glasses—all giving us several profiles. Additionally, this collection of film includes several shots taken at the beginning of his funeral procession and at the cemetery, just before burial in 1918.

Additionally, he was one of the first Presidents of the Church to have his voice recorded for a new generation of Latter-day Saints who did not have the privilege to hear him in person.[12]

Thus, the written record, the photographic record, the motion-picture record, and the voice record allow us to have a fuller view of Joseph F. Smith than of any other prophet before him.

NOTES

1. There are many articles and books chronicling Joseph F. Smith's life and ministry that may be of interest for further reading. These include the following:

Joseph Fielding Smith, *Life of Joseph F. Smith: Sixth President of The Church of Jesus Christ of Latter-day Saints* (Salt Lake City: Deseret Book, 1938).

Preston Nibley, "Joseph F. Smith," *The Presidents of the Church* (Salt Lake City: Deseret Book, 1941), 222–69.

Richard S. Van Wagoner and Steven C. Walker, "Joseph F. Smith," *A Book of Mormons* (Salt Lake City: Signature Books, 1982), 295–302.

Norman S. Bosworth, "Remembering Joseph F. Smith: Loving Father, Devoted Prophet," *Ensign* 13 (June 1983): 21–24.

Leonard J. Arrington, "Joseph F. Smith: From Impulsive Young Man to Patriarchal Prophet," John Whitmer Historical Journal 4 (1984): 30–40.

Francis M. Gibbons, *Joseph F. Smith: Patriarch and Preacher, Prophet of God* (Salt Lake City: Deseret Book, 1984), (Macmillan Publishing Company, 1992).

Bruce Van Orden, "Joseph F. Smith," in *Encyclopedia of Mormonism*, 5 vols, (New York: Macmillan Publishing Company, 1992), 3:1349–52.

Amelia Smith McConkie, "Grandpapa Joseph F. Smith," *Ensign* 23 (1993): 12–15.

Scott Kenney "Joseph F. Smith," in *Utah Encyclopedia* (Salt Lake City: University of Utah Press, 1994), 505.

Jill Mulvey Derr and Heidi S. Swinton, "Joseph F. Smith: Following the Prince of Peace," *Ensign* 30 (January 2000): 37–43.

2. Joseph Fielding Smith, comp., *Life of Joseph F. Smith: Sixth President of The Church of Jesus Christ of Latter-day Saints* (Salt Lake City: Deseret Book, 1938); hereafter cited as *LJFS*, 3.

3. While all of these events are significant, the effort to organize the priesthood quorums was one of Joseph F. Smith's greatest administrative legacies; see William G. Hartley, "The Priesthood Reform Movement, 1908–1922," *BYU Studies* 13 (winter 1973): 137–56.

4. *Journal of Discourses*, 11:307.

5. Written on a small scrap of paper apparently stored in an envelope addressed to "Pres. Joseph F. Smith" from Joseph Smith, Lamoni, Decatur Co., Iowa, 1896, A. S. McConkie Collection.

6. Leonard J. Arrington, "Joseph F. Smith: From Impulsive Young Man to Patriarchal Prophet," *John Whitmer Historical Journal* 4 (1984): 33.

7. Joseph F. Smith to Joseph Smith III, 7 November 1896, Joseph F. Smith Letter Copy Book, Joseph Fielding Smith Papers, 1856–1918, LDSCA.

8. Ibid.

9. Joseph F. Smith to George Q. Cannon, 16 October 1896, Joseph F. Smith Letter Copy Book, Joseph Fielding Smith Papers, 1856–1918, LDSCA.

10. Ezra Taft Benson, "Receive All Things with Thankfulness," *New Era* 6 (November 1976): 5.

11. Davis Bitton, *Images of the Prophet Joseph Smith* (Salt Lake City: Aspen Books, 1996), 123.

12. Wilford Woodruff is the first President of the Church to have his voice recorded. At this time, there is no known recording of Lorenzo Snow.

CHAPTER ONE

The Legacy of a Name

Joseph F. Smith, the sixth President of The Church of Jesus Christ of Latter-day Saints, was born into the cauldron of intense persecution on 13 November 1838 at Far West, Missouri. Named after his uncle (Joseph Smith the Prophet) and after his mother (Mary Fielding Smith), Joseph Fielding Smith was known as Joseph F. Smith during his lifetime.

To Be Known for Good and Evil

When the Angel Moroni visited Joseph Smith in 1823, he told the young man that his "name should be had for good and evil among all nations, kindreds, and tongues, or that it should be both good and evil spoken of among all people" (Joseph Smith—History 1:33). Later events proved the prophecy to be true.

Joseph F. inherited not only his uncle's name but also his legacy of having his name known "for good and evil." The name *Joseph*, which brought both comfort and joy along with ridicule and hatred, was not selected without some thought. His mother and father chose his name as a way to honor each of their families—and the young infant as well.

Of all the modern presidents of the LDS Church, only Joseph Smith, Brigham Young, and Joseph F. Smith experienced intense and continuous personal attacks during most of their ministry, having, as it were, their names known "for good and evil." John Taylor, Wilford Woodruff, and Lorenzo Snow rarely were exposed to the personal abuse Joseph Smith and Brigham Young experienced during their lives. John Taylor, along with the other Latter-day Saints, was persecuted during his presidency, yet he was rarely personally vilified by enemies of the Church as his predecessors had been before him. Those men who followed President Joseph F. in the First Presidency, beginning with Heber J. Grant and George Albert Smith, rarely were faced with the kind of defamation of character that Joseph Smith, Brigham Young, and Joseph F. Smith were subjected to during their lives. In most cases, the Church leaders who followed Joseph F. Smith were generally honored in the press (George Albert Smith appeared on the cover of *Time* in 1947 with a very complimentary article about the Church).

Never since the days of Brigham Young did newspapers, magazines, and books (both authors and publishers) direct such vicious and cruel attention on the President of the Church as they did during Joseph F.'s presidency.

Loyalty to His Name

Despite the persecution, most people, even his enemies, admitted there were good qualities about Joseph F. Loyalty was one of the main character attributes most people identified him with, even his enemies. Joseph F. declared during a general conference address: "We should set an example; we should be true to the faith, as Brother Stephens sings to us; true to the faith! We should be true to our covenants, true to our God, and true to one another and to the interests of Zion, no matter what the consequences may be, no matter what may result. I can tell you that the man who is not true to Zion and to the interests of the people will be the man who will be found bye and bye, left out and in a pitiable spiritual condition. The man who stays with the kingdom of God, the man that is true to this people, the man that keeps himself pure and unspotted from the world, is the man that God will accept, that God will uphold, that he will sustain and that will prosper in the land, whether he be in the enjoyment of his liberty or be confined in prison cells; it makes no difference where he is, he will come out all right."[1]

Loyalty was indeed important to Joseph F. Smith, and loyalty to the Prophet Joseph Smith, after whom he was named, was a constant throughout his life. One former missionary companion recalled a story that demonstrated Joseph F.'s loyalty to that name. The story deals with Joseph F. Smith's experience shortly after boarding a ship for his Hawaiian mission: "After working two months in the harvest field to earn his passage money, Joseph with the other elders, sailed steerage passage, on the bark Yankee, for the islands. As soon as the ship was clear from the wharf, the passengers were lined up on the deck and their names read off to see if there were any stowaways. When the purser called, 'Joseph Smith' the captain asked, 'Any relation to old Joe Smith?' 'No, sir,' was the prompt answer, 'I never had a relative by that name; but if you had reference to the Prophet Joseph Smith, I am proud to say, he was my uncle.' 'Oh, I see,' said the captain, and he did see a man who had the nerve and manhood to demand that proper respect be shown to the name of the Prophet, whom he loved and honored."[2]

This loyalty to the name "Joseph" explains, in part, both the honor and the animosity Joseph F. experienced in his life.

Vilified in the Press

Shortly following President Lorenzo Snow's funeral (October 1901) and before Joseph F. Smith was sustained as his successor (November 1901), Juab Utah Stake President James W. Paxman

PLATE 4
Political Cartoon from *The Salt Lake Tribune*
26 March 1905, Bunker Collection. The main caption states: "Blocking Progress."
The cartoon depicts an oversized head of Joseph F. Smith blocking the advance of a railroad, which represented progress in the early twentieth century.

reported a recent dream he had experienced foretelling, in part, the struggles and final victory laying ahead of the next President of the Church: "He had beheld a mighty struggle between [Joseph F. Smith], the [Salt Lake] Tribune & Herald which wore ugly mask, worn by men. [President] Smith conquered and crushed the life out of both of them."³

From the beginning of his presidency and through 1912, President Smith was in a mighty struggle with the press, especially the *Salt Lake Tribune*, the leading anti-Mormon newspaper in America at the time. Gary L. Bunker and Davis Bitton wrote: "In terms of sheer numbers no other newspaper could equal the *Salt Lake Tribune* when it came to cartoons about Mormonism. Some eight hundred cartoons focused on

PLATE 5
POLITICAL CARTOON FROM THE SALT LAKE TRIBUNE
23 AUGUST 1905, BUNKER COLLECTION.
THE MAIN CAPTION STATES: "UNDER WHICH SOVEREIGNTY?!" THE CARTOON DEPICTS JOSEPH F. SMITH WEARING CHECKERED PANTS AND DARK GLASSES.

the Mormons during this period [1890–1914] with more than six hundred of these appearing in the four years from 1905 to 1909."[4]

Although different aspects of the Church and, in some cases, different individuals were targeted, more than three hundred of the cartoons appearing at this time depicted President Joseph F. Smith. Bunker and Bitton noted: "His conservative appearance was frequently caricatured, and he often appeared in a butterfly bow tie, dark glasses, checked pants, striped cuffs, a top hat, and spats. In many illustrations a battered halo dangles over his head. He was drawn as a spider, rat, elephant, turtle, and turkey or referred to as 'profit.' Joseph F. Smith became, as Brigham Young had, the focus for much of the hostility that was intended for the Mormon religion."[5]

What was true in Utah was true in the United States as well during this particularly ugly period of yellow journalism. LDS historians James B. Allen and Glen M. Leonard summarize the situation at the time: "In this climate the Church did not escape renewed criticism and a revival of many old charges. The most direct attack came in the years 1910 and 1911 in such popular magazines as *Pearsons*, *Everybody's Magazine*, *McClure's*, and *Cosmopolitan*. . . . A *Cosmopolitan* series entitled 'The Viper on the Hearth,' by Alfred Henry Lewis, accused the Church of laying plans to subvert the family structure of America and take over the country both politically and economically."[6]

Although the *Salt Lake Tribune* was among President Smith's most vocal critics, attacking him almost daily during some periods of his ministry, the tone and tenor slowly changed. By 1912, the *Salt Lake Tribune* printed fewer and fewer of its vindictive cartoons and dropped most of its personal attacks on Joseph F. Smith. By 1918, the climate had changed so drastically that the *Salt Lake Tribune* honored Joseph F. Smith at the time of his passing with this tribute:

"It seems but a little while since President Joseph F. Smith was a familiar figure on the streets of Salt Lake City. With his alert glance, his erect figure, his brisk walk, his benign countenance, his dignified bearing and his cordial greeting, he was a striking personality wherever he went. For many years, even before he reached a place of high authority, he was the idol of his people, a zealous champion and a fearless crusader, ever ready to meet all comers without counting the odds, believing in himself, in his creed, in his organization, in its leaders and in the traditions of his church.

"Born eighty years ago, amid the scenes of conflict which marked the forced migrations of his relatives, he was thought to have inherited much of the bitterness of those times. In his earlier days he was fiery, fearless, impetuous and uncompromising, and was therefore looked upon as a fanatic intolerant of moderation and irreconcilable to opposition. But with the coming of age, the assumption of authority, the increase of responsibility and the consequent contact with his fellow men, came a broadening of vision and a softening of his nature which gained for him a recognition of those sterling qualities for which he will be remembered longest and best.

"Joseph F. Smith was sincere and intense in whatever he believed; he was loyal and courageous under whatever banner he marched, whether as a churchman, as a partisan, as an advocate of war or of peace, as a business associate or as a personal friend.

"In later years he made many friends in every walk of life, in every circle of society, in every cult or congregation with which he came in contact. He was a preacher of the gospel as he understood it, and an orator of exceptional power and eloquence. He was a leader upon whom his people leaned because of the simplicity of his character and the frankness of his disposition. Against his doctor's orders he arose from bed during his fatal illness to take his dying message to the general conference of the Mormon people last month.

"As president of the Church and trustee-in-trust of its many holdings and undertakings, and because of the influence of this position, Joseph F. Smith was identified with many commercial concerns. He was not regarded by his closest friends as a business man, in the ordinary understanding of that term, but his integrity, his interest and his sympathy made him a welcome and influential member of every board on which he served.

"He will be mourned throughout the west and missed by all classes of our citizens, because, after all is said and done, he was very much a man, with the courage of his convictions and a sincere affection for his followers; he exhorted them to obey the laws, to honor the flag, to aid and defend the government in the war just ended, and he goes now to his final rest covered with all the earthly glory he ever sought or that his people could bestow.

"Even those who differed radically from him in the past have doubtless forgotten it in the presence of death, if it had not already passed from their memories in close acquaintance through mutual interests and activities of later years."[7]

Given a common name at birth, Joseph F. Smith proved to be more than a common person. Preserved and prepared by the Lord in significant and miraculous ways, he led the Latter-day Saints from 1901 until his death in 1918. During his lifetime, he remained loyal to his name, his uncle (the Prophet Joseph Smith), and the gospel of

Jesus Christ. And, like the Prophet, his name was literally known for "good and evil."

However, before he died in November 1918, those who once hated and abused him in print had, for the most part, silenced their voices. Of them, many, in fact, joined in honoring him as one of the greatest leaders of the twentieth century. Of course, during this same period, hundreds of thousands honored him as a mighty apostle, prophet, seer, and revelator. Their testimonies, letters, diaries, and reminiscences speak of his name with reverence, fulfilling the prophecy that his name would also be known for "good" among many people and nations. By the time he passed from this life, Joseph F. had become "a tender father figure for a whole generation of Western Latter-day Saints who grew up in the first two decades of the twentieth century."[8]

NOTES

1. In CR, October 1906, 9.

2. John R. Young, *Memoirs of John R. Young* (Salt Lake City: Deseret News Press, 1920), 275–76.

3. Abraham O. Woodruff Journal, 16 October 1901, Special Collections, Harold B. Lee Library, Brigham Young University.

4. Gary L. Bunker and Davis Bitton, *The Mormon Graphic Image, 1834–1914: Cartoons, Caricatures, and Illustrations* (Salt Lake City: University of Utah Press, 1983), 57.

5. Ibid., 68.

6. James B. Allen and Glen M. Leonard, *The Story of the Latter-day Saints* (Salt Lake City: Deseret Book, 1992), 476.

7. As cited in *LJFS*, 483–84.

8. Leonard J. Arrington, "Joseph F. Smith: From Impulsive Young Man to Patriarchal Prophet," *John Whitmer Historical Journal* 4 (1984): 33.

CHAPTER TWO

FROM BIRTH TO THE APOSTLESHIP 1838–1867

Joseph F. Smith was born during one of the most difficult periods of Latter-day Saint history on 13 November 1838 at Far West, Missouri.

Far West, a Mormon community located in northwestern Missouri amidst the rolling countryside, was the site of turmoil and distress. Just two weeks before Joseph F.'s birth, Missouri Governor Lilburn W. Boggs issued an order that all Mormons should be driven from the state.

On 31 October, George Hinkle, commander of the Caldwell County Militia and a member of the Church, negotiated an agreement with state militia officers under which the leaders of the Church at Far West were to be surrendered and tried. According to this agreement, members of the Church were required to forfeit their property to pay for damages and costs involved in the so-called Mormon War, give up all their arms, and leave the state.

On 1 November 1838, Joseph F.'s father, Hyrum Smith, was arrested and summarily tried by a military court for treason. He was ordered to be shot the following day at the public square at Far West.

Through the intervention of Alexander W. Doniphan, another Missouri militia officer, Hyrum Smith and other Church leaders, including the Prophet Joseph Smith, were saved from the firing squad. A day later, Hyrum, along with his brother Joseph, Sidney Rigdon, Parley P. Pratt, Lyman Wight, Amasa Lyman, and George W.

PLATE 6
HYRUM SMITH PORTRAIT
KING COLLECTION. JOSEPH F. SMITH'S FATHER, PATRIARCH HYRUM SMITH, WAS KILLED WITH THE PROPHET JOSEPH SMITH IN CARTHAGE JAIL ON 27 JUNE 1844 WHEN JOSEPH F. SMITH WAS FIVE YEARS OLD.

Robinson, all of whom had been arrested earlier, were taken to the public square of Far West, Missouri. There they were allowed a brief visit with their families before being taken under shackle to Independence, Missouri, to await a civil hearing.

When Hyrum left, there was no assurance that Mary Fielding Smith would see her husband again; and now, within days of the delivery of her first child, she was left to fend for herself.

Physically and emotionally exhausted, Mary fell gravely ill and was utterly defenseless during this period. She had to rely on family members and friends for help. It was at this trying time that Joseph F. Smith was born.

Not long afterward, a local Methodist minister entered the Smith family home with a group of men and ransacked it. Joseph F. explained: "I, being an infant, and lying on the bed, another bed being on the floor, was entirely overlooked by the family . . . during the fright and excitement. So when the mob entered the room where I was, the bed on the floor was thrown on to the other completely smothering me up, and here I was permitted to remain until after the excitement subsided. When thought of, and discovered, my existence was supposed to have come to an end; but subsequent events have proven their suppositions erroneous, however well founded!"[1]

Childhood in Illinois (1839–1844)

The Smith family made its way to Illinois and found shelter and hospitality in Quincy, Adams County. In the meantime, following nearly six months of incarceration in Liberty Jail, the prisoners were allowed to escape the dark and dirty prison. Hyrum finally joined his family in Illinois on 22 April 1839 and, within a short time, moved them upriver to Commerce, Illinois, the new Mormon gathering place, later known as Nauvoo.

Despite the persecution suffered by his family, Joseph F. experienced a relatively happy childhood until the time he was five and a half years old. On 27 June 1844 his father and uncle were murdered, and that experience, as Leonard J. Arrington noted, "was imprinted indelibly on the memory of little Joseph."[2] Years later, Joseph F. still recalled his mother's screams when she heard the awful news and then the weeping and sobbing that lasted through the terrible night.

While standing inside Joseph and Emma Smith's home on a visit to Nauvoo in 1906, President Joseph F. remembered: "In this room the bodies of the martyrs lay in their coffins, after they had been brought from Carthage and dressed for burial. I remember my mother lifting me up to look upon the faces of my father and the Prophet, for the last time."[3]

At forty-three, Mary Fielding Smith was left alone with five children of Hyrum's from his first marriage and two of her own—Joseph F. and a little girl, Martha Ann, born on 14 May 1841.

After a short lull in the storm of conflict in Hancock County, attacks and counterattacks increased to an extent that the Latter-day Saints knew they could not remain in western Illinois. By mid-February of 1846, Church leaders initiated an exodus from Nauvoo, hoping to avoid a catastrophe similar to the one experienced by the Saints in Missouri. Hyrum Smith's family remained in Nauvoo until the summer of 1846, however. As pressure mounted against the remaining Saints in the city, Mary Fielding loaded her few possessions on a wagon and, with her children, crossed the Mississippi River to Iowa, beginning the long trek to the Missouri River Valley.

Exodus to Winter Quarters (1846)

Though Joseph F. was only eight years of age at this time, he drove one of the ox teams most of the way from Montrose to Winter Quarters, some three hundred miles. The family remained in the Mormon staging ground in the Missouri River Valley until spring of 1848.

According to his own recollections, Joseph F. learned some important lessons about life while in Winter Quarters. On one occasion, he went looking for some lost cattle but was unable to locate them. As he approached the wagon to report his failure, Joseph F. found his mother in the attitude of prayer. While standing there, he heard her plead with the Lord to help them recover their cattle so they could continue their journey in safety. As she arose from praying, Joseph F. recalled, "The first expression I caught upon her precious face was a lovely smile, which discouraged as I was, gave me renewed hope and an assurance that I had not felt before."[4]

This provided him with one of the "first practical and positive demonstrations of the efficacy of prayer" and was a pivotal moment in his spiritual development that became a guide throughout his life.[5]

On to the Salt Lake Valley (1848)

The family struggled, after two winters in the Missouri River Valley, to prepare for the journey to the Great Basin, where Church leaders established the new Latter-day Saint gathering place. Joseph F.'s reminiscences tell of hardship and suffering during the trek west. Although he was only ten years of age, his family depended upon his help, and he worked hard during the journey.

Joseph F. felt that those in charge of their particular group not only were unhelpful but also made the family's trip more difficult than it should have been. Years later, in speaking of this situation to a group of Boy Scouts, President Joseph F. Smith remarked that the leader told Mary Fielding: "If you start out in this manner, you will be a burden on the company the whole way, and I will have to carry you along or leave you on the way."[6] Mary responded that the Smith family would not burden the company and forcibly prophesied that they would beat the company to Salt Lake City.

Despite the tension between Mary Fielding and the company's captain, the trip was full of adventures. It was during this trip that the family ox was healed—a story that has become a legend. Finally, the company reached the top of East Mountain just east of Salt Lake City from where they glimpsed their first view of the Valley. Near here, the Smith family spent its last night on the trail. As they awoke the next morning, they discovered that their cattle and oxen had strayed away from the campsite.

While family members were searching for the lost animals, the pioneer company began its march to the valley. As Joseph F. sat considering all they had been through, a large, dark, and heavy cloud suddenly arose in the northwest and headed directly into the path of the slowly moving wagon train. Within minutes, the cloud burst with such anger that the cattle in the train could not face the storm. Out of necessity, the company's captain ordered the company to halt and settle in for the mountain storm. The unhitched cattle bolted and headed down into Parley's Canyon. By this time, the Smith family cattle had been found and reclaimed. As they began to move out, Joseph F. asked his mother if they should wait for the company, to which she replied: "Joseph . . . they have not waited for us, and I see no necessity for us to wait for them."[7] And so Mary Fielding did indeed "beat the company" to the Valley. Such were the experiences that helped shape Joseph F.'s mind, attitude, and personality.

In the Salt Lake Valley (September 1848)

On 23 September 1848, the Smith family entered the Salt Lake Valley, reaching the old fort around ten o'clock in the evening. At a Pioneers' Day celebration on 24 July 1917 at Ogden, Utah, Joseph F. noted that it had been sixty-nine years since he drove his team into the Valley. He fondly recalled:

"My team consisted of two pairs, or yokes, of oxen. My leaders' names were Thom and Joe—we raised them from calves, and they were both white. My wheel team were named Broad and Berry. Broad was light brindle with a few white spots on his body, and he had long, broad, pointed horns, from which he got his name. Berry was red and boney and short horned. Thom was trim built, active, young, and more intelligent than many a man. Many times while traveling sandy or rough roads, long, thirsty drives, my oxen, lowing with the heat and fatigue, I would put my arms around Thom's neck, and cry bitter tears!

That was all I could do. Thom was my favorite and best and most willing and obedient servant and friend. He was choice!"[8]

Like many other pioneer families, the arrival in the Salt Lake Valley did not end all the trials and struggles for the family. Locating in Millcreek south of Salt Lake City, the family began to scratch out a living from the soil.

It was during this period of time that another story—now engraved into the institutional memory of the Saints—occurred. Joseph F. recalled that Mary Fielding had the boys load up the best of the potatoes to take to the tithing office as her offering to the Lord. Joseph F. recalled that upon their arrival, one of the clerks came out and said, "'Widow Smith, it's a shame that you should have to pay tithing.' He . . . called her anything but wise and prudent; and said there were others able to work that were supported from the tithing office."[9] She, of course, stood firm and indicated that she planned to pay her tithing and expected to receive the blessings promised for the faithful.

Recalling the incident with the tithing clerk, Joseph F. went on to say: "When [he] told my mother that she ought not to pay tithing, I thought he was one of the finest fellows in the world. I believed every word he said. I had to work and dig and toil myself. I had to help plow the ground, plant the potatoes, hoe the potatoes, dig the potatoes, and all that sort of thing, and then to load up a big wagon-box full of the very best we had, leaving out the poor ones, and bringing the load to the tithing office. I thought in my childish way that it looked a little hard, especially when I saw certain of my playmates and early associates of childhood, playing, riding horses and having good times, and who scarcely ever did a lick of work in their lives, and yet were being fed from the public crib. . . . Well, after I got a few years of experience, I was converted, I found that my mother was right and that [he] was wrong."[10]

PLATE 7
MARY FIELDING SMITH PORTRAIT

KING COLLECTION. THIS ILLUSTRATION APPEARED IN JAMES T. JAKEMAN, ALBUM: "DAUGHTERS OF THE UTAH PIONEERS AND THEIR MOTHERS," (SALT LAKE CITY: WESTERN ALBUM PUBLISHING COMPANY, [1916]). JOSEPH F. SMITH'S MOTHER, MARY FIELDING SMITH, HAD A MORE PROFOUND IMPACT UPON HIS LIFE THAN ANY OTHER PERSON.

A Year of Tragedy (1852)

At age thirteen, Joseph F. was baptized a member of the Church in City Creek (near the northeast corner of the Temple Block in Salt Lake City) on 21 May 1852. He later recalled:

"I felt in my soul that if I had sinned—and surely I was not without sin—that it had been forgiven me; that I was indeed cleansed from sin; my heart was touched, and I felt that I would not injure the smallest insect beneath my feet. I felt as if I wanted to do good everywhere to everybody and to everything. I felt a newness of life, a newness of desire to do that which was right. There was not one particle of desire for evil left in my soul. I was but a little boy, it is true, when I was baptized; but this was the influence that came upon me, and I know that it was from God, and was and ever has been a living witness to me of my acceptance of the Lord."[11]

It was an important day for him, but another event during the year shook the very foundation of his world. Only four months after his baptism, his beloved mother died, leaving him and his sister orphans, without parents or grandparents. Joseph F. was less than fourteen years of age, and his sister, Martha Ann, was less than twelve.

Joseph F. remembered this period in a candid letter to Samuel L. Adams, written in May 1888:

"It was in 1852 that my blessed Mother passed away; leaving me fatherless & motherless, but not altogether friendless at the early age of 13 years. . . . After my mother's death there followed 18 months—from Sept 21st, 1852 to April, 1854 of perilous times for me. I was almost like a comet or fiery meteor, without attraction or gravitation to keep me balanced or guide me within reasonable bounds."[12]

It was during this period that a now-famous confrontation between Joseph F. and a teacher took place in a little one-room school on the Utah frontier. Joseph F. saw the school master pulling out a leather strap to punish his younger sister, Martha Ann. When the principal told Martha to hold out her hand Joseph spoke up: "Don't whip her with that!"[13] Without warning, the school master turned on Joseph F. However, the young teenage boy "licked him good and plenty."[14] Naturally, Joseph was immediately expelled from school.

Apparently, Church leaders and relatives were concerned what might become of a teenager who had experienced the personal tragedies and struggles Joseph F. had gone through in his short life. In a brilliant stroke of inspiration, Brigham Young and other leaders decided to call him on a full-time mission.

Continuing on with the theme that this was a "perilous time," Joseph F. added: "My four years mission to the Sandwich Islands restored my equilibrium, and fixed the laws and metes and bounds which have governed my subsequent life. I shall always thank God and Pres. Heber C. Kimball for that mission, altho' it was the hardest one I ever performed."[15]

Others agreed that the mission redirected his energy. George A. Smith stated at the time of Joseph F.'s call to the apostleship: "His father and mother left him when he was a child, and we have been looking after him to try and help him along. We first sent him to school, but it was not long before he licked the schoolmaster, and could not go to school. Then we sent him on a mission, and he did pretty well at it. I think he will make good as an Apostle."[16]

First Mission to the Sandwich Islands— Hawaii (1854–1857)

After the call was announced from the pulpit at general conference, Joseph F. was ordained an elder by his uncle, George A. Smith, received his endowments, and was set apart for his mission by Parley P. Pratt.

Of twenty-one Pacific Islands missionaries, Joseph F. was the youngest among them. He left Salt Lake on 27 May 1854, taking the southern route out of Utah. During the journey to southern California, the party slept on blankets in the great western outdoors. During a visit

PLATE 8
GEORGE A. SMITH, CA. 1870

C. R. SAVAGE, LDSCA. GEORGE A. SMITH WAS THE PATRIARCHAL LEADER OF THE SMITH FAMILY IN UTAH UNTIL HIS DEATH IN 1875. KNOWN AS "UNCLE GEORGE," HE WAS A SURROGATE FATHER FOR JOSEPH F. SMITH, WHO WAS HIS FIRST COUSIN ONCE REMOVED. ADDITIONALLY, ESPECIALLY DURING THE 1860S AND 1870S, GEORGE A. SMITH WAS A COUNSELOR, CONFIDANT, AND CLOSE ASSOCIATE TO JOSEPH F. SMITH.

to central Utah in 1917, President Joseph F. remembered one of the nights on the journey: "I lay there and looked up at the stars, rather a home-sick youth, realizing for the first time in my life that I was just about to cut loose entirely from all the associations that I loved and honored and revered in all the world; to go out into the world—I knew not where, nor did I know the circumstances in which I would be placed."[17]

In southern California and later in San Francisco, the missionaries worked to earn the necessary money to continue their journey. Finally, in early September, they took passage on a clipper ship, *Vaquero*, which left San Francisco Harbor on 8 September 1854.

As Joseph F. first caught sight of the shoreline of the beautiful Hawaiian Islands, he could never imagine how his life would be intertwined with the native people he was about to be introduced to on this very first trip across the Pacific. His first mission lasted until 1857; he returned again on a special mission in 1864; as Church president, he visited the islands in 1915, 1916, and 1917; and he dedicated the first temple site in the Pacific there.

Early in his mission, Joseph F. became quite sick, probably with yellow fever. A local woman, Ma Mahuhii, nursed him back to health and became, in a real sense, the orphan's second mother. Years later, during a visit to the islands, President Joseph F. met her again in a very heartfelt and joyous reunion. Bishop Charles W. Nibley, one of Joseph F.'s dearest friends and constant traveling companion during this period, provided a word-picture of the occasion:

"I noticed a poor, old blind woman tottering under the weight of about ninety years, being led [into the meetinghouse where the Saints were gathering to greet President Joseph F.]. She had a few choice bananas in her hand. It was her all—her offering. She was calling 'Iosepa, Iosepa!' Instantly, when he saw her, he ran to her and clasped her in her arms, hugged her, and kissed her over and over again, patting her on the head saying, 'Mama, Mama, my dear old Mama!'

"And with tears streaming down his cheeks he turned to me and said, 'Charley, she nursed me when I was a boy, sick and without anyone to care for me. She took me in and was a mother to me!'"[18]

Joseph F. noted his appreciation for the mission experience and his gratitude for the kindness shown him by the people with whom he lived and worked: "I shall never cease to be grateful for that experience, hard though it was at times, and shall ever remember the kindness manifested towards me by many of the good native people of Hawaii."[19]

Mission life was difficult. Living conditions were rather crude, North American missionaries struggled with a new diet and a significant language barrier, and there was always rejection of the message and even a lack of commitment by some of the converts. Sometime during this mission, Joseph F. received an important manifestation that helped him overcome the challenges he faced in Hawaii—and, in a real sense, the challenges he faced in his life. Joseph F. recalled:

"I was very much oppressed, once, on a mission.... I felt as if I was so debased in my condition of poverty, lack of intelligence and knowledge, just a boy, that I hardly dared look a white man in the face.

"While in that condition I dreamed that I was on a journey.... Finally I came to a wonderful mansion.... As I passed towards it, as fast as I could, I saw a notice, 'Bath.' I turned aside quickly and went into the bath and washed myself clean. I opened up this little bundle that I had, and there was a pair of white, clean garments, a thing I had not seen for a long time. . . . And I put them on. . . . I knocked and the door opened, and the man who stood there was the Prophet Joseph Smith. He looked at me a little reprovingly, and the first word he said: 'Joseph, you are late.' Yet I took confidence and said: 'Yes, but I am clean—I am clean!'"

He concluded, "When I woke up I felt as if I had been lifted out of a slum, out of despair, out of the wretched condition that I was in."[20]

Joseph F.'s spirituality was taking shape, as a letter to his uncle George A. Smith, reveals:

"I know that the work in which I am engaged is the work of the living and true God, I am ready to bear my testimony of the same, at any time, or at any place, or in whatsoever circumstances I may be placed; and hope and pray that I ever may prove faithful in serving the Lord, my God. I am happy to say that I am ready to go through thick and thin for this cause in which I am engaged; and truly hope and pray that I may prove faithful to the end."[21]

Though young and inexperienced, he was recognized as one of sound judgment; and the natives, as well as the missionaries, respected his prudence, wisdom, and discernment. He was also blessed with gifts of the Spirit. Writing home, he said, "Of the many gifts of the Spirit which were manifest through my administration, next to my acquirement of the language, the most prominent was perhaps the gift of healing, and by the power of God, the casting out of evil spirits which frequently occurred."[22]

During his mission, he experienced a significant trial when the Church's storehouse burned down. In the fire, Joseph F. lost his clothing, family photographs, personal papers, and precious copies of the scriptures that had belonged to his father. Yet he wrote stoically in his diary: "Well these dear earned few things are gone and not one saved, and now I am destitute, but with old Job exclaim, 'The Lord giveth and the Lord taketh away, blessed be the name of the Lord,' I am confident that he has and will provide for his servants, so all is well."[23]

On 28 June 1856, he wrote: "We found also some Poi in the house and after hunting we made [?] of one or two onions and sat down to eat. (As we had had nothing to eat for two or three days) when we was about to cry enough some of the brethren came with a large fine chicken which after it had been cooked, we despatched (all but the feathers) with but very little ceremony."[24] A few weeks later, he noted: "Begged a little for our selves. As we have no shoes, clothing &c our Trunks being destroyed by the fire."[25]

Another entry in his Hawaiian diary, dated 9 February 1857, provides a vivid description of the situation following the fire: "I bought enough stuff to day to make a pair of garments. I being destitute on account of the loss of my trunk and clothes by fire at Lanai."[26]

Another famous story was born at this time when Joseph F. and his companion shared one suit between them. On any given day, one of the elders would, of necessity, remain in bed while the other, wearing the suit, went to the meetings to preach. The next day, the venue was reversed, and the elder who had gone off to the meetings remained in bed while the other wore the suit and preached.

Home Again to Utah (1857–1858)

On 6 October 1857, Joseph F., along with six other missionaries, set sail for San Francisco on the ship *Yankee*. These early trips across the oceans were not enjoyable. Later, he recalled this particular passage: "Things have changed since I was a boy and crossed the seas with the Divine message you bear. Experience is better possessed than to be gained. It is like a bruise, it feels better after it quits hurting."[27]

In late 1857, the Church was under attack in the press, and a large army was marching toward Utah to occupy the Mormon settlements. It was during this time that another famous incident occurred in his life. Joseph F. was making his way back to Utah. One evening, he was away from the camp looking for firewood when a group of drunken men rode into the camp on horseback, cursing and looking for Mormons to kill. Unaware of what waited for him in camp, Joseph F. headed back with an armful of wood. While still a distance off, Joseph F. soon realized there was a problem. He recalled: "Why should I run from these fellows?" Feeling a bit emboldened, he marched back into camp and became the first to meet the armed group of hostile men. As he was depositing the recently acquired firewood, one of the leaders of the group, still holding a gun, came toward Joseph F. cursing and declaring in drunken speech that he was duty bound to exterminate any Mormon he found. The inebriated scoundrel shouted, "Are you a Mormon?" Without a moment of hesitation and looking the ruffian in the eye, Joseph F. Smith boldly answered, "Yes, siree; dyed in the wool; true blue, through and through."[28]

"The answer was given boldly and without any sign of fear, which completely disarmed the belligerent man, and in his bewilderment, he grasped the missionary by the hand and said: 'Well, you are the _____ _____ pleasantest man I ever met! Shake, young fellow, I am glad to see a man that stands up for his convictions.'"[29]

PLATE 9
JOSEPH F. SMITH, CA. 1858
COPY PRINT PROBABLY BASED ON AN EARLIER DAGUERREOTYPE, KING COLLECTION. ACCORDING TO FAMILY TRADITION, THIS IMAGE WAS TAKEN WHEN JOSEPH F. SMITH WAS NINETEEN YEARS OF AGE, FOLLOWING HIS RETURN FROM HIS FIRST MISSION TO THE SANDWICH ISLANDS (HAWAII).

Defending the Saints (1858)

When Joseph F. reached home in 1858, the Latter-day Saints in Utah were facing another difficult moment in their history—a large military force was at their very doorsteps, east of Salt Lake City. This force was bent on occupying the region, arresting Church leaders, and diverting the attention of the nation from the real crisis of escalating tension between the North and the South. Joseph F., like other missionaries arriving home, reported to Brigham Young. He was assigned to join territorial militia units located in Echo Canyon for military duty. Joseph F. remembered: "I sat up all night molding rifle bullets from a pig of lead I had brought with me from a 'Mormon' smelter at Las Vegas."[30] Later, he was assigned to the front where he performed faithful service under the direction of Porter Rockwell.[31]

Shortly after the conclusion of the conflict, Joseph F. fell in love with Levira Smith, a sixteen-year-old cousin. She was the daughter of Samuel Harrison Smith, one of Hyrum Smith's brothers. During this time, it was not unusual for first cousins to marry, and Joseph F. and Levira did so on 5 April 1859.

First Mission to Great Britain (1860–1863)

Joseph F. found employment as the sergeant-at-arms of the territorial legislature. During this time, he was ordained a seventy on 20 March 1858 and soon thereafter a high priest, being called to the Salt Lake Stake High Council. The pace of change continued when, at the April general conference in 1860, Joseph F. was called to serve another mission. Before the month was out, Joseph F. bid his wife good-bye and left for England. He was accompanied by Levira's brother, Samuel Harrison Bailey Smith, who was also going to the British Isles to serve a mission.

It was a difficult separation from family and friends, especially as Joseph F. reflected upon the death of his mother and the breakup of her household following her death. He noted in one diary entry during this period, "I [am now] 5,000 miles from what only a short time before was a peaceful lovely home, now broken up and its inmates scattered."[32]

Joseph F. recalled his missionary assignment shortly after becoming

PLATE 10
JOSEPH F. SMITH, CA. 1860
COPY PRINT FROM UNKNOWN SOURCE, WADSWORTH COLLECTION.

President of the Church: "I prize very highly my many pleasant reminiscences of the Saints in the European mission, where I labored successively as a traveling Elder in the Leeds conference, as president of the Sheffield conference, and as pastor of the Sheffield district, comprising the Sheffield, Leeds, Hull and Lincolnshire Conferences. Towards the latter part of my mission, while Apostle George Q. Cannon was presiding in that land, I accompanied him, by his invitation, on a tour through the Scandinavian conferences; a very pleasant trip, lasting about six weeks."[33]

PLATE 11
JOSEPH F. SMITH, CA. 1861

LDSCA. THIS PHOTOGRAPH WAS GIVEN TO JOSEPH F. SMITH'S WIFE, EDNA LAMBSON SMITH, YEARS AFTER IT WAS TAKEN. THIS EARLY IMAGE OF JOSEPH F. SMITH PROVIDES US A VIEW OF THE YOUNG MISSIONARY WHILE HE WAS IN ENGLAND ON HIS FIRST MISSION TO THE BRITISH ISLES.

ECOND MISSION TO HAWAII (1864)

Brigham Young asked Joseph F. to accompany Apostles Ezra T. Benson and Lorenzo Snow, as well as Elders William W. Cluff and Alma L. Smith, on a special mission to Hawaii in 1864. It was a difficult mission because he went not to baptize but to reclaim the flock. Walter M. Gibson, the leader of the mission at the time, apostatized and set up another church organization in the islands. Joseph F. noted, "We confronted him, charged him with his misdeeds, and labored faithfully to reclaim him, but he proved obdurate and impenitent and was therefore cut off from the Church."[34]

This mission not only provided Joseph F. with an opportunity to observe closely the seasoned Church leaders who accompanied him to the islands but also provided them an opportunity to witness for themselves his growing strengths and administrative abilities. Joseph F. recalled: "I was given charge, with Elders Cluff and Smith as my assistants; the two Apostles returning to Utah. . . . We worked energetically against the imposture, and gradually won back those whom Gibson had deceived."[35]

Joseph F. proposed to Brigham Young through a letter that the Hawaiian Saints gather to Oahu. Following the acceptance of the plan, a site was identified and soon work began to build up the Laie plantation and Church headquarters. During a later visit, President Joseph F. dedicated the Hawaiian temple site at this location.

PLATE 12
Church Historian's Office, ca. 1865

LDSCA. Brigham Young announced the appointment of Joseph F. Smith to work at the Historian's Office on 22 January 1865, replacing Thomas Bullock. The office was attached to George A. Smith's home on South Temple just across the street from the present-day Joseph Smith Memorial Building. This assignment strengthened the close association Joseph F. Smith already had with George A. Smith (Church historian) and allowed him to become more familiar with Wilford Woodruff (Assistant Church historian).

New Opportunities and Responsibilities (1865–1866)

In January 1865, within a few weeks of his arrival home, Joseph F. became a clerk in the Church Historian's Office. This experience gave him the opportunity to become well acquainted with Church history through conversations with those who had participated in the events, especially with George A. Smith, Church historian, and Wilford Woodruff, assistant Church historian.

The following extracts from the Historian's Office journal, covering the period from 24 January through 2 July 1865, reveal the nature of his work and his activities during the first months of his assignment:

[24 January 1865] Joseph F. Smith—Writing letters under G.A.S's dictation and for W. Woodruff.[36]

[18 February 1865] J. F. Smith—Cleaned up the Office. putting papers in order. P.M, filed away 10 letters into Geo. A. S's box, on historical notation.[37]

[20 February 1865] J. F. Smith, Shoveled Snow off front Steps. Posted the Office Journal, polled his vote for the Canal. P.M. on historical Notation. adding to the Same for Prest. Young's large letter book.[38]

[16 March 1865] J. F. S. in the Office writing letter for Geo. A. S. copying &c. went on an errand to bookbinder's, & post Office. posted the Journal.[39]

[12 April 1865] R. L. C. & J. F. S. Getting out items for Gen. Epistle.[40]

[7 May 1865] Meeting in Tabernacle—Several of the Missionaries preached. Afternoon, Joseph F. Smith preached.[41]

[17 June 1865] J. F. S. at Endowment house—keeping records.[42]

[2 July 1865] Pres. B. Young, John Taylor, W. Woodruff, Geo. A. Smith, F. D. Richards, Geo. Q. Cannon, John W. Young & Jos. F. Smith met and prayed, this p.m.[43]

The above quotations not only reveal Joseph F.'s activities in the Historian's Office but also reveal the additional responsibility to labor in the Endowment House, keeping records of the important ordinances performed there under the direction of President Brigham Young and Elder Heber C. Kimball. Located on the northwest corner of the Temple Block, the Endowment House was a temporary temple in Salt Lake City, used to perform baptisms for the dead, endowments, sealings, and so forth. This particular assignment eventually caused President John Taylor to assign Joseph F., his counselor at the time in the First Presidency, to go on the "underground" during the federal government's efforts to prosecute Latter-day Saints for violation of

PLATE 13
ENDOWMENT HOUSE, CA. 1885
F. I. MONSEN & COMPANY, LDSCA. DEDICATED IN MAY 1855, THE ENDOWMENT HOUSE STOOD IN THE NORTHWEST CORNER OF THE TEMPLE BLOCK UNTIL IT WAS TORN DOWN IN NOVEMBER 1889. JOSEPH F. SMITH WAS SEALED TO LEVIRA SMITH, DAUGHTER OF SAMUEL HARRISON SMITH, ON 5 APRIL 1859 BY HEBER C. KIMBALL IN THE ENDOWMENT HOUSE. LATER, IN 1865, JOSEPH F. WAS CALLED TO WORK IN THE SACRED BUILDING. HE WAS PUT IN CHARGE OF RECORDS AND, FROM TIME TO TIME, ASSISTED IN THE ORDINANCES GIVEN THERE FOR THE LIVING AND THE DEAD.

antipolygamy laws in the 1880s. Joseph F. was the most knowledgeable Church leader about such sacred ordinances, and President Taylor wanted him to avoid arrest.

Additionally, the Historian's Office journal provides insights to Joseph F.'s Sabbath activities, including attending Sunday meetings at the Tabernacle (speaking from time to time at those meetings) and participating in the private prayer circles of the leading brethren of the Church. Eventually, as noted in the 2 July 1865 journal entry, Joseph F. participated in Brigham Young's prayer circle where he acted as the clerk, keeping records of attendance and minutes of discussions.

At the end of 1865, Joseph F. began serving in the Territorial Legislature. He continued in this office for several terms, stepping down in 1874 to serve another mission. (Later, in 1880 and 1882, he served in the Council, or Senate; in 1882, he also presided over a constitutional convention to formulate plans for Utah statehood.) In early 1866, Joseph F. was elected to the Salt Lake City Council.

It was a busy time for Joseph F., as he continued attending Salt Lake Stake high council meetings and the First Presidency and Quorum of the Twelve weekly prayer circles.

Marriage to Julina Lambson (May 1866)

At this period of busy community and ecclesiastical labors, President Young asked Joseph F. to marry a second wife. Apparently, Joseph F. was happily married and had not considered such a move at the time. While working in the Historian's Office, Joseph F. met Julina Lambson, the niece of George A. and Bathsheba Smith. In the

PLATE 14
JOSEPH F. SMITH AND WIVES JULINA, SARAH, AND EDNA

C. R. SAVAGE. THE SMITHS' FAMILY BIBLE, WALKER COLLECTION. SEVERAL FAMILY PHOTOGRAPHS, INCLUDING THIS PAGE THAT FEATURES THREE OF JOSEPH F. SMITH'S WIVES, ARE FOUND IN THE ALBUM SECTION OF THE FAMILY BIBLE BELONGING TO JULINA LAMBSON SMITH. TOP FROM LEFT: JOSEPH F. SMITH AND JULINA LAMBSON SMITH (MARRIED ON 5 MAY 1866). BOTTOM FROM LEFT: SARAH ELLEN RICHARDS SMITH (MARRIED ON 1 MARCH 1868) AND EDNA LAMBSON SMITH (MARRIED ON 1 JANUARY 1871). ALL THE PHOTOGRAPHS WERE PRINTED ON C. R. SAVAGE CARD STOCK.

presence of Levira, he was sealed to his first plural wife, Julina, on 5 May 1866 by Heber C. Kimball.

Julina and Joseph F. eventually had eleven children, one of whom died during Joseph F.'s lifetime: Mercy Josephine, born 14 August 1867 (she died 6 June 1870). The other children were Mary Sophronia, born 7 October 1869; Donette, born 17 September 1872; Joseph Fielding, born 19 July 1876; David Asael, born 24 May 1879; George Carlos, born 14 October 1881; Julina Clarissa, born 10 February 1884; Elias Wesley, born 21 April 1886; Emily, born 11 September 1888; Rachel, born 11 December 1890; and Edith Eleanor, born 4 January 1894. They also adopted two children: Marjorie Virginia, born 7 December 1906, and Edward Arthur, born 1 November 1858.

Ordained an Apostle (July 1866)

A few weeks later, on the first day of July 1866, Elder Woodruff recorded having attended President Brigham Young's prayer circle that day and made note of a singular event:

"I met at the Prayer Circle with President Young John Taylor W. Woodruff G. A. Smith G. Q. Cannon & Joseph F Smith. John Taylor Prayed & . . . Presidet Young arose from his knees. . . . Of a sudden he stoped & Exclaimed hold on, 'Shall I do as I feel led? I always [feel] well to do as the Spirit Constrains me. It is my mind to Ordain Brother Joseph F Smith to the Apostleship, and to be one of my Councillors.'

"He then Called upon Each one of us for an Expression of our Feelings and we Individually responded that it met our Harty approval. . . . After which Brother Joseph F Smith knelt . . . we laid our hands upon him, Brother Brigham being mouth & we repeating after him in the usual Form He Said:

"'Brother Joseph F. Smith, we lay our hands upon your head in the name of Jesus Christ, and By virtue of the Holy Priesthood we ordain you to be An Apostle in the Church of Jesus Christ of Latter Day Saints, And to be a special witness to the Nations of the Earth. We seal upon your head all the Authority, Power & keys of this Holy Apostleship, and we ordain you to be a Councillor unto the First Presidency of the Church & Kingdom of God upon the Earth. These Blessings we seal upon you in the name of Jesus Christ & By the Authority of the Holy Priesthood Amen.'"[44]

Although this was a momentous Sunday for the twenty-seven-year-old son of the martyred Patriarch, the ordination was not publicly announced until the following year.

During his lifetime, Joseph F. served longer than any other man as a counselor to Presidents of the Church, including Brigham Young, John Taylor, Wilford Woodruff, and Lorenzo Snow—a total of thirty-eight years.

Broken Heart (June 1867)

On 10 June 1867, Joseph F.'s marriage to Levira ended in divorce. This was a most difficult time for him. Although it is impossible to know all the details, it appears that Levira suffered physically and mentally during her lifetime and was unwilling or unable to bear the rigors of the frontier life in Utah and the common sacrifices that young Mormon couples faced together, especially plural marriage. Additionally, as in many marriages, Joseph F. and Levira often struggled to communicate; and, having failed, Levira ended the marriage by asking for a divorce. She moved to California shortly thereafter and died heartbroken herself.

One of the poignant aspects of this experience is the love and concern Julina Lambson Smith had for her sister-wife Levira. Apparently, Julina was very solicitous to Levira, helping and comforting her during Levira's sicknesses and troubles. When Levira decided to leave the family, Julina recalled, "This was a very sad experience for both Joseph and me."[45]

Later, Levira visited Julina in Salt Lake City. Julina recalled: "Some time later I was happily surprised to have a caller. Here was Levira. She said she was on her way through Salt Lake on her way East, but could not go without first seeing me and my baby. We again parted in sadness, but friendly, and my heart surely went out to her."[46]

Julina also knew how much her husband loved Levira. She asked and eventually was able to stand as proxy for Levira in a temple sealing to Joseph F. Smith.[47]

Notes

1. Joseph Fielding Smith, comp., *Life of Joseph F. Smith: Sixth President of The Church of Jesus Christ of Latter-day Saints* (Salt Lake City: Deseret Book, 1938); hereafter cited as *LJFS*, 124.

2. Leonard J. Arrington, "Joseph F. Smith: From Impulsive Young Man to Patriarchal Prophet," *John Whitmer Historical Journal* 4 (1984): 32.

3. Preston Nibley, *Presidents of the Church* (Salt Lake City: Deseret Book, 1941), 229.

4. *LJFS*, 132.

5. Ibid., 133–34.

6. Ibid., 148.

7. Ibid., 155.

8. Ibid., 155–56.

9. Ibid., 158–59.

10. Ibid., 159–60.
11. Joseph F. Smith, *Gospel Doctrine: Selections from the Sermons and Writings of Joseph F. Smith, Sixth President of The Church of Jesus Christ of Latter-day Saints* (Salt Lake City: Deseret Book, 1966); hereafter cited as GD, 96.
12. Joseph F. Smith to Samuel L. Adams, 11 May 1888, as cited in *TC*, 6.
13. *LJFS*, 229.
14. Ibid.
15. Joseph F. Smith to Samuel L. Adams, 11 May 1888, as cited in *TC*, 6.
16. *LJFS*, 229.
17. F. W. Otterstrom, "A Journey to the South," *Improvement Era* 21 (December 1917): 106.
18. *LJFS*, 185–86.
19. Joseph F. Smith, "My Missions," *Deseret Evening News*, 21 December 1901, 57; James R. Clark, comp., *Messages of the First Presidency of The Church of Jesus Christ of Latter-day Saints*, 6 vols. (Salt Lake City: Bookcraft, Inc., 1965–75), hereafter cited as MFP, 4:18.
20. *LJFS*, 445–47.
21. Ibid., 176–77.
22. Ibid., 179.
23. Joseph F. Smith Diary, 26 June 1856, typescript, Joseph F. Smith Papers, 1856–1918; LDSCA.
24. Ibid., 28 June 1856.
25. Ibid., 6 July 1856.
26. Ibid., 9 February 1857.
27. *LJFS*, 187–88.
28. Ibid., 189
29. Ibid.
30. *MFP*, 4:19.
31. Ibid.
32. Joseph F. Smith Diary, 13 November 1860, Joseph F. Smith Papers, 1856–1918, LDSCA; as cited in typescript extracts, Scott G. Kenney Collection, BYU.
33. Joseph F. Smith, "My Missions," *Deseret Evening News*, 21 December 1901, 57; *MFP*, 4:20.
34. Ibid.; *MFP*, 4:21.
35. Ibid.; *MFP*, 4:21.
36. Historian's Office Journal, 24 January 1865, typescript, LDSCA.
37. Ibid., 18 February 1865.
38. Ibid., 20 February 1865.
39. Ibid., 16 March 1865.

40. Ibid., 12 April 1865.
41. Ibid., 7 May 1865.
42. Ibid., 17 June 1865.
43. Ibid., 2 July 1865.
44. Wilford Woodruff Journal, 1 July 1866, LDSCA; as cited in Scott G. Kenney, ed., *Wilford Woodruff's Journals, 1833–1898*, 9 vols. (Midvale, Utah: Signature Books, 1983–85), 6:289–90.
45. "Wives of Joseph F. Smith," typescript, 1; USHS.
46. Ibid.
47. Vivian McConkie Adams to Richard Neitzel Holzapfel, 7 February 2000, in author's possession.

CHAPTER THREE

THE QUORUM OF THE TWELVE AND THE FIRST PRESIDENCY 1867–1901

The period from 1868 to 1901 was an important chapter in the life of Joseph F. Smith, as well as in the Church. During this period he became a prominent spokesman for the Church and an important counselor to three different Presidents of the Church.

PLATE 15
JOSEPH F. SMITH'S FAMILY, CA. 1868
COPYPRINT OF AN ORIGINAL TINTYPE; KING COLLECTION. FROM LEFT: JOSEPH F. SMITH, MARTHA ANN SMITH HARRIS, MERCY FIELDING THOMPSON, AND MARY JANE THOMPSON TAYLOR. MARTHA ANN WAS JOSEPH F. SMITH'S YOUNGER SISTER, WHO WAS MARRIED TO WILLIAM J. HARRIS IN 1857. MERCY FIELDING THOMPSON WAS JOSEPH F. SMITH'S AUNT (SISTER OF MARY FIELDING SMITH) AND THE WIDOW OF THE PROPHET JOSEPH SMITH'S CLERK, ROBERT B. THOMPSON, WHO DIED IN NAUVOO. MARY JANE THOMSON WAS JOSEPH F. SMITH'S COUSIN (DAUGHTER OF MERCY FIELDING THOMPSON).

Despite the increased role he played in the Church and community, Joseph F. never forgot his family, especially his sister Martha Ann and his aunt Mercy Fielding Thompson. Their lives were intertwined not only because of their blood relationship but also because they shared the same commitment to the kingdom of God.

Marriage to Sarah Ellen Richards (1 March 1868)

Joseph F. married Sarah Ellen Richards, daughter of Willard and Sarah Longstroth Richards, on 1 March 1868. Sarah died on 22 March 1915, three years before Joseph F. died in 1918. The couple had eleven children, five who died before Joseph F.'s death: Sarah Ella, born 5 February 1869 (died 11 February 1869); Leonora, born 30 January 1871 (died 23 December 1907); Joseph Richards, born 22 February 1873; Heber John, born 3 July 1876 (died 3 March 1877); Rhoda Ann, born 20 July 1878 (died 6 July 1879); Minerva, born 30 April 1880; Alice, born 27 July 1882 (died 29 April 1901); Willard Richards, born 20 November 1884; Franklin Richards, born 12 May 1888; Jeanetta, born 25 August 1891; and Asenath, born 28 December 1896.

A Member of the Council of the Twelve (October 1868)

President Brigham Young set apart Joseph F. as a member of the Quorum of the Twelve Apostles, replacing Amasa Lyman, on 8 October 1868. Joseph F. continued to serve as a counselor to the First Presidency, which assignment he received in July 1866, an assignment that lasted until the death of President Young in August 1877.

Joseph F.'s loyalty to the Prophet Joseph Smith and Brigham Young

PLATE 16
JOSEPH F. SMITH, CA. 1867–68
C. R. SAVAGE; LDSCA. TAKEN NEAR THE TIME OF HIS APOSTOLIC ORDINATION BY BRIGHAM YOUNG.

PLATE 17

LDS CHURCH FIRST PRESIDENCY AND COUNCIL OF THE TWELVE, 9 OCTOBER 1869

C. R. SAVAGE; USHS (PHOTO #27673). FROM LEFT: ORSON HYDE, ORSON PRATT, JOHN TAYLOR, WILFORD WOODRUFF, GEORGE A. SMITH, EZRA T. BENSON, CHARLES C. RICH, BRIGHAM YOUNG, LORENZO SNOW, DANIEL H. WELLS, ERASTUS SNOW, FRANKLIN D. RICHARDS, GEORGE Q. CANNON, BRIGHAM YOUNG JR., AND JOSEPH F. SMITH. THIS REMARKABLE IMAGE CAPTURES THE ENTIRE FIRST PRESIDENCY AND THE QUORUM OF THE TWELVE, THE FIRST PHOTOGRAPHIC IMAGE OF THIS BODY OF CHURCH LEADERS.

is underscored in a talk he gave in the Tabernacle, recorded by a Protestant visitor to Salt Lake City in 1868. Reverend E. P. Willard quoted Joseph F. as saying, "I know myself that Joseph is a true prophet of God, and that Brigham Young is his lawfully appointed successor to establish the government of God throughout the world."[1]

A Trial and Struggle (June 1870)

Joseph F. experienced firsthand the heartache of losing loved ones through death beginning with his own father in 1844 and mother in 1852. Additionally, two of his wives preceded him in death: Levira Annett Clark (1888) and Sarah Ellen Richards (1915). Of particular anguish is the death of a child. Between 1869 and 1918, Joseph F. buried thirteen children, nine of whom were young. They included six-day-old Sarah Ella (died on 11 February 1869); two-year-old Mercy Josephine (died on 6 June 1870); eight-month-old Heber John (died on 3 March 1877); one-year-old Alfred Jason (died on 6 April 1878); one-year-old Rhoda Ann (died on 6 July 1879); one-year-old Albert Jesse (died on 25 August 1883); two-year-old Robert (died on 4 February 1886); one-year-old John Schwartz (died on 3 August 1889); four-year-old Ruth (died on 17 March 1898); nineteen-year-old Alice (died on 29 April 1901); thirty-six-year-old Leonora (died on 23 December 1907); twenty-five-year-old Zina (died on 25 October 1915); and forty-six-year-old Hyrum Mack (died on 23 January 1918). (Hyrum's wife, Ida Elizabeth Bowman Smith, died eight months later on 24 September 1918, leaving five children orphans, including newly born Hyrum Mack Smith Jr.) And while he mourned for all his lost loved ones, the death of his firstborn child, Mercy Josephine (named after

PLATE 18
SARAH ELLEN KIMBALL SMITH AND MERCY JOSEPHINE SMITH, 15 AUGUST 1869

C. R. SAVAGE, NICHOLS COLLECTION. JOSEPH F. SMITH'S PLURAL WIFE, SARAH, POSES WITH JULINA LAMBSON AND JOSEPH F. SMITH'S DAUGHTER, MERCY JOSEPHINE. SHE WAS BORN ON 14 AUGUST 1867 AND DIED NEARLY THREE YEARS LATER ON 6 JUNE 1870.

him with the feminine form of his name), may well have been one of his hardest challenges.

Mercy Josephine was very ill in late May 1870. Joseph F.'s diary provides a detailed and emotionally laden account of this period. On 30 May, he noted: "At E[ndowment] H[ouse]. 70—endowments. President B. Young sealed 10 coups for the dead. I sealed 48. & Prest. Wells 45 total 103. My little Josephine was taken very sick last evening."[2] The following day, he recorded: "At the office writing, copying &c. All night up watching and tending my little girl: symtoms of the measles, rained and Snowed this morning. very cold. 'Dodie' [Mercy Josephine] very sick all day. high fever. cough. rattling in the throat."[3] On a hopeful note, he wrote on 2 June: "My little 'Dodo' was some better, but far from well."[4] He recorded on 3 June: "Up all night with my little girl. I think She is better. At the H[istorian's] Office, copying S[ealing] record and writing biographical Sketch of Asa Lyman."[5] On the following day, he noted the departure of his sister Martha Ann and a request for the united prayers of the Saints who were in the Endowment House, located on the Temple Block, in his daughter's behalf:

"Joseph[ine] very sick all night I could not feel to leave her, accompanied Martha Ann to the Station & saw them off, waited on my little daughter all day, gave her two packs, and put warm corn-meal and hops poultice on her chest. She seemed somewhat relieved in her lungs. & breathed easier. But is very languid & weak. I got her a few Straw-berries which She would eat, She takes but little except cold water, or lemon juice. I left a request at the E[ndowment] House for her to be prayed for, and got bro. Tingy to administer to her."[6]

On 5 June, Joseph F. wrote:

"I slept from 10.30 till 1.30. The remainder of the night attending my little Sick girl. At 5 a.m. took the cars for Brigham City. bro. Jos. A. Young giving me pass. to & from Brigham City and home. arrived at 8:35. William Pierce met me at the Station. Took breakfast at bro. L. Snow's. Attended meeting in the bowery at 10. a.m. opening prayer by myself. . . . I dined along with bros. Taylor & wife. Jos. Horn & wife, Jesse Fox and wife, and Samuel H. B. Smith & wife at bro. Samuel Smiths. I have no appetite, my sympathy & solicitude for my darling little Josephine, has greatly bowed my spirit. Notwithstanding I think I have received a testimony that she will not die. Still, She is a sensitive, delicate, and tender little creature and loves her 'Papa.' . . . Reached home about 9 evening, and found my baby much lower than in the morning. I went for Dr. Lee, who came & fixed her some acid drink. Geo. A. Bathsheba and others called."[7]

On 6 June, Joseph F. struggled:

"Sarah and I sat up and watched and attended my little girl all night. She gradually Sank, I became very anxious. Early in the morning sent for Bro. Reed & Tingey who with me anointed and laid hands on her, also sent for Dr. Lee. who came and gave her a catharic I said to her in the morning 'you did not sleep good all night my "Dodo."' She replied 'I'll <u>sleep</u> today Papa.' Oh, how these little words shot thro' my heart, I knew, yet I would not fully believe, that she <u>meant</u> the sleep of death. And she did sleep! O, my 'Dodo' my heart is nearly broken for the loss of you. You came to me when my heart was wrung in a time of deep trouble, sorrow and affliction. Like a golden Sun-beam of joy. Thou wert a green oasis in my hitherto desert life, my first born lovely—beautiful as the rose, bright intelligent beyond thy age—and possessed of noble mein & heart. Thou art the priceless Jewel & the brightest gem of earth nearest to my heart. Thou didst live in my thoughts and dwelt ever in my hearts purest & best love. O! Thou wert the Joy & the light of my heart and home. 'Dodo' my babe, I loved thee! My ambition was to see the[e] shine pure and bright amid earths noblest & best. I loved thy innocent prattle, and thy little footsteps echoed in my heart. Thy voice was as the music of an holy angel. And thy little cunning ways more pleasant and endearing than the voice of love. thy bright black eyes were as jet. & more lovely than the summers eve, speaking the intelligent language of thy soul more fluently than thy forward little tongue. Oh thou wert lovely, Sweet—all in all to me. thou wert a heavenly gift directly to my heart of hearts—I loved thee more than tongue can tell, more than the Soul can speak through mortal agency. Thou didst make me a better man, for thy sake I loved humanity, earth—and Heaven—more—Thou didst draw me nearer

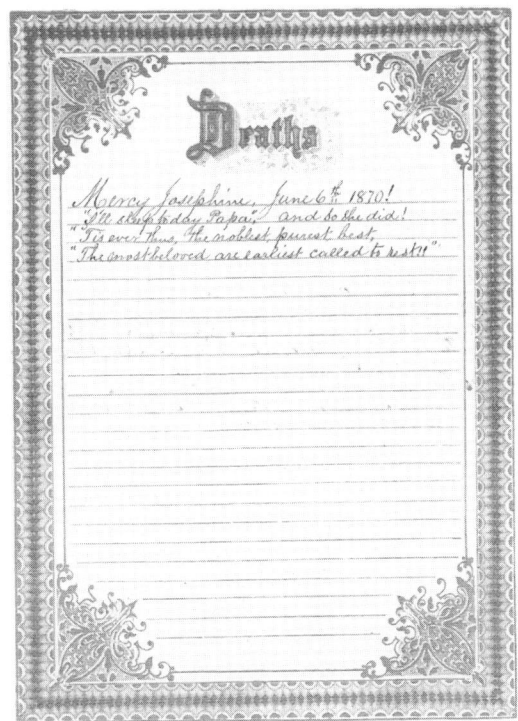

PLATE 19
PAGE FROM JULINA LAMBSON SMITH'S FAMILY BIBLE
WALKER COLLECTION. JOSEPH F. RECORDED A TRIBUTE TO HIS AND JULINA'S DAUGHTER: "MERCY JOSEPHINE, JUNE 6TH 1870! 'I'LL SLEEP TODAY PAPA.' AND SO SHE DID! 'TIS EVER THUS, THE NOBLEST, PUREST BEST, THE MOST BELOVED ARE EARLIEST CALLED TO REST!!'"

unto God—and purify my heart—for thy sake I besought God with greater faith and ferver on behalf of all children. & my sympathy was aroused more keenly for those bereaved. Thy bright Spirit lighted all my cares, and made all earth to me, seem good. O! my darling how I miss thee.

I was obliged to go to the E[ndowment] H[ouse] and, as I was about leaving I said, 'My baby look at papa and kiss me once more,' and She threw up her little arms, as if to clasp my neck, and Smiled Oh, how sweetly. And then how Sad. And kissed me. This was her last <u>kiss</u> for 'papa.' I went to the E[ndowment] H[ouse] attended to the lectures, and [sealed] 7 coups. . . . when I went home and found my loved darling sweet cherub asleep. Alas. That last long 'sleep,' and my heart was almost broken. O! the bitter grief that wrung my very soul. Not that she slept—not that she had gon to heaven, not that she had escaped the woes of earth, but that the light Joy and glory of my heart and Home, had faded from my Sight. My little earthly angel gon, my heaven on earth removed, the bright star of my hopes obscured, darkening all the [horoscope?] of my mortal existence. My heart rent to the core, the tenderest fibers shred by the cold & cruel hand of death. O! my Soul, how thou didst love that babe! O! God forgive me I am stricken with grief."[8]

As was the custom in pioneer Utah, Joseph F. made the necessary preparations for burial: "I called at the store with Aunt Priscinda, and then I called on bro. Jos. Taylor, to obtain materials and & coffin for burial. I obtained a very beautiful one with glass top almost the whole length—cost 14$. I telegraphed to Julina's mother, and made arrangements for funeral to take place tomorrow at 2 P.M."[9]

The following day, Joseph F. recorded:

"Mary S. is just 8 months old to day, & she was born Just 8 months after the birth of my little Sarah Ella, who died the 6th day after she was born, and now my own sweet Josephine is to be laid away. I spent the fore noon, in grief at home, At 2 P.M. quite a large number of my friends came in. meeting was opened by sing, prayer & singing—when Prest. Geo. A. Smith made a few remarks & was followed by bro. Geo. Q. Cannon, both speaking very comfortingly. We then proceeded to the cemetery and deposited our little treasure in her last long resting place on earth. O! Sleep my babe, in peace, but in thy spirit visit me, let thy sweet purifying influence Still be over me, in thy sleepless, immortal life watch over us. Thy 'papa,' thy 'mama.' 'Little Sister' and 'Aunt Sarah.' Oh forsake us not, and give me to <u>feel</u> that thou art nigh. and bring with you 'little Sister Ella' with whose sweet spirit you have met. I have one on earth & two in heaven. O! how desolate my home, yet here are 'mama,' 'baby' and 'Aunt Sara.' and 'Edward,' I love them none the less because I love my 'Dodo' more.

Julina seems to miss her more now she is buried. & grieves very much. Oh, her little toys, & vacant chair!"[10]

On 8 June, he noted: "I wrote the following to put on to 'Dodo's' grave stone. 'In memory of Mercy Josephine—daughter of Joseph F. & Julina Smith born Aug. 14, 1867. Died June 6th 1870. 'I'll Sleep today, papa'—and another treasure was laid up in heaven. . . . This every thus, the brightest, purest, best, The most beloved are earliest called to rest."[11]

Years later, Julina provided this insight about Joseph F.'s feelings regarding Mercy Josephine's death:

"He loved them all, but never got over losing his firstborn. She was an extra bright child and clung to her papa. She always ran to meet him and would ask so many questions that sometimes he would almost tire of answering. She came to us when he needed comfort, and she filled the bill, although when she died we had another baby girl, Mamie, which he used to take in his arms, walk the floor and cry. I have had eleven children; he has loved them all with as great a love as human could, but he never got where he could talk of his 'Dodo' without tears in his eyes."[12]

The result of such experiences caused Joseph F. to be a most devoted father to his children, especially when they were ill. On one occasion, while away from home, he received notice that one of his children was sick. Joseph F. wrote to Julina: "I received this morning your penciled letter of 26th and 28th. I had just sent you a letter written yesterday. Your letter this morning has almost 'broke me up.' I am of course, as you well know, almost useless when anything ails the children. O! I hope all will be well with them and you. I feel now that you will get along, but I cannot help worrying."[13]

He added: "If I am not mistaken, Alvin was the last one of the children who had the scarlet fever. If so, then Joseph, David, George, Wesley, Nerva, Alice, Willard, and Melissa, as well as Ina are in danger.

O! my soul, what could you do with half a dozen or more of them, all sick and that terrible disease. Heaven have mercy upon us and deliver us from affliction and sorrow.... Well what can I do? If I was there I could not do much, and might be in the way, but it is hard to know my pets are sick and I cannot minister to them."[14]

Personal trials brought to Joseph F.'s character a sincere and deep compassion for others in similar distress. One such example is found in a letter to Joseph H. Dean, a missionary in Hawaii, when Joseph F. wrote him in 1888:

"I heard with deep sympathy of the death of your baby at home. I knew how to sympathize, for I passed thro' the same kind of bitter experience myself while there.... The Lord truly knows best and we know that the innocents who have been recalled from earth, so soon after their coming untainted by the sordid elements of this fallen world, return to Him from whom they came, pure and holy, redeemed from the foundation, by the sacrifice of one who said 'of such is the kingdom of heaven.' My most earnest, heartfelt prayer is, O! God help me to live and be worthy to join my innocent children in their home with thee!"[15]

PLATE 20
JOSEPH F. SMITH, CA. 1869
EDWARD MARTIN, LDSCA. THIS RARE PORTRAIT BY EDWARD MARTIN CAPTURES JOSEPH F. SMITH SEVERAL YEARS BEFORE HE BEGAN WEARING A BEARD CONTINUOUSLY.

Marriage to Edna Lambson (January 1871)

On 1 January 1871, Joseph F. married Edna Lambson, sister of his wife Julina. Joseph F. and Edna had ten children, of whom six died before Joseph F.'s death in 1918: Hyrum Mack, born 21 March 1872 (died 23 January 1918); Alvin Fielding, born 7 August 1874; Alfred Jason, born 13 December 1876 (died 6 April 1878); Edna Melissa, born 6 October 1879; Albert Jesse, born 16 September 1881 (died 25 August 1883); Robert, born 12 November 1883 (died 4 February 1886); Emma, born 21 August 1888; Zina, born 11 October 1890 (died 25 October 1915); Ruth, born 21 December 1893 (died 17 March 1898); and Martha, born 12 May 1897.

More Missions to England (1874–1875 and 1877)

At the October 1873 general conference, Joseph F. was called by President Young on another mission. This time, he was appointed to preside over the European Mission.

In April 1877, President Young appointed Joseph F. to return to England as the presiding officer of the European Mission again. During this missionary assignment, he was able to have Sarah accompany him. His cousin Alma L. Smith and Charles W. Nibley also went with him. A long and trusted friendship developed with C. W. Nibley.

Joseph F. recalled: "Between the spring of 1874 and the fall of 1877 I filled two more missions to Europe, where I was called to preside; being summoned home in 1875 on account of the death of President Geo. A. Smith, and in 1877 on account of the death of President Brigham Young."[16]

PLATE 21
JOSEPH F. SMITH, CA. 1874
C. W. CARTER, LDSCA.

PLATE 22 (LEFT)
CHURCH HEADQUARTERS, LIVERPOOL, ENGLAND, CA. 1880

C. R. SAVAGE, LDSCA. THE BUILDING, LOCATED AT 42 ISLINGTON STREET, SERVED AS THE HEART OF THE MISSION FROM 1855 TO 1904.

PLATE 23 (RIGHT)
JOSEPH F. SMITH, CA. MAY 1874, COPENHAGEN, DENMARK

LDSCA. A NOTATION ON THE BACK OF THIS IMAGE STATES: "DIARY ENTRY STATES MAY 27, 1874; IN COPENHAGEN," BUT ANOTHER NOTATION INDICATED IT WAS TAKEN ON 25 MAY.

PLATE 24 (OPPOSITE PAGE)
JOSEPH F. SMITH, 25 SEPTEMBER 1874

RICHARD BROWN AND A. VANDYKE, LIVERPOOL, LDSCA.
JOSEPH F. SMITH INSCRIBED THIS IMAGE TO A FRIEND: "YOURS TRULY. JOS. F. SMITH."

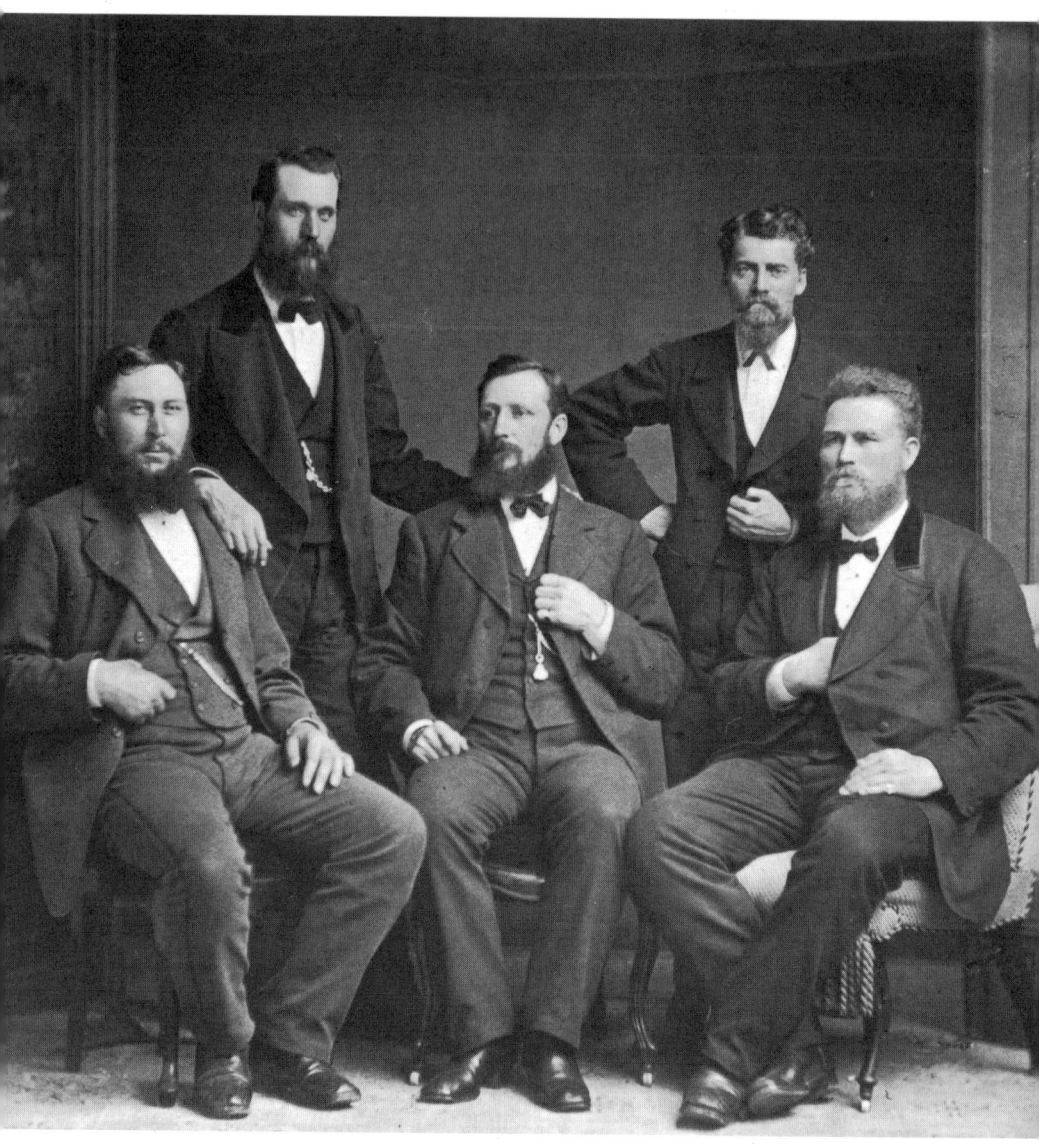

PLATE 25

JOSEPH F. SMITH AND EUROPEAN MISSIONARIES, 27 MAY 1875, COPENHAGEN, DENMARK

LDSCA. FROM LEFT: JOHN H. SMITH, E. G. FREEMAN, JOSEPH F. SMITH, MILTON H. HARDY, FRANCIS M. LYMAN. WHEN ORIGINALLY PUBLISHED IN JOSEPH FIELDING SMITH'S *LIFE OF JOSEPH F. SMITH* (1933), THE CAPTION IDENTIFIED E. G. FREEMAN AS SAMUEL H. B. SMITH. ANOTHER COPY OF THE PHOTOGRAPH, LOCATED IN THE UTAH STATE HISTORICAL SOCIETY, ALSO SHOWS THIS INDIVIDUAL AS SAMUEL H. B. SMITH. THE WRITING ON THIS IMAGE APPEARS TO BE IN A NINETEENTH-CENTURY HAND, CONTEMPORARY WITH THE ACTUAL SITTING.

The Death of Brother Brigham (August 1877)

Unexpectedly, Joseph F. was summoned home following the death of President Young in August 1877. Joseph F. and Sarah arrived in Salt Lake City on 27 September. At this time he was appointed, along with three other members of the Twelve, to form a committee to resolve problems regarding the settlement of the Brigham Young estate.

A Special Church History Mission (1878)

A year later, in September 1878, Joseph F. and Orson Pratt left Salt Lake City for a very unusual mission. President John Taylor, Wilford Woodruff, George Q. Cannon, and A. Carrington set them apart to "take a mission to the states to gather up records and data relative to the early history of the Church."[17]

They traveled to Mormon historical sites in Missouri, Illinois, Ohio, and New York. While there, the two apostles interviewed William E. McLellin, David Whitmer, and Jacob Whitmer. Joseph F. noted of this trip: "In 1878 I accompanied Brother Pratt to the states during which trip we called upon David Whitmer at Richmond, and upon William E. McLellin at Independence, Missouri; also touching at Far West, Plano and Kirtland. At New York I wrote an account of our journey for publication, and returned home in time to attend the October conference."[18]

Joseph F. enjoyed interviewing David Whitmer, who eventually became the most interviewed witness of the Book of Mormon. Joseph F. was moved by his "strong and undeviating testimony to the truth of the Book of Mormon.... Nothing could be more earnest, more sincere, than that aged man's solemn affirmation that he saw the angel and heard his voice declaring that the characters upon those plates had been divinely translated."[19]

Joseph F.'s visit with former apostle William E. McLellin was less uplifting. Joseph F. noted: "[He] seemed to be all unsettled in his feelings and convictions, at one moment praising the Prophet Joseph to the skies, and at the next casting reflections upon him and the other Church leaders of his period. I never saw the sad effects of apostasy more plainly manifested."[20]

New First Presidency (October 1880)

On 10 October 1880, Joseph F. became the second counselor in the First Presidency to President John Taylor at the age of forty-one. He served with George Q. Cannon, an association that lasted until 1901, when President Cannon died. As one historian noted, "Selecting Joseph F. Smith was an inspired stroke, for the outspoken young apostle would now work directly in the new First Presidency, where for twenty-one years he gained invaluable experience before becoming Church president in 1901."[21]

Second Counselor in the First Presidency

OCTOBER — 1880

PLATE 26
LDS CHURCH FIRST PRESIDENCY, CA. 1880

LDSCA. FROM LEFT: GEORGE Q. CANNON, JOHN TAYLOR, AND JOSEPH F. SMITH. THESE THREE MEN FACED SOME OF THE GREATEST CHALLENGES TO CONFRONT THE LATTER-DAY SAINTS DURING THE SECOND HALF OF THE NINETEENTH CENTURY. EARLIER, THE CHURCH STRUGGLED TO SURVIVE MOB ATTACKS, EXTERMINATION ORDERS, THE DEATHS OF THEIR LEADERS, AND A CONFRONTATION WITH FEDERAL OFFICIALS. HOWEVER, IT WAS DURING THE 1880S THAT THE ENTIRE UNITED STATES GOVERNMENT, WITH THE GENERAL SUPPORT OF THE MAJORITY OF THE CITIZENS OF THE COUNTRY, MOVED TO DESTROY THE CHURCH.

ANOTHER PROPHECY (JANUARY 1881)

This important period of Church service was another stage of preparation for Joseph F.'s future responsibilities. Those responsibilities were revealed again to the Saints during a stake conference meeting in Ogden. In January 1881, Joseph F. accompanied Wilford Woodruff to visit Weber County, several miles north of Salt Lake City. While

> *... would be President of the Church of Jesus Christ of Latter Day Saints in his Day.*

there, they attended the stake quarterly conference held on Saturday and Sunday, 22–23 January. Wilford Woodruff noted in his journal, reflecting events in the morning service: "Statistics of the Stake read. Then Joseph F. Smith spoke in much power for one hour and 35 M[inutes]."[22]

In the afternoon session, Wilford Woodruff addressed the Saints: "Bore testimony to the work of God and what Joseph F. Smith had said and . . . his remarks . . . [and declared] Joseph F. Smith was One of the first Presidency and would be Preside[n]t of the Church of Jesus Christ of Latter Day Saints in his DAY."[23]

Marriages to Alice Ann Kimball and Mary Taylor Schwartz (1883 and 1884)

President John Taylor asked Joseph F. to increase his family obligations by marrying two additional plural wives. On 6 December 1883, Joseph F. married Alice Ann Kimball, daughter of President Heber C. Kimball. They raised seven children, four of whom were their own. The children were Alice May, born 11 October 1877; Heber Chase, born 19 November 1881; Charles Coulson, born 19 November 1881; Lucy Mack, born 14 April 1890; Andrew Kimball, born 6 January 1893; Jesse Kimball, born 21 May 1896; and Fielding Kimball, born 9 April 1900.

PLATE 27
JOSEPH F. SMITH, CA. 1880
C. R. SAVAGE, USHS (PHOTO #13685).

Plate 28
Joseph F. Smith, ca. 1880
C. R. Savage, Ashworth Collection.

Plate 29
Alice Ann Kimball (Smith), ca. 1880
Nichols Collection. Joseph F. Smith married Alice Ann Kimball on 6 December 1883.

PLATE 30
MARY TAYLOR SCHWARTZ SMITH, CA. 1884
NICHOLS COLLECTION. JOSEPH F. SMITH MARRIED MARY TAYLOR SCHWARTZ ON 13 JANUARY 1884.

Joseph F. married his last plural wife, Mary Taylor Schwartz, in 1884. Mary was President John Taylor's niece. Sealed on 13 January 1884, the couple had seven children, one of whom died before Joseph F.'s death in 1918: John Schwartz, born 20 August 1888 (died 3 August 1889); Calvin Schwartz, born 29 May 1890; Samuel Schwartz, born 26 October 1892; James Schwartz, born 13 November 1894; Agnes, born 3 November 1897; Silas Schwartz, born 3 January 1900; and Royal Grant, born 2 May 1906.

ON THE UNDERGROUND: 1884–1891

During the difficult period of the late 1880s, Joseph F. went on the "underground" in an effort to avoid arrest by federal officers; this lasted from 1 October 1884 until 10 September 1891. It was a difficult period for Joseph F. and his family. President John Taylor was anxious to have Joseph F. far away from Utah because of his knowledge regarding the records of sealings performed in the Endowment House in Salt Lake City.

Joseph F. left Salt Lake City to begin his exile on 29 August 1884. With other Church leaders, including Erastus Snow, they visited the Saints living in eastern, central, and southern Utah, Colorado, New Mexico, Arizona, and other parts, traveling twenty-nine miles by stage coach, nearly five hundred miles by wagon, and thirty-two hundred miles by rail before ending the journey on 1 October in Salt Lake City.[24]

Because of efforts to capture him and other Church leaders at the time, Joseph F. did not attend the October general conference of the Church.

On 4 December 1884, President John Taylor specifically asked Joseph F. to "remain concealed" until arrangements could be made for

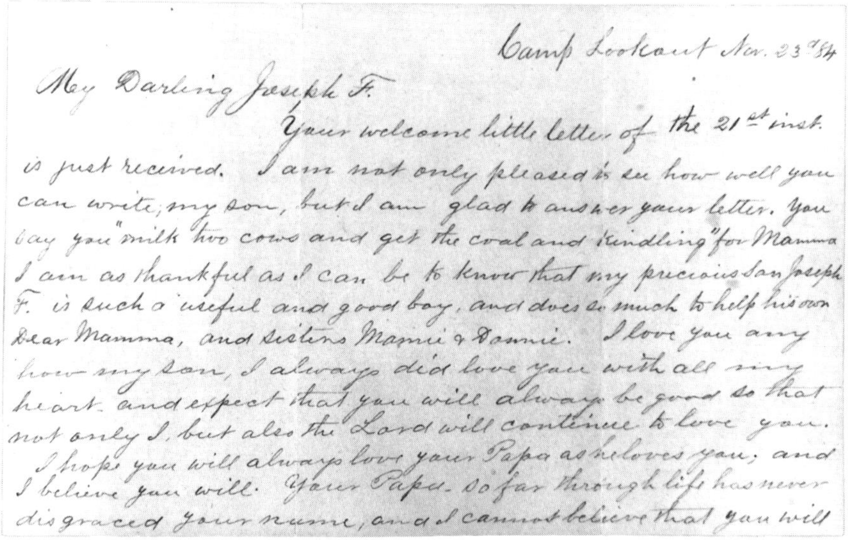

PLATE 31
PAGE OF A LETTER FROM JOSEPH F. SMITH TO JOSEPH FIELDING SMITH, DATED 23 NOVEMBER 1884

A. S. MCCONKIE COLLECTION. JOSEPH F. SMITH USED SEVERAL DESIGNATIONS FOR HIS HIDEOUTS WHILE ON THE "UNDERGROUND." THIS ONE IS IDENTIFIED AS "CAMP LOOKOUT." THIS LETTER TO HIS YOUNG SON, "MY DARLING JOSEPH F.," IS FULL OF ADVICE FOR HIS RECENTLY BAPTIZED SON.

> ever do it. I never can tell how much I love you and all my
> loving children and I pray and hope and hope and pray
> that I may live to see them all grown up to be good and
> noble men and women. You know you have been
> baptized and will soon be a big boy, and the greatest desire
> of my heart for you, my son, is that you may be a good, pure
> and wise man, so that if the Lord needs you for any good
> work in the church and Kingdom of God, you will be worthy
> of Gods pleasure and commands, and willing always to respond
> the authority of the Priesthood, and the requirements of heaven.
>   You must never swear, nor lie nor steal, nor speak evil of your
> associates or neighbors. Shun the company of swearing boys.
> never chew or smoke tobacco, nor drink whiskey nor do anything
> dishonorable. If you will shun all these evil things and love your
> Parents and your Aunties & brothers & sisters, and do good to the
> poor and needy, then Papa, & Mamma, and the Lord and every good person
> in this world and in heaven will love you and bless you. Your loving Papa.

PLATE 32
PAGE OF A LETTER FROM JOSEPH F. SMITH TO JOSEPH FIELDING SMITH, DATED 23 NOVEMBER 1884
A. S. McCONKIE COLLECTION.

---

another mission to Hawaii. After meeting privately with family members, Joseph F. bid his family good-bye.

This sad story is aptly told in his son's biography, written by Joseph F.'s grandson, Joseph Fielding Smith Jr., and John J. Steward:

"It was just a week before Christmas, December 18, 1884, but instead of it being a time of pleasant anticipation and excitement, as it should be for a youngster, it was for eight-year-old Joseph Fielding Smith a dreaded, lonely day.

"He along with his several brothers and sisters sat quietly in the big parlor of the Smith home while his father gave each of them in turn a blessing. His four 'aunties'—his father's other wives—each received a departing blessing too. But not his mother, nor his baby sister Julina, ten months old, for they were going with Papa this time, on a long journey far away, for a very long time."²⁵

However, the trip to the Hawaiian Islands was postponed. In January 1885, President John Taylor and his two counselors, George Q. Cannon and Joseph F. Smith, Elders Brigham Young, Moses Thatcher, Francis M. Lyman, Charles W. Penrose, John Q. Cannon, George Reynolds, Lot Smith, Charles Barrell, John Sharp, and Brigham Randall made their way to Denver and continued on to Pueblo where they were joined by Erastus Snow.

During the next weeks, they visited Albuquerque, St. Joseph, Woodruff, Snowflake, Taylor, Holbrook, Deming, Benson, St. David, and Nogales and crossed the Mexican border going to Magdalena, Hermosillo, Guaymas, and back to St. David. From there, the party retraced its steps, also visiting Tucson, Mesa, and other points in Arizona.

Eventually, the party continued to California, through San Bernardino, Los Angeles, and on up to Oakland and San Francisco. They considered returning to Salt Lake, but President Taylor had second thoughts and decided then and there that Joseph F. should immediately prepare for a mission to Hawaii.²⁶

*To J. F. and Susia Napukapa.
With my love. Joseph.
Laie, May 17, 1886.*

PLATE 33
JOSEPH F. SMITH, CA. 1885
C. R. SAVAGE, NEBEKER COLLECTION. JOSEPH F. SMITH INSCRIBED A GREETING IN HAWAIIAN ON THE BACK OF THIS PHOTOGRAPH, A GREETING TRANSLATED AS "TO J. F. AND SUSIA NAPUKAPA. WITH MY LOVE. JOSEPH. LAIE, MAY 17, 1886."

PLATE 34
CHURCH PLANTATION AT LAIE, CA. 1885
LDSCA. THE CHURCH PURCHASED A SIX-THOUSAND- ACRE PLANTATION AT LAIE ON THE ISLAND OF OAHU IN 1865, AND IT IMMEDIATELY BECAME A GATHERING PLACE FOR THE CHURCH. DURING HIS EXILE TO HAWAII BETWEEN 9 MARCH 1885 AND 1 JULY 1887, JOSEPH F. SMITH PERFORMED NUMEROUS ECCLESIASTICAL DUTIES AS WELL AS A SIGNIFICANT AMOUNT OF MANUAL LABOR AT THE MORMON COLONY AT LAIE. WHILE ON THE "UNDERGROUND" IN HAWAII, JOSEPH F. WAS KNOWN AS J. F. SPEIGHT.

During all the time of his third mission to Hawaii, Joseph F. directed the affairs of the Church in Hawaii. He also worried about his family and friends in Utah. On 12 February 1885, he wrote in his journal:

"Sam. Gilson and three other deputy marshals made a raid on my houses on Saturday, Feb. 7th. They found Aunt Melissa L. Smith and Albert J. Davis and subpoenaed them to appear before either commissioner McKay or the grand jury, which was not stated, but I suppose the grand jury. Bertie refused to give his name, he was subpoenaed as 'John Doe,' but up to the 12th he did not appear. Five of my children were at home at the time; three of Julina's and one each of Sarah's and Edna's, whom the deputies interrogated but could get no information from them; they refusing to give their names, telling the marshals it was 'none of their business.' Sarah and Edna and the children had to leave home to avoid being subpoenaed. Where they went was not stated. This was but one of many raids. Well and long will they be remembered by those children who were home and forced to listen to the abuse and threats of the occasion."[27]

On 25 February 1885, he wrote: "These are scary times for me and mine. God be merciful to my wives and children."[28] On 1 March, he prayed:

"O God, may this month see thy people relieved from this oppression and power and persecutions of their enemies in Zion. May all be well with my family and all the families of thy persecuted servants this morning and henceforth and forever. Unto thee, O my Father, I commend, and into Thy hands I commit my wives and my children and beseech Thee to be a present help and a Father and a Friend unto them and Thy unworthy servant in this time of oppression and need."[29]

Eventually, Joseph F. returned to Salt Lake City when news came of John Taylor's failing health. In July 1887, he arrived at the home of Thomas F. Roueche at Kaysville, Davis County, where President Taylor was in hiding. President George Q. Cannon joined him—it was the first time since December 1884 that the members of the First Presidency were together.

President Taylor died on 25 July 1887, dissolving the First Presidency. The Council of the Twelve Apostles, with President Wilford Woodruff at the head, took charge of the affairs of the kingdom.

Joseph F. later recalled these days:

"My most recent foreign mission was performed under somewhat peculiar circumstances. It began in the midst of what is known as 'the crusade' under the Edmunds law, enacted by Congress in March, 1882. Since the 10th of October, 1880, I had been second counselor in the First Presidency, and when the anti-polygamy crusade began I went with President John Taylor and other Church leaders, into exile, owing to the extreme bitterness that then prevailed. I remained 'on the underground' from October 1, 1884, to September 10, 1891, and spent much of this time in the Sandwich Islands, returning just before the death of President Taylor, July 25, 1887. I attended him during his last moments, still in exile."[30]

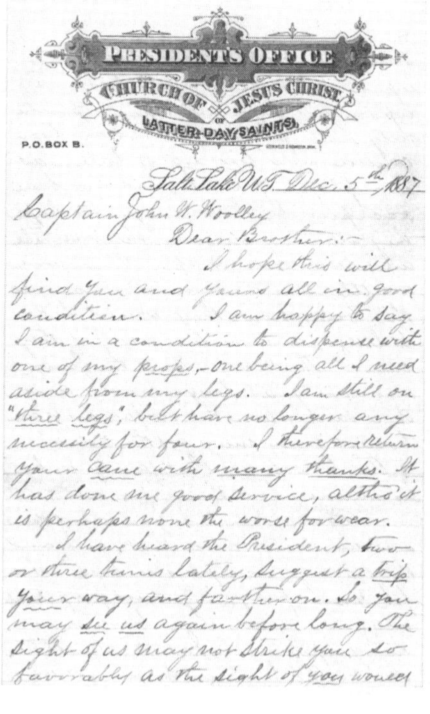

PRESIDENTS OFFICE
CHURCH OF JESUS CHRIST OF LATTER-DAY SAINTS
P.O. BOX B.

Salt Lake U.T. Dec. 5th 1887

Captain John W. Woolley
Dear Brother:—
I hope this will find you and yours all in good condition. I am happy to say I am in a condition to dispense with one of my props,—one being all I need aside from my legs. I am still on "three legs", but have no longer any necessity for four. I therefore return your cane with many thanks. It has done me good service, altho' it is perhaps none the worse for wear.
I have heard the President, two or three times lately, suggest a trip your way, and farther on. So you may see us again before long. The sight of us may not strike you so favorably as the sight of you would

PLATE 35

JOSEPH F. SMITH LETTER (PAGE ONE), DATED 5 DECEMBER 1887

ASHWORTH COLLECTION. ADDRESSED TO CAPTAIN JOHN W. WOOLLEY. JOSEPH F. TALKS ABOUT A VISIT AND OTHER MATTERS REGARDING THIS PERIOD WHEN HE WAS ON THE "UNDERGROUND."

A NEW FIRST PRESIDENCY AND THE END OF THE CONFLICT (1888–1890)

On 2 February 1888, President Woodruff decided to send Joseph F. to Washington, D.C., to help the Church. Eight days later, Wilford Woodruff, Franklin D. Richards, and George Q. Cannon blessed and set him apart for this new mission. Once again, Joseph F. left his family to serve the Lord on a mission. When he returned to Salt Lake, he remained out of the public eye.

During this time, Joseph F., using the pseudo-name of Jason Mack (the name of Joseph F. Smith's grandmother's—Lucy Mack Smith—brother), wrote John Henry Smith regarding Joseph F.'s feelings about avoiding capture by federal officers. Apparently, there were even some

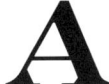

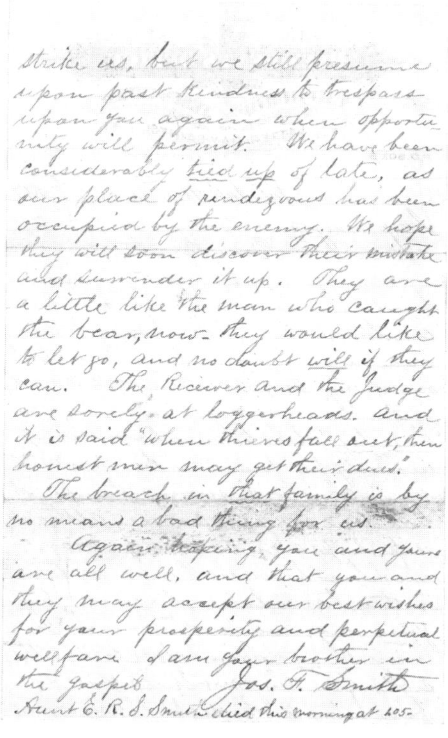
strike us, but we still presume
upon past kindness to trespass
upon you again when opportunity will permit. We have been
considerably tied up of late, as
our place of rendezvous has been
occupied by the enemy. We hope
they will soon discover their mistake
and surrender it up. They are
a little like the man who caught
the bear, now- they would like
to let go, and no doubt will if they
can. The Reciever and the Judge
are sorely at loggerheads. and
it is said "when thieves fall out, then
honest men may get their dues."
The breach in that family is by
no means a bad thing for us.
Again hoping you and yours
are all well, and that you and
they may accept our best wishes
for your prosperity and perpetual
wellfare I am your brother in
the gospel Jos. F. Smith
Aunt E. R. S. Smith died this morning at 405-

PLATE 36

JOSEPH F. SMITH LETTER (PAGE TWO), DATED 5 DECEMBER 1887

ASHWORTH COLLECTION. AT THE END OF THE LETTER, JOSEPH F. NOTED THE PASSING OF ELIZA R. SNOW, WITH THE ADDED "SMITH" BECAUSE SHE WAS THE PLURAL WIFE OF JOSEPH SMITH THE PROPHET.

Latter-day Saints who were critical of their leaders' efforts to avoid arrest. Joseph F. penned: "Now if I should be caught and thrust into the 'lions den' or the 'fiery furnace,' I hope to be able to endure it like a man. But I am not hankering after that sort of thing. I pray, 'O, My Father let this cup pass, if it be possible, but not my will, but thine be done.'"[31] A few weeks later, he wrote his brother-in-law on the same theme, adding:

"When God requires my life as he did that of my Father and uncle and the cause will be aided by it, He is welcome it. But if I can maintain my liberty and use my tongue or pen for good, and employ my free agency in helping to forward the cause, it will perhaps be as acceptable to God and the Church as to make a martyr of myself. Besides that, I

PLATE 37
JOSEPH F. SMITH AND UTAH LOBBYISTS IN WASHINGTON, D.C., 1888
LDSCA. STANDING FROM LEFT: GEORGE F. GIBBS, L. JOHN NUTTALL, AND CHARLES W. PENROSE. SEATED FROM LEFT: JOHN T. CAINE, MARGARET NIGHTINGALE CAINE, JOSEPH F. SMITH, EMILY S. RICHARDS, AND FRANKLIN S. RICHARDS.

PLATE 38
JOSEPH F. SMITH, CA. 1889–90

C. R. SAVAGE, LDSCA. JOSEPH F. SMITH APPARENTLY SENT THIS PHOTOGRAPH TO AN "AUNT." HE WROTE ON THE BOTTOM: "YOURS TRULY JOSEPH F. SMITH TO AUNT 'SEND' DEC. 25. 1893." THE PHOTOGRAPH WAS TAKEN BEFORE 1893, AS ANOTHER COPY OF THIS IMAGE, IN PRIVATE POSSESSION, WAS GIVEN "TO MY FRIENDS, OCT. 13TH 1890." ADDITIONALLY, THE INSCRIPTION ON THE BACK OF THIS PHOTOGRAPH INDICATES THAT IT WAS TAKEN DURING THE "UNDERGROUND DAYS," AGAIN SUGGESTING AN 1889–90 DATE FOR THE ORIGINAL SETTING. FINALLY, OTHER IMAGES, APPARENTLY TAKEN ON THE SAME DAY, HAVE "AGE 51" WRITTEN BY JOSEPH F., INDICATING IT WAS TAKEN BETWEEN 13 NOVEMBER 1889 AND 13 NOVEMBER 1890.

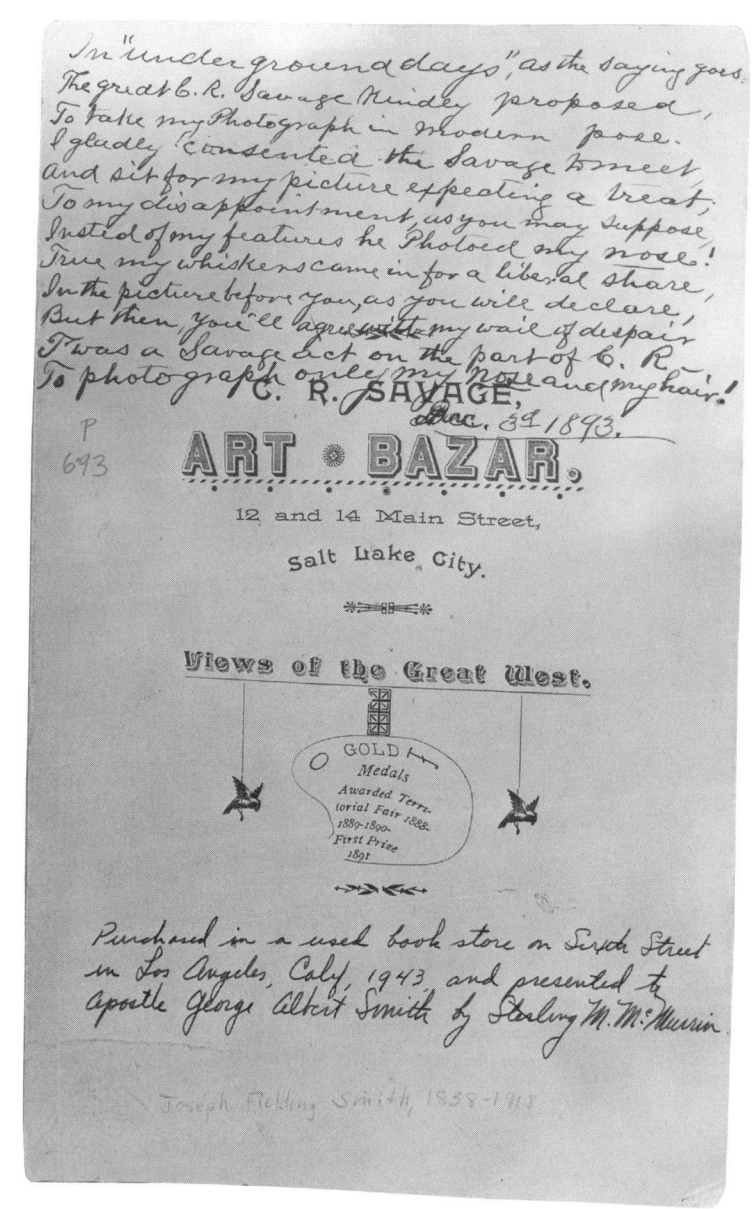

PLATE 39
BACK SIDE OF PREVIOUS PORTRAIT

LDSCA. JOSEPH F. SMITH WROTE: "IN 'UNDERGROUND DAYS,' AS THE SAYING GOES. THE GREAT C. R. SAVAGE KINDLY PROPOSED, TO TAKE MY PHOTOGRAPH IN MODERN POSE. I GLADLY CONSENTED THE SAVAGE TO MEET, AND SIT FOR MY PICTURE EXPECTING A TREAT; TO MY DISAPPOINTMENT, AS YOU MAY SUPPOSE, INSTEAD OF MY FEATURES HE PHOTOED MY NOSE! TRUE MY WHISKERS CAME IN FOR A LIBERAL SHARE, BUT THEN, YOU'LL AGREE WITH MY WAIL OF DESPAIR. T'WAS A SAVAGE ACT ON THE PART OF C. R., TO PHOTOGRAPH ONLY MY NOSE AND MY HAIR! DEC. 3D 1893."

have no hankering for the Mud Pen, nor its ordinary occupants, nor to be branded with the 'Stripes' without the 'Stars.' Still to meet the devil at his gate has a greater charm to the natural man within me, than to be beating him round the bush. I am satisfied that all will come out just right in the end."[32]

In April 1889, Joseph F. was again in Salt Lake City, when President Wilford Woodruff announced it was the will of the Lord to reorganize the First Presidency. Those in attendance sustained the move, and President Woodruff was chosen President with George Q. Cannon and Joseph F. as counselors.

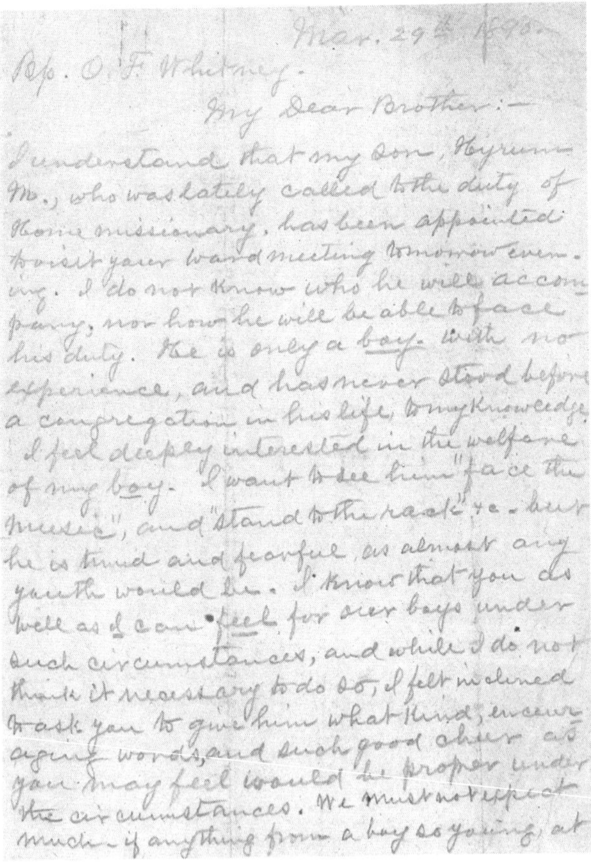
Mar. 29th 1890.
Bp. O. F. Whitney.
My Dear Brother:—
I understand that my son, Hyrum
M., who was lately called to the duty of
Home missionary, has been appointed
to visit your ward meeting tomorrow evening. I do not know who he will accompany, nor how he will be able to face
his duty. He is only a boy. with no
experience, and has never stood before
a congregation in his life, to my knowledge.
I feel deeply interested in the welfare
of my boy. I want to see him "face the
music", and "stand to the rack" &c. but
he is timid and fearful, as almost any
youth would be. I know that you as
well as I can feel for our boys under
such circumstances, and while I do not
think it necessary to do so, I felt inclined
to ask you to give him what kind, encouraging words, and such good cheer as
you may feel would be proper under
the circumstances. We must not expect
much - if anything from a boy so young, at

PLATE 40

JOSEPH F. SMITH LETTER (PAGE ONE), DATED 29 MARCH 1890

ASHWORTH COLLECTION. LETTER ADDRESSED TO SALT LAKE CITY BISHOP ORSON F. WHITNEY. APPARENTLY, JOSEPH F. AND EDNA LAMBSON SMITH'S SON, HYRUM MACK SMITH, WAS ASSIGNED AS A "HOME MISSIONARY," CORRESPONDING TO A STAKE MISSIONARY IN THE CURRENT CHURCH ORGANIZATION, AND WOULD BE SPEAKING IN THE WARD ON SUNDAY. THE LETTER DEMONSTRATES JOSEPH F.'S CONCERN FOR HIS SON, WHO WILL BECOME KNOWN AS A POWERFUL SPEAKER IN THE FUTURE.

Sometime later, President Woodruff issued the Manifesto, which began the process of ending new plural marriages in the Church. At the general conference in October 1890, the Manifesto was presented to the members of the Church and unanimously accepted by them.

This move brought relief from the persecution and prosecution by the federal government. Within a year, on 27 September 1891, Joseph F. attended conference services in the Tabernacle—the first time in seven years. It was a joyful time for him. He said:

"The house was full to the gallery. I spoke briefly, for I was so overcome by my feelings that I could scarcely restrain them. A good spirit

PLATE 41
JOSEPH F. SMITH LETTER (PAGE TWO), DATED 29 MARCH 1890
ASHWORTH COLLECTION.

PLATE 42
JOSEPH F. SMITH FAMILY MEMBERS AT HOME IN SALT LAKE CITY, 1891

EM. MARTIN, LDSCA. LOCATED AT 333 FIRST NORTH (200 NORTH) STREET, SALT LAKE CITY, THIS WAS THE CENTER OF JOSEPH F. SMITH'S WORLD UNTIL HE BECAME PRESIDENT OF THE CHURCH AND MOVED INTO THE BEEHIVE HOUSE, AT THE TIME THE HOME OF THE PRESIDENT OF THE CHURCH. PHOTOGRAPHED SOMETIME IN THE SUMMER OF 1891 BY EM. MARTIN OF SAN FRANCISCO. JULINA LAMBSON SMITH ORDERED COPIES OF THE IMAGE ON 12 JANUARY 1892, RECEIVING A COPY ON 22 JANUARY.

was present. President George Q. Cannon then addressed the meeting at length and, after a short beginning, had excellent liberty. This is a memorable day for me, and no words at my command can express my gratitude to God. I spent the evening at home. I called on Aunt Thompson, and came back to the office to sleep."[33]

The Church's general conference was held a few days later, and the entire First Presidency was present. A new day dawned.

ALT LAKE TEMPLE (1892–1893)

The First Presidency was anxious to complete the Salt Lake Temple during President Woodruff's administration. A great and glorious event occurred when the capstone was laid on 6 April 1892. Within the year, plans were made to dedicate the building. All the General Authorities gathered with the Saints in the upper auditorium of the temple on 6 April 1893 to dedicate the building to the Lord.

One of the participants provided this word-picture of Joseph F. at the first dedication service in the temple: "Prest. Joseph F. Smith also expressed his feelings, he too was melted and sobbed & wept like a child before the assembled hosts of Israel."[34] Another participant noted: "Prest. Joseph F. Smith spoke 12 minutes very feeling, the congregation melted to tears at his words and spirit I never felt so well in my life. I cannot express my feelings."[35] A local newspaper provides the summary of his remarks on this occasion:

"President Joseph F. Smith spoke of the great amount of work that had been done upon the Temple since April, 1892. It had been accomplished by the labor and offerings of the Saints. He also alluded in terms of commendation to the efficient services of Architect Joseph Don Carlos Young, and the assiduous labors, faith, persistency and watchfulness of Bishop John R. Winder, who was entitled to the gratitude and blessing of the whole people, and he, the speaker, pronounced a blessing upon him to endure in time and eternity. President Smith next spoke of the united condition of the Priesthood and of the nature of his feelings, which were deeply stirred and many of the congregation were also moved to tears. In response to a request made by him for an expression as to whether those present felt that the Lord had accepted of the house dedicated to Him, a tremendous and unanimous shout was given.

The [Spirit] of God filled the house during the services."[36]

PLATE 43
JOSEPH F. SMITH, CA. 1893
CHARLES ELLIS JOHNSON, BYU (P-6/3524). COPY PRINT REPRODUCED FROM THE ORIGINAL GLASS-PLATE NEGATIVE (NOTE CRACK).

PLATE 44
Joseph F. Smith, ca. 1893
Charles Ellis Johnson, BYU (P-418). Copy print reproduced from the original glass-plate negative (note crack).

PLATE 45
LDS CHURCH FIRST PRESIDENCY, 6 APRIL 1893
SAINSBURY AND JOHNSON, USHS (PHOTO 00043B).
FROM LEFT: GEORGE Q. CANNON, WILFORD WOODRUFF, AND JOSEPH F. SMITH.

On 8 April 1893, Joseph F. provided his feelings about the cessation of plural marriages and the eternal covenant that he entered into with his wives: "Now if any man shall forsake and abandon his loved ones, he shall wither away and die. Obey the laws of the land but do not forsake your covenants."[37]

In this same session he said "that every man, woman, and child who were living in a manner so that they knew that their lives were acceptable to God, would know that this house is accepted. Was pleased to witness the completion of this house not withstanding the predictions of apostates that it would never be completed. Advised the people 'to prophesy not evil concerning Zion.' Had seen this house in the hands of the enemy. The leaders were in exile. . . . The people hedged about on every hand. Now everyone was at his post. Who had brought about this change? God Almighty."[38]

During the eleventh session of dedication, held on 10 April, he said: "Oh that Pres. Joseph Smith could have lived to see the little that we have accomplished in the erection of this house."[39]

On 12 April, Joseph F. spoke: "I have felt as though my heart would burst during these services, I have felt so full of joy. . . . There is no reason why we should not have the ministration of angels if we were worthy. If you have carried bitterness here in your hearts, go out from here without it."[40]

In his remarks on 16 April, Joseph F. "read from Sec. 110 of the Doc. & Cov. For every gift, and every blessing which we enjoy we should be thankful. The door of the Gospel is open to every creature whether white or black. This is the sixth temple, but it is not the end. There is a temple to be built in the center Stake of Zion which will surpass this as much as this surpasses others."[41]

At a special meeting held on 20 April for priesthood leaders, Joseph F. spoke to those gathered in the celestial room before the sacrament was administered: "We lose nothing in remaining here waiting on the Lord. We must learn to wait upon the people, the Spirit of the Lord has reclaimed us from the cares of the world. The love of God casts out all bitterness, I am the brother of Christ. I love you because the Lord can speak through you and save the people. God is love, we must love God and our neighbour, read from 3rd Nephi how Jesus administered the sacrament, how we are to eat and drink in the presence of God, oh what joy." At the end of the meeting, Joseph F. arose and blessed those present:

"May peace be unto you, may the Holy Ghost never forsake you, may you be true and faithful and come up on the morning of the first resurrection with your wives, children and your children's children to reign among the Gods. The Circle formed today was the largest ever formed in this dispensation. He said the sins of the brethren were forgiven them, they would remember this day and that they were one of the 115 privileged and blessed."[42]

In addition to addressing the assembled Saints in the upper floor of the temple, Joseph F. also read the prayer of dedication at the 7 April morning session, 13 April morning session, and 23 April afternoon session.

During a special Friday evening dedication service, Emma Bennett of Provo, Utah, arrived early to stand in line as nearly twenty-five hundred Saints waited at the gates of the Temple Block. She was in her last month of pregnancy at the time. In the same group of Saints, another sister, Amanda P. Savage Cook, a midwife from Garden City, Utah, noticed the young, pregnant woman. As they conversed, Sister

Bennett confided to Sister Cook that "maybe she should not have come." She admitted that she had been "so anxious to be at the dedication that she had taken the chance." The experienced and kind midwife assured Emma that if "she should need any help, she should call for her and she would help."[43]

The services began at eight o'clock in the evening. President Woodruff offered the prayer of dedication, the choir sang the hymn, "The Spirit of God," and the congregation joined together in the sacred "Hosanna Shout" as the meeting proceeded. For Emma Bennett, the evening ended in a dramatic and unexpected way. Sometime before 10 p.m., she began to feel labor begin. She quickly signaled Sister Cook that her time had come. The experienced midwife escorted the young woman from the main Assembly Hall to a side room nearby. As Sister Bennett lay on the floor "fast in labor," another

PLATE 46
EMMA BENNETT AND SON, JOSEPH TEMPLE BENNETT, CA. 1893
COPY PRINT FROM UNKNOWN SOURCE, BALLS COLLECTION. BENJAMIN AND EMMA BENNETT OF PROVO WERE THE PARENTS OF A YOUNG BOY, BORN DURING ONE OF THE DEDICATION SESSIONS AT THE SALT LAKE TEMPLE AND GIVEN A NAME AND A BLESSING BY JOSEPH F. SMITH SHORTLY THEREAFTER.

PLATE 47
JOSEPH F. SMITH AND JOHN SMITH, 4 JUNE 1895

C. R. SAVAGE, LDSCA. PATRIARCH AND FIRST PRESIDENCY COUNSELOR, JOHN AND JOSEPH F. SMITH WERE HALF BROTHERS, SONS OF HYRUM SMITH, THE MARTYRED PATRIARCH OF THE CHURCH. LATER, WHEN JOSEPH F. SMITH BECAME PRESIDENT OF THE CHURCH IN 1901, IT WAS ONLY THE SECOND TIME IN THE CHURCH'S HISTORY THAT TWO BROTHERS OCCUPIED THE POSITIONS OF PRESIDENT AND PATRIARCH OF THE CHURCH AT THE SAME TIME. ANOTHER VIEW TAKEN ON THE SAME DATE HAS PREVIOUSLY BEEN PUBLISHED.

woman entered the room and exclaimed, "What is she doing here? She can't have a baby here!" Amanda Cook replied politely, but firmly, "She can and will, because she can't be moved now."⁴⁴

Eight days later, on 15 April, Emma Bennett returned to the temple with her husband, Benjamin, and new son for a special blessing. In the blessing, Joseph F. named the baby boy Joseph Temple Bennett: Joseph after himself, Temple after the place of his birth, and Bennett after the young couple who had the privilege of having him come to them on such a special occasion in such a special place.

Trip to Alaska (July 1895)

In an effort to find some necessary relief from the heavy duties resting upon him, President Wilford Woodruff decided to take a trip to the Northwest. He invited his counselors, George Q. Cannon and Joseph F., to accompany him. During this trip, several photographs were taken on board a ship as they sailed along the coast of Alaska. President Woodruff noted on 15 July: "We passed the first glacier today on the east of us some ten miles away, about 500 feet high. We saw a good many ducks. It was quite cold, so we sat by the pilot house while going through the straits. In the afternoon we saw two whales sporting. At the same time we passed two ice bergs."⁴⁵

On 18 July, the group "found hundreds of ice bergs all around us. Saw a pair of porpoises plunging in ten feet down, and remaining for some time. They were about four feet long. We also [saw] several whales. It was cloudy and quite cold."⁴⁶

President Woodruff continued his narrative: "We then started for the Mina Glacier. The whole ocean was covered with ice bergs, from very large ones down to small ones. The sea was covered in this way as far as the eye could see. We stayed three hours at the glacier. . . . The body of ice measured 400 feet high and 1,700 feet under water. There were huge bodies of the glacier continually breaking off."⁴⁷

On 21 July, the group held a meeting aboard ship: "President George Q. Cannon spoke, and Prest Jos. F. Smith prayed. Mr. Sterling spoke in the evening. The captain took the steamer up Gardner Inlet or the passengers to see the water falls. The scenery there was wonderful. The largest fall fell some 500 feet."⁴⁸

PLATE 48
LDS CHURCH LEADERS IN ALASKA, 13–22 JULY 1895
RLUA (ACCESSION #97-196-04). FROM LEFT: CAPTAIN ROBERTS, JOSEPH F. SMITH, GEORGE Q. CANNON, WILFORD WOODRUFF, AND GUS NORTH (FIRST MATE).

PLATE 49
LDS CHURCH LEADERS IN ALASKA, 13–22 JULY 1895
RLUA (ACCESSION #97-196-05). FROM RIGHT: JOSEPH F. SMITH AND GEORGE Q. CANNON.

President Woodruff continued to struggle with his health. On 22 July, he noted: "I have been greatly distressed in my health for the last three nights. Presidents Cannon and Smith administered to me this morning."[49] The party returned to Utah, arriving in Salt Lake City on 27 July 1895. The next days, weeks, months, and years were filled with heavy responsibilities. The Church was still under economic stress resulting from the persecution and prosecution of its members and leaders at the hands of the government.

A Letter to a Friend (November 1895)

In 1895, Joseph F. wrote Susa Young Gates, a longtime associate. The letter is enlightening on several accounts, not the least of which is his sincere humility. It is no more evident than in the opening lines of this personal correspondence:

"My Dear Sister, Susa Y. Gates:—Your very welcome letter of the 9th inst. I found awaiting me this morning on my return from attending the Bear Lake Stake Conference. I thank you sincerely for the warm, sisterly affection and confidence expressed and implied therein toward me and my honored and beloved superiors and associates. I feel assured that your

PLATE 50
Joseph F. and Mary Taylor Schwartz Smith Family, CA. 1895
NICHOLS COLLECTION. FROM LEFT: MARY TAYLOR SCHWARTZ, CALVIN, SAMUEL, JAMES, AND JOSEPH F. SMITH.

PLATE 51
JOSEPH F. AND EDNA LAMBSON SMITH FAMILY, CA. 1895
NICHOLS COLLECTION. FRONT FROM LEFT: ZINA, JOSEPH F., RUTH, EDNA L., AND EMMA.
BACK FROM LEFT: HYRUM, MELISSA, AND ALVIN.

PLATE 52
JOSEPH F. SMITH AND SONS, CA. 1898
C. R. SAVAGE, LDSCA. JOSEPH F. IS SEATED IN THE MIDDLE OF NINE OF HIS SONS, INCLUDING DAVID A., JOSEPH FIELDING, ALVIN F., GEORGE C., HYRUM M., E. WESLEY, FRANKLIN R., WILLARD R., AND JOSEPH R.

confidence and friendship are not displaced so far, at least, as relates to our file-leaders. Personally I thank you with all my heart for your 'love, faith and blessing,' and, unworthy as I am, by the help of the Lord I will constantly endeavor to prove myself worthy of the belief that my greatest desire is to serve God and His people, as an honest man. However much I may lack ability or err in Judgment let no one doubt the rectitude of my purpose, nor the sincerity of my heart."[50]

A Letter to a Missionary Son (May 1896)

In a modern day, society would have excused Joseph F. from virtually all responsibilities as an adult based on a difficult childhood.

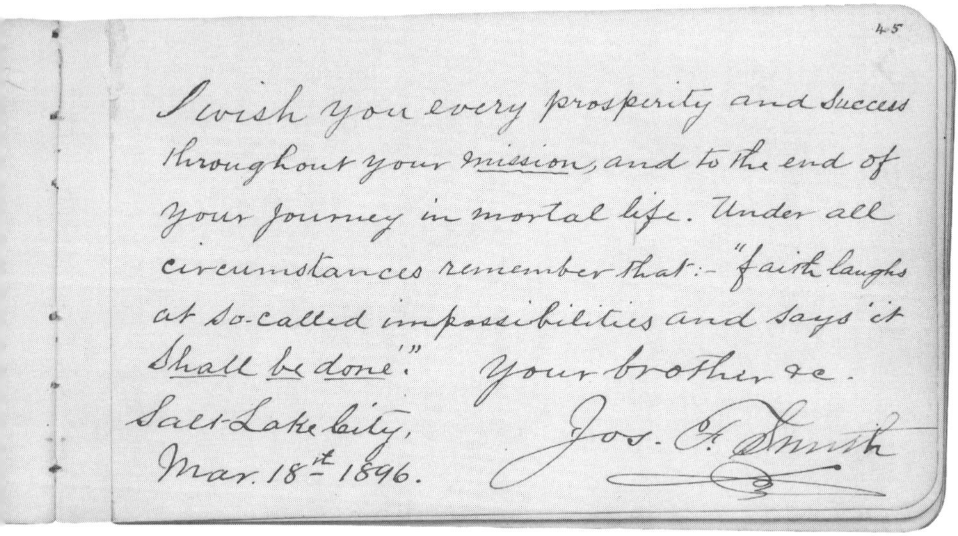
45

I wish you every prosperity and Success throughout your mission, and to the end of your journey in mortal life. Under all circumstances remember that:- "faith laughs at so-called impossibilities and says 'it Shall be done'." Your brother &c.

Salt Lake City, Mar. 18th 1896.

Jos. F. Smith

PLATE 53

Joseph F. Smith's Greeting in L. C. Snow's Autograph Album, Dated 18 March 1896

Ashworth Collection. Many people owned autograph albums during this period, and it was customary to have friends, relatives, and notable individuals sign an album. This inscription is to LeRoi C. Snow, President Lorenzo Snow's son.

However, Joseph F. did not excuse himself and sought to change and improve as he grew to manhood. This is one of the most remarkable aspects of his life—truly he wanted to become a Saint. In two frank letters to a missionary son, Joseph F. attempted to help the zealous missionary reign in his actions that may have been against the spirit of the gospel. The advice, as revealed in the letters, came from his own personal experiences.

The first letter deals with Joseph F.'s encounter with an English mob while on his first mission to the British Isles:

"I never but once was the cause of a disturbance. That was in Sheffield, during my first experience in speaking in English. (Previous to that I had been to the Islands.) We had a large audience. . . . I said that 'the authority of the Apostles of today was the same as that held by the Apostles of Christ's day, and that the word of the modern Apostles was as good as the word of ancient Apostles.' Somebody in the audience cried out 'blasphemy!' This was too much for my boyish temper to bear; the proposition I had made seemed so clear, so plain and so indisputable to my mind, I could not brook a shout of 'blasphemy,' and I let loose on my opponent, upon apostate Christianity, hireling ministers, and upon those who opposed the truth in general, in my best licks, and by the time I got through, I had stirred up the emissaries of his Satanic Majesty until they were red-hot, and the parrot and monkey show began in good shape! Bro. Gibson tried to quell the riot, but the excited mob would not listen to him—would not hear any more, and made for our stand! We slipped through the crowd, and made for home. But some of the leaders were aching to get hold of me, and hung round for hours to get a chance. Well, this experience taught me a good lesson. Thereafter I moderated my fervor—

became more diplomatic in the presence of a mixed crowd, and avoided showing any temper when reviled. In fact I learned to be reviled without reviling back again, to take an insult without retorting, except in meekness and gentlemanly candor."[51]

In another letter, Joseph F. provides another story with his advice about contention with those holding different religious views:

"There is great difference between reasoning and contention.

Discussion nearly always runs into contention, and that is not of the Lord, nor at all wise. I can understand you well, and I know how hard it is to decline a banter to discuss questions. I have been in it myself, and your disposition is much like my own. Experience has taught me that where calm statements of fact, and mild reasoning, will not prevail or succeed, there is no use to enter into discussions and arguments. . . . You must take care that your earnestness be not carried to the extent, as mine has often been, to be mistaken for anger. Of course you will have to learn by experience all these things."[52]

As part of this long letter, Joseph F. provided his son with an enlarged view of missionary work:

"We should always aim to help them to victory—not to defeat them! Our aim is life eternal—our object to lift up mankind—not to debase them. The enemy of the truth always seeks to dishonor and debase the truth and its advocates, the friend of truth who would pursue a similar course descends to the level of the enemy of truth at least in his efforts, and so far is no wiser, nor better than he."[53]

Joseph F.'s copy letter books are filled with hundreds of such letters to his missionary sons. Because they were away from home on missions they often received more letters than their sisters. However, there are letters to wives and daughters who were away from him when he was

THE QUORUM OF THE TWELVE AND THE FIRST PRESIDENCY

gone on missions and while on the underground. There even are letters for daughters who were away from Salt Lake City, as is the case of his daughter Donnette. In the first letter written following his departure for New York City, Joseph F. wrote: "To my Darling Daughter Donnette: Scarcely an hour has passed since I parted you at the station that I have not thought about you."⁵⁴

NEW FIRST PRESIDENCY (SEPTEMBER 1898)

PLATE 54
LDS CHURCH FIRST PRESIDENCY AND COUNCIL OF THE TWELVE, CA. 1898
FOX AND SYMONS, LDSCA.

PLATE 55
LDS CHURCH FIRST PRESIDENCY, POSSIBLY 10 OCTOBER 1898
FOX AND SYMONS, LDSCA. FROM LEFT: GEORGE Q. CANNON, LORENZO SNOW, AND JOSEPH F. SMITH.

PLATE 56
JOSEPH F. AND SARAH ELLEN RICHARDS SMITH FAMILY, CA. 1898
FOX AND SYMONS, NICHOLS COLLECTION. FRONT FROM LEFT: FRANKLIN, LEONORA, JOSEPH F., ASENATH, SARAH ELLEN RICHARDS, AND JEANETTA. BACK FROM LEFT: WILLARD, ALICE, JOSEPH RICHARDS, AND MINERVA.

PLATE 57
JOSEPH F. SMITH FAMILY, 13 NOVEMBER 1898

FOX AND SYMONS, LDSCA. JOSEPH F. SMITH'S FAMILY, INCLUDING HIS FIVE WIVES SEATED CENTER FROM LEFT: MARY TAYLOR SCHWARTZ, EDNA LAMBSON, JULINA LAMBSON, JOSEPH F., SARAH ELLEN RICHARDS, AND ALICE ANN KIMBALL. APPARENTLY TAKEN ON JOSEPH F. SMITH'S SIXTIETH BIRTHDAY CELEBRATION IN SALT LAKE CITY, UTAH.

President Wilford Woodruff died 2 September 1898 in San Francisco. However, the length of time between the death of the President of the Church and the reorganization of the First Presidency was not delayed, as had been the custom in the past. On 13 September, just eleven days following President Woodruff's death, Lorenzo Snow was sustained as President of the Church. He chose George Q. Cannon and Joseph F. to serve as counselors.

Missionary Calls and Recommendations (1900–1901)

During his service as counselor to Lorenzo Snow, Joseph F. responded to missionary calls and recommendations as a member of the Missionary Committee. He made notes at the bottom of letters received from prospective missionaries. These responses provide insights into Joseph F.'s personality; the comments demonstrate especially his concern for the condition of a man's family, economic situation, level of literacy and gospel competence, and personal feeling toward the gospel.

A member of the Church from St. Johns, Arizona, wrote in early 1900: "It is something over a year since I received a call to the Northern States. At the time I received my call, I was in the service of Volunteer Army of the United States. At that time I wrote you, that I would be glad to accept the mission as soon as I could get my discharge and get ready, but did not know at that time when I would get my discharge." Joseph F. wrote: "This is very good, If he is needed in or consigned to any of the U.S. missions July will be all right. Let him be appointed to the field where he is or will be most needed. J. F. S."[55]

A Brother Morse, who was willing to serve, had his bishop respond to a mission call. Brother Morse did not know how to read or write. Joseph F. wrote: "Let him, bro. Morse, be honorably excused from going on a mission. But the one who recommended him for a mission should not be so excused, provided he knew bro. Morse's condition. J. F. S."[56]

In March, Parley Peterson Jr. wrote:

"In response to your letter of inquiry I can find no reasonable excuse except that I am ignorant of the first principles of the gospel having never taken active parts in Young Men's Mutual, Sunday

Schools or Priesthood meetings always having been very indifferent as to religious matter. I am also very ignorant in every respect not having attended school for five years. But I am willing to start to school and try to become interested in my religion and try also to make something of myself as I think this was the object of the local authorities in sending my name."

Joseph F. responded: "Very good, I hope he will profit by this opportunity to study the gospel. I suppose he will go to school in Ephraim, if not, in Provo. He does not say where. We shall expect further word when he has taken his courses. J. F. S."[57]

One Latter-day Saint responded to a call, indicating he was "not capeabal af goin at present. As I have not studed the bible. And have no edacation. I would be glad to be exused. For the presant. I will close hoping that the Lord will help me to do my duty at all times." Joseph F., realizing the struggle this fellow Saint had with reading and writing, responded: "Excuse him J. F. S."[58]

Utah Stake President Edward Partridge wrote the First Presidency concerning the wife of Elder Zobell, who was seeking permission to accompany her husband on a mission to Scandinavia. President Partridge noted: "She is a very fine intelligent woman and I know of no reason why she should not accompany her husband on a mission to Denmark." Joseph F. stated: "Very good, let her go with her husband. J. F. S."[59]

A sister wrote President Snow in May 1901, responding to a mission call:

"At the time [George Reynolds, secretary to the First Presidency] spoke to me about [a mission call], I thought that my father could furnish the necessary means, which I knew he would be glad to do if it were possible. Last night I received a letter from my father saying that owing to changes in circumstances which came unexpected, his means was gone and he had not enough left to pay the expenses of a mission. I spoke to Brother Brimhall about it. He told me to write and explain the circumstance, and then to do as you thought best. (Which was also the advice of my father). I am willing to go if you will sanction my going without being sure of enough money to keep me on my mission, but I am sure of some help. If it is the desire of the authorities that I should go, I have full faith that the means will be provided. I want to do what ever is in my power in helping to roll on the work of the Lord."

Joseph F. responded: "We admire her courage and her faith, May they never diminish. Still I think she had better see what arrangements, if any, she can make so soon as convenient, for means to take her to and help her while on a mission. And if she can do so to her own satisfaction she can so report. And we will make the call. J. F. S."[60]

A missionary laboring in Spokane, Washington, wrote the First Presidency asking permission to be transferred to the British Mission: "My father went to England at the same time [I began my mission], and has done an excellent work among relatives and acquaintances, and has been really impressed of late that there is a labor for me there, and is desirous of me being transferred. About the same time the impressions crossed his mind, I was also under the same impression. And I feel that such have arose from the spirit of the Lord." Joseph F. wrote George Reynolds, the secretary, "I think I would send him (bro. Astele) his release from his present mission and an appointment to Great Britain. J. F. S."[61]

In August 1901, the First Presidency received a letter from a brother living in Pocatello, Idaho, indicating that his mother had just died, that his wife's health was not good, and that he had the major responsibility to take care of his five children. Nevertheless, he noted: "I want to do the will of the Lord. Either go or stay at home." Joseph F. wrote: "What does the Bp. Say about his circumstance and the propriety of his going on a mission? If the Bp and the Ward will look after the wife & children in his absence, All right. Otherwise perhaps he ought not to go at present. Let us hear from his presiding officers. J. F. S."[62]

Letters of Fatherly Counsel (1899–1901)

During his lifetime, Joseph F. wrote hundreds of letters to family members. Now found in private family hands and in various institutional repositories, these constitute a rich source in learning more about Joseph F.'s feelings, attitudes, and concerns. Among these treasures are many letters to children serving on missions for the Church. In 1899, two of Joseph F.'s sons, Joseph Richards and Joseph Fielding, were called to the British Mission. During their service, Joseph F. often wrote them separate letters. However, when answering doctrinal questions, he sometimes sent one son a carbon copy of the letter he had written to the other.[63]

In June 1899, shortly after the arrival of Joseph Richards in England, his father wrote him a letter of encouragement:

"It was with feelings of great joy mingled with sadness that we received your favors of the 4th and 5th inst. . . . We pray for you earnestly and most sincerely desire that you may humble yourself, obtain the spirit of your calling and of the ministry to which you have been sent, that you may be instrumental in the hands of the Lord of not only convincing yourself of the truths of the Gospel of everlasting life, but that you may be instrumental in bringing others to a knowledge of the same. It is for these reasons you have been called and sent forth, and I esteem the good which may result to you through your obedience to the call, and your effort to fulfill it honorably as being of greater consequence to me and to your mother, and above all, to yourself, than to any other living creature, although you might succeed in bringing many to the knowledge of the Gospel. If you can see, by the prompting of the Holy Spirit, and also by the prompting of your own judgement that the world is in sin and in transgression of the laws of God, then it should follow that the world ought to be warned of the consequences of sin and be taught to return [to] the laws of God and to works of righteousness, and blessed indeed is he who may be the instrument in the hand of the Lord of bringing even one soul out of darkness into the light, and out of the bonds of iniquity into the marvelous liberty of the Gospel.

"Christ rules by the principle of love; God's method of ruling is by that of love, and upon the principle of intelligence he has given us our agency, he has set before us, practically speaking, the tree of knowledge of good and of evil, and in the Gospel he has pointed out to us the glorious consequences of obedience to the laws of righteousness, the partaking of the good fruit of the tree of knowledge, and of the dreadful consequences of partaking of the fruit of evil of its tree. And having pointed out the consequences, he leaves us free as individuals to choose our own course. In the language of the poet, as you will find in the hymn book, 'Know this, that every soul is free, to choose his

82nd section of the Doctrine and Covenants

course and what he'll be; for this eternal truth is given, that God will force no man to heaven. He'll call, persuade, direct him right, bless him with wisdom, love and light; in nameless ways be good and kind, but never force the human mind.'

"I would call your attention to the 82nd section of the Doctrine and Covenants, paragraph four; also paragraphs five to ten, and I pray you to remember these words: 'I the Lord am bound when ye do what I say. But when ye do not what I say, ye have no promise.' It will do no good to fast or pray unless it is with a sincere and earnest desire in the heart to learn the will of the Lord with an unalterable determination to do it. . . .

"May God bless you my boy and help you, and preserve you from the fear of the world, and help you to overcome your own timidity and to find out God, to know him, and Jesus Christ whom He hath sent into the world, whom to know is life eternal.

"With love and hope, and abiding faith, I am, Affectionately, your father, Jos. F. Smith.

"[P.S.] My own Dear Son: I had to close at this point in order to attend a meeting. . . . I know it was and is the *will* of God, our Heavenly Father that you should take this mission. And it is His will that you should succeed, but it is your duty to see and acknowledge His hand therein and to do your best to meet His will and purpose concerning it. It is also *my will, nay more,* my *earnest desire* and my *hope,* my *faith* and most *fervent prayer* to God, my Father, that you shall succeed in this mission. . . . You must not fail! And you will not, no you cannot fail, if you will but do your duty. My God, bless and help my son! Think of us. Ever. Papa."[64]

On the same day that he wrote Joseph Richards, Joseph F. wrote his other missionary son, Joseph Fielding. And while the same news from home was reported to each, such letters often contained specific counsel and direction to each, as is the case of the two letters written on 29 June 1899:

"I am glad to hear that the people of the ship treated you kindly and that you did not see any occasion to find fault with anything except the slow progress of the voyage. As for scoffing unbelievers, it is not worth your while to waste time or the energy of your thought on them. Let your mind turn as it naturally does upon the duties of your mission and calling. Do not stop to trouble yourself about what the world may think of you, or what enemies may say about you. Of one thing be sure, that is, that you are in fellowship with the Almighty, and have a conscience void of offence towards all men. Do not seek to excel men, only seek to do your duty faithfully and well, leaving all the results in the hands of the Lord. It will then be well with you both in time and in eternity. . . .

"There is nothing that could give me more joy and satisfaction than the realization which I have that you possess the spirit of the Gospel and have received the testimony of its truth. God bless you forever in this regard, my son, and cause you to develop in mind and to grow in understanding and in the knowledge of His truth until you shall know as you are known and see as you are seen. And withal, I admonish you to use judgement and cultivate patience and humility; be not censorious or arbitrary, rather be yielding and humble in your spirit and assert the truth by moral suasion and gentle fervor than by dogmatic force. Write as often as you can, not to interfere with your duties. A good letter to me will be one to all the family except Louie, who will expect to have her own correspondence from you. We want

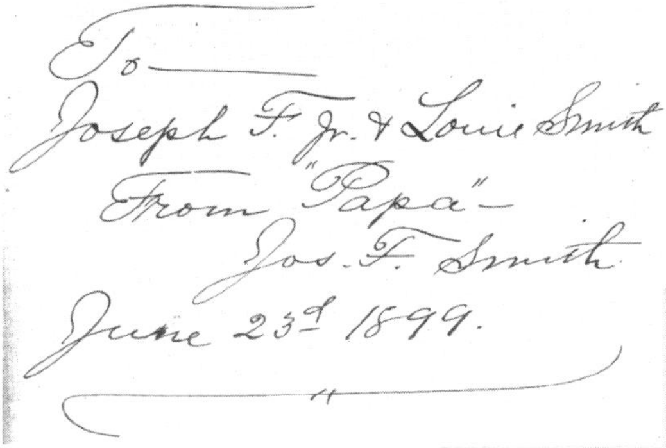

PLATE 58 (ABOVE)
JOSEPH F. SMITH'S INSCRIPTION
IN ANDREW JENSON'S CHURCH CHRONOLOGY (SALT LAKE CITY: DESERET NEWS, 1899), ASHWORTH COLLECTION. THE NOTATION TO HIS SON AND DAUGHTER-IN-LAW READS: "TO JOSEPH FIELDING AND LOUIE SMITH. FROM 'PAPA' JOS. F. SMITH. JUNE 23D 1899." JOSEPH FIELDING SMITH DEPARTED FOR A MISSION TO THE BRITISH ISLES ON 13 MAY 1899, LEAVING HIS WIFE OF JUST ONE YEAR. JOSEPH F. SMITH GAVE THIS RECENTLY RELEASED BOOK TO HIS DAUGHTER-IN-LAW WHILE HER HUSBAND WAS STILL ON HIS MISSION.

PLATE 59 (ABOVE)
JOSEPH FIELDING SMITH, CA. 1900
J. T. HILLEN, A. S. MCCONKIE COLLECTION. TAKEN DURING HIS MISSIONARY SERVICE IN ENGLAND.

her to feel that your home is not broken up. Your rooms are at her service and command at any moment, and she is welcome to come and occupy them whenever and as long as she pleases. . . . She is a good girl, and we confidently expect the Lord will bless her and you so that you both shall accomplish a glorious mission in all its fulness on the earth, and I don't want either of you to feel the least discouraged in any possible way, but to continue to put your trust in the Lord and he will most assuredly open your way. I feel so confident in my spirit in making this promise that I would almost pronounce it an inspired prediction, but never mind, we will trust in the Lord and we feel sure that He will do all things right."[65]

Several months later, Joseph F. wrote to Joseph Fielding in response to his son's letter concerning anti-Mormon activity in England, which was apparently on the increase at the time:

"I was very sorry that you have been subjected to such an unmerciful siege of mobbing in that boasted land of freedom and equal rights. I hope you will be very cautious to avoid such hornets' nests of anti-Mormonism and hatred and viciousness on the part of the Jarmanites or anybody else. While it is evident the adversary is afraid of some good being done in such places it is well not to invite such treatment if you can reasonably avoid it. I am sincerely thankful that you escaped without injury, and pray that God will always deliver you from the wrath of the wicked. It is always prudent, under such circumstances, and as a general thing, to keep together. One should never travel alone. The Lord has provided that the elders should travel two and two, and there should never be less than two of you together. Mamma was considerably worried after she read your letter for she feels that you are the apple of her eye and if turned loose on those that would molest you she would scarcely leave a grease spot of them."[66]

In early January 1900, Joseph F. wrote to Joseph Fielding, providing advice on how a missionary should act toward ministers of other faiths. It should be noted that Protestant clergymen were active in their opposition to the Church at the time:

"It gives me pleasure to acknowledge the receipt of your esteemed favors of December 2nd and 18th, the first of which reached me December 19th, and the latter this morning. I am pleased to say that it gives me pleasure to read your letters and to discern as I do between the lines the excellent spirit which pervades your thoughts and accompanies you in your ministrations. I was interested in your communications to the reverend gentleman you name in reference to the principles of the Gospel, and while it is all right to get after those gentlemen in the true spirit of inquiry and of hope of enlightening them, it is always well to be brief and pointed and courteous in such communications, as I think you have been. As a rule, the more you say to such people, the more opportunity is given to them for criticism and fault-finding. It is very seldom that gentlemen of *the cloth*, whose living depends upon their ecclesiastical position, will listen to reason or will yield to the persuasions of the good Spirit. They are blinded by the spirit of the world, and the profits of their calling. Besides they are thoroughly committed to their profession, for it is but a profession with them. Much labor and pains may be bestowed without good effects upon that class of people, still it is consistent and proper that they should receive admonition and warning and the testimony of the servants of the Lord, which should always be given in great humility and then they should be left in the hands of the Lord."[67]

On 14 May 1900, Joseph F. wrote to Joseph R. about the death of his daughter: "Your welcome letter of April 30th has just come to hand.

Your letter was written just one day after our Darling 'Alibo's' death. It came to my hand today. And I suppose my brief note to you of April 29th will have reached you yesterday or today, conveying to you and to Joseph F. the sad news of our irreparable earthly loss. Our hearts are still bowed down in the earth where the remains of our sweet girl'and those of her little Brothers and Sisters repose in the dust. The blow was hard upon all of us, but it fell with mighty force upon the frail of her beloved and precious Mother. May the merciful Father sustain and preserve the mortal life of our darling 'Mamma.' She is not strong at best, and this crucial ordeal has drawn heavily upon the little she had. But we will do the best we can, by the help of the Lord, and from our hearts we feel that our sleeping treasures are all in His holy keeping and will soon

PLATE 60

SMITH THREE GENERATIONS, 30 MARCH 1900

FOX AND SYMONS, KING COLLECTION. FROM LEFT: HYRUM M. SMITH, JOSEPH F. SMITH JR., AND JOSEPH F. SMITH. INSCRIBED ON THE BACK, JOSEPH F. SMITH WROTE: "JOSEPH F. SMITH AND SON, HYRUM M.—AND GRANDSON, JOS. F. TAKEN MARCH 30TH 1900. FOR AUNT MARTHA A. HARRIS. FROM HER BROTHER JOSEPH F."

PLATE 61
BRIGHAM YOUNG ACADEMY
FOUNDERS' DAY CELEBRATION, 16 OCTOBER 1900

USHS (PHOTO #6936). TAKEN AT THE CONCLUSION OF A PARADE AS PART OF THE TWENTY-FIFTH ANNIVERSARY OF THE FOUNDING OF BRIGHAM YOUNG ACADEMY, KNOWN TODAY AS BRIGHAM YOUNG UNIVERSITY. THE RECENTLY ORGANIZED "DARTON BAND" IS PICTURED AT THE EXTREME LEFT OF THE VIEW. NOTE THE TWO HORSEMEN, ONE HOLDING AN AMERICAN FLAG WHILE THE OTHER HOLDS THE BYA FLAG (WHITE AND BLUE). SEVERAL OF THE CLASSES AT THE SCHOOL MADE BANNERS RANGING IN COST FROM $20 TO $40. THE MOTTOES INSCRIBED ON THEM INCLUDE "CHARACTER IS POWER," "SELF EFFORT EDUCATES," AND "TO THINE OWN SELF BE TRUE." HONORED GUESTS INCLUDED PRESIDENT JOSEPH F. SMITH, SEATED IN THE FIRST CARRIAGE (DRAWN BY TWO WHITE HORSES), ALONG WITH FORMER BYA PRESIDENT KARL G. MAESER (IN THE FRONT ON THE RIGHT), DR. GEORGE H. BRIMHALL (IN THE FRONT ON THE LEFT), AND A REPRESENTATIVE OF THE BRIGHAM YOUNG FAMILY, SUSA YOUNG GATES (SEATED NEXT TO JOSEPH F. SMITH).

---

awake from dust to immortality and eternal life. But for the precious assurance and hope in the Gospel of Christ, life would not only *not* be worth the living, but it would be an infamous and damning *farce*! But, 'O, what joy this sentence gives, I *know* that *my Redeemer* lives!' Thank God. He is 'the resurrection and the life,' and his word is true. 'He that believeth in me, tho he were dead, yet shall he live; and whosoever liveth and believeth in me shall *never die*.' "[68]

He wrote that same day to Joseph Fielding: "She knew no sin against God or man. Too good, it seems, to live in this poor sin-cursed world. And so the good Father who gave her to us, has taken her to himself again. We shall meet again 'beyond the river where the surges cease to roll.' O! what happifying thought! She came to us under the Holy Bond of the New and everlasting Covenant. Whosoever God hath joined together neither man, nor time, nor distance, nor even death can sever. How grateful I am for God's truth and power unto salvation."[69]

The letters to his missionary sons reveal the depth of concern and love for his family. Additionally, they reveal his deepest beliefs and commitments—a window to his heart, mind, and soul.

Founders' Day at BYA (October 1900)

Joseph F. was in Provo participating in the twenty-fifth anniversary of the founding of Brigham Young Academy (known today as Brigham Young University) on 16 October 1900.

The *Deseret Evening News* reported: "At 9 o'clock the parade commenced with about seven hundred students participating. First came a horseman carrying the Stars and Stripes, followed by Darton's silver band. Then followed another horseman with the academy flag, white and blue, after which came the classes in their order of seniority, led by their class presidents and standard bearers. Lastly come the faculty. All together they made a very imposing appearance. Distinguished visitors rode back and forth in a carriage."[70]

The local BYA newspaper noted that the recently formed "Darton's brass band hastened the flagging feet and gave the procession a military appearance."[71]

BRIGHAM YOUNG ACADEMY

Finally, the group arrived at the BYA building located on Academy Avenue (known today as University Avenue), where a historic photograph was taken on a beautiful autumn day in Utah Valley.[72] Following the shooting of the photograph, students, faculty, staff, and local community members joined the school leaders and Joseph F. and the other dignitaries in the "college hall" for a celebration.[73]

The student newspaper reported: "After the invocation by President [Edward] Partridge and a short opening address by Dr. [George H.] Brimhall, President Joseph F. Smith spoke of the financial condition of the academy. Although the school had passed through hard struggles, he thought the Lord had overruled them for the school's good. He felt thankful that Brigham Young had been inspired to found the church schools, which are doing a mighty work in Zion. The maintenance of them had severely taxed the church, but the results accomplished have been sufficient reward. He saw a brighter day coming—a day when the school would not longer be cramped financially. The students were advised with all their getting to get the spirit of the Lord and obey His priesthood, then they would succeed. 'If these were my last words on earth' he said in closing, 'I would want to bear testimony that God lives, and that He has restored His priesthood to those who now act with authority in His name. President Young was led to found this school that the spiritual side of young men and young women might be educated in the things of God.'"[74]

A New Century (April 1901)

With the death of George Q. Cannon on 12 April 1901, Joseph F. was called and sustained but was never set apart as the first counselor in the First Presidency.[75] He served in this position until October 1901, when President Snow died in Salt Lake City. By the end of the first year of a new century, Joseph F. stood as the senior apostle of The Church of Jesus Christ of Latter-day Saints.

Notes

1. Reverend E. P. Willard, "Mormon Preaching at Salt Lake City," *The Independent*, 17 September 1868, 6.
2. Joseph F. Smith Diary, 30 May 1870, typescript, Joseph F. Smith Papers, 1856–1918; LDSCA.
3. Ibid., 1 June 1870.
4. Ibid., 2 June 1870.
5. Ibid., 3 June 1870.
6. Ibid., 4 June 1870.
7. Ibid., 5 June 1870.
8. Ibid., 6 June 1870.
9. Ibid.
10. Ibid., 7 June 1870.
11. Ibid., 8 June 1870.
12. Julina Lambson Smith Journal, 1912; as cited in Joseph Fielding Smith, comp., *The Life of Joseph F. Smith: Sixth President of The Church of Jesus Christ of Latter-day Saints* (Salt Lake City: Deseret Book, 1938); hereafter cited as *LJFS*, 458–59.
13. Joseph F. Smith to Julina Lambson Smith, 2 April 1888; as cited in

Joseph Fielding McConkie, ed., *Truth and Courage: Joseph F. Smith Letters*; hereafter cited as *TC*, 56.

14. Ibid.; as cited in *TC*, 57.

15. Joseph F. Smith to Joseph H. Dean, 5 April 1888; as cited in *TC*, 55.

16. Joseph F. Smith, "My Missions," *Deseret Evening News*, 21 December 1901, 57; James R. Clark, comp., *Messages of the First Presidency of The Church of Jesus Christ of Latter-day Saints*, 6 vols. (Salt Lake City: Bookcraft, Inc., 1965–75); hereafter cited as *MFP*, 4:22.

17. Joseph F. Smith Diary, 2 September 1878, Joseph F. Smith Papers, 1856–1918, LDSCA; as cited in *LJFS*, 237.

18. "My Missions," 57; *MFP*, 4:22.

19. Ibid.

20. Ibid; *MFP*, 4:23.

21. Davis Bitton, *George Q. Cannon: A Biography* (Salt Lake City: Deseret Book, 1999), 239.

22. Wilford Woodruff Journal, 23 January 1881; LDSCA; as cited in Scott G. Kenney, ed., *Wilford Woodruff's Journals, 1833–1898*, 9 vols. (Midvale, Utah: Signature Books, 1983–85), 8:8.

23. Ibid.

24. See *LJFS*, 255–56.

25. Joseph Fielding Smith Jr. and John J. Steward, *The Life of Joseph Fielding Smith: Tenth President of The Church of Jesus Christ of Latter-day Saints* (Salt Lake City: Deseret Book, 1972), 36.

26. See *LJFS*, 259–60.

27. Ibid., 282.

28. Ibid.

29. Ibid., 282–83.

30. "My Missions," 57; *MFP*, 4:23.

31. Jason Mack [Joseph F. Smith] to John H. Smith, 21 March 1888; as cited in *TC*, 30.

32. Joseph F. Smith to Joseph A. Harris, 16 April 1888; as cited in *TC*, 32.

33. *LJFS*, 300.

34. Francis Asbury Hammond Journal, 6 April 1893, LDSCA.

35. L. John Nuttall Diary, 6 April 1893, typescript, BYU.

36. "Annual Conference," *Deseret News Weekly*, 15 April 1893, 516.

37. Joseph West Smith Journal, 8 April 1893, LDSCA.

38. Francis Asbury Hammond Journal, 10 April 1893, LDSCA.

39. As cited in Brian H. Stuy, *Collected Discourses Delivered by President Wilford Woodruff, His Two Counselors, The Twelve Apostles, and Others*, 5 vols. (Sandy, Utah: B. H. S. Publishing, 1989), 3:279.

40. Joseph West Smith Journal, 12 April 1893, LDSCA.

41. Ibid., 16 April 1893.

42. L. John Nuttall Journal, 20 April 1893, typescript, BYU.

43. Amanda Cook Personal History, in possession of Pat Balls, Hyde Park, Utah.

44. Ibid.

45. Wilford Woodruff Journal, 15 July 1895, LDSCA; as cited in *Wilford Woodruff's Journals, 1833–1898*, 9:360.

46. Ibid., 9:361.

47. Ibid.

48. Ibid., 9:362.

49. Ibid.

50. Joseph F. Smith to Susa Young Gates, 11 November 1895; as cited in *TC*, 62–63.

51. Joseph F. Smith to Hyrum M. Smith, 18 May 1896; as cited in *TC*, 44–45.

52. Ibid., 20 May 1896; as cited in *TC*, 46.

53. Ibid.; *TC*, 49–50.

54. Joseph F. Smith to Donnette Smith, 18 September 1896, Joseph F. Smith Letter Copy Books, Joseph F. Smith Papers 1838–1918, LDSCA.

55. Andrew C. Peterson to President Lorenzo Snow, 11 February 1900, First Presidency Missionary Calls and Recommendations, 1877–1918; LDSCA.

56. Daniel E. Price to George Reynolds, 27 February 1900, First Presidency Missionary Calls and Recommendations, 1877–1918; LDSCA.

57. Parley Peterson Jr. to President Lorenzo Snow, 19 March 1900, First Presidency Missionary Calls and Recommendations, 1877–1918; LDSCA.

58. Joseph Peterson to First Presidency, 13 June 1900, First Presidency Missionary Calls and Recommendations, 1877–1918; LDSCA.

59. Edward Partridge to George Reynolds, 1 October 1900, First Presidency Missionary Calls and Recommendations, 1877–1918; LDSCA.

60. Amelia Carling to President Lorenzo Snow, 7 May 1901, First Presidency Missionary Calls and Recommendations, 1877–1918; LDSCA.

61. William W. Astle to President Lorenzo Snow, 17 July 1901, First Presidency Missionary Calls and Recommendations, 1877–1918; LDSCA.

62. David Clark to First Presidency, 22 August 1901, First Presidency Missionary Calls and Recommendations, 1877–1918; LDSCA.

63. *The Life of Joseph Fielding Smith: Tenth President of The Church of Jesus Christ of Latter-day Saints*, 116.

64. Joseph F. Smith to Joseph R. Smith, 20 June 1899; as cited in Hyrum M. Smith III and Scott G. Kenney, *From Prophet to Son: Advice of Joseph F. Smith to His Missionary Sons* (Salt Lake City: Deseret Book, 1966); hereafter cited as FPS, 60–62.

65. Joseph F. Smith to Joseph Fielding Smith, 20 June 1899; as cited in FPS, 62–64.

66. Ibid., 27 September 1899; as cited in FPS, 64.

67. Ibid., 2 January 1900; as cited in FPS, 65–66.

68. Joseph F. Smith to Joseph R. Smith, 14 May 1901; as cited in FPS, 75–76.

69. Joseph F. Smith to Joseph Fielding Smith, 14 May 1901; as cited in FPS, 76.

70. "Twenty-fifth Anniversary," *Deseret Evening News*, 17 October 1900, 2.

71. "The New Features of the Parade," *The White and Blue*, 15 October 1900, 19.

72. See description on the back of plate 61, found in the collection of photographs of BYU buildings (Box 2, Folder 28) by Dyke Walton, BYU.

73. "Founders Day Exercises," *The White and Blue*, 15 October 1900, 12. The student newspaper, which was to be published on 15 October, was released after the Founders' Day event held on 16 October. Nevertheless, the date of 15 October appears on the masthead, though it was actually published later in the month.

74. Ibid.

75. Rudger Clawson was called and sustained as the second counselor but was not set apart before President Lorenzo Snow's death on 10 October 1901.

CHAPTER FOUR

The Twentieth-Century Prophet 1901–1918

While nursing a cold, President Lorenzo Snow spoke at the October general conference in 1901. It would be his last address to the Saints. At the same conference, his counselor Joseph F. also addressed the Saints. It was a Spirit-filled address, and some in the congregation could see that the mantel of the prophet was already beginning to fall upon him. As he stood at the pulpit on this occasion, a stake president in attendance noted, "I looked at him and he appeared to me to be Prest. Snow, and I looked several times and each time he appeared like that."[1]

A few days later, President Snow's cold turned into pneumonia. The Twelve were summoned to his bedside on 10 October at 5 A.M. In the afternoon, with family, friends, and Church leaders nearby, the President of the Church died.

Sustained as the Sixth President of the Church (October 1901)

One week later, the Twelve met in the Salt Lake Temple. Elder John Henry Smith proposed that the Twelve "proceed at once to the organization of the First Presidency."[2] Elder Rudger Clawson recorded the events on this momentous day:

"Apostle Brigham Young said that he was heartily in favor of reorganizing the First Presidency, and nominated Pres. Jos. F. Smith as president of the Church of Jesus Christ of Latter-day Saints in all the world. Carried by unanimous vote. Pres. Smith accepted the action of the brethren and remarked that the time was ripe to sustain Brigham Young as president of the Twelve Apostles. Pres. Smith said that he had selected his counselors and named Bp. Jno. R. Winder as the first and Apostle Anthon H. Lund as the second counselor."[3]

Elder Abraham O. Woodruff noted in his diary that the motion was "carried with a hearty united vote of all."[4]

In addition to being sustained as "president of the Church of Jesus Christ of Latter-day Saints in all the world," President Joseph F. was also "sustained as trustee-in-trust" and as "president of the Salt Lake Temple."[5] Finally, President Joseph F. was sustained as the head of the Young Men's Mutual Improvement Association (YMMIA).

According to Elder John Henry Smith, "John Smith Patriarch was mouth in setting apart Joseph F. Smith as President of the Church. John R. Winder was called in and ordained an Apostle under the hands of us all, President Smith being mouth and also set apart as first Councillor. Anthon H. Lund was set apart as second Councilor by Joseph F. Smith and Brigham Young as the President of the Twelve."[6]

Elder Abraham O. Woodruff told those gathered in the temple that his father, President Wilford Woodruff, prophesied that "Jos. F. Smith would one day be president of the church. Apostle Woodruff predicted that his administration would be eventful."[7] One such occasion was on 23 January 1881, as noted in Wilford Woodruff's journal.[8]

Elder John Henry Smith reflected on the event with these words—making a poignant phrase: "The spirit of [the] Lord was with us in power."[9] President Joseph F. was sixty-two years of age. Thus began the ministry of the first President of the Church born of Latter-day Saint parents in this dispensation.

News spread quickly of the action throughout the settlements of the Latter-day Saints. L. John Nuttall noted in his diary on 17 October 1901: "Announcement is made today of the re-organization of the First Presidency. Joseph F. Smith is made President of the Church. . . . Wise and God-fearing men have been chosen, and I look for great developments under the presidency of Brother Smith."[10]

A few days later in Provo, Church leaders and school officials at the Brigham Young Academy (BYU today) gathered for the annual "Founders' Day" celebration. Utah County Stake President David John noted: "Joseph F. Smith was elected President of the Academy."[11]

In the monthly fast meeting in the temple, President Joseph F. presided for the first time as President. Emmeline B. Wells, General Relief Society secretary, noted in her diary: "Rose early and went to the Temple. . . . President Joseph F. Smith was presiding as President of the Church and very impressive were the words he spake."[12]

The *Improvement Era* provided its readers a description of the new Church president:

"President Joseph F. Smith has an imposing physical appearance. He has completed his sixty-third year; he is tall, erect, well-knit and symmetrical in build. He has a prominent nose and features. When speaking, he throws his full, clear, brown eyes wide open on the listener who may readily perceive from their penetrating glimpse the wonderful mental power of the tall forehead above. His large head is crowned with an abundant growth of hair, in his early years dark, but now, like his full beard, tinged with a liberal sprinkling of gray. In onversation, one is forcibly impressed with the sudden changes in

JOSEPH F. SMITH
SIXTH PRESIDENT OF THE CHURCH OF JESUS CHRIST
OF LATTER-DAY SAINTS

appearance of his countenance, under the different influences of his mind; now intensely pleasant, with an enthusiastic and childlike interest in immediate subjects and surroundings: now absent, the mobility of his features set in that earnest, almost stern, majesty of expression so characteristic of his portraits—so indicative of the severity of the conditions and environments of his early life."[13]

Calling New Leaders (1901–1918)

One of the most important assignments of the Presidents of the Church is to choose, under the direction of the Lord, new apostles to fill the vacancies in the Council of the Twelve. In his first opportunity, President Joseph F. chose twenty-nine-year-old Hyrum M. Smith to fill the vacancy in the Council of the Twelve caused by the calling of Anthon H. Lund to the First Presidency.

During his presidency, President Joseph F. called George Albert Smith (1903), Charles W. Penrose (1904), George F. Richards (1906), Orson F. Whitney (1906), David O. McKay (1906), Anthony W. Ivins (1907), Joseph Fielding Smith (1910), James E. Talmage (1911), Stephen L Richards (1917), and Richard R. Lyman (1918) to the Twelve.

The significance of these calls cannot be underestimated, as three of them, George Albert Smith, David O. McKay, and Joseph Fielding Smith, eventually were sustained as Presidents of the Church themselves.

PLATE 62 (LEFT)
JOSEPH F. SMITH, CA. 1901
PUBLISHED IN IMPROVEMENT ERA 5 (DECEMBER 1901). JOSEPH F. WAS BE BETWEEN 80 AND 81 YEARS OLD.
THE ERA STATED THAT THIS ENGRAVING WAS JOSEPH F. SMITH'S FAVORITE PORTRAIT;
IMPROVEMENT ERA 5 (DECEMBER 1901): 132.

EDITOR'S TABLE.

REDEMPTION BEYOND THE GRAVE.

A missionary writing to the editor of the ERA is troubled upon this subject, and asks to have the matter explained. He refers to II Nephi 9: 27-38, and Alma 11: 40, 41, which passages appear to give him the impression that there is no redemption beyond the grave.

Let me say in explanation that Alma is evidently speaking to those who have received a knowledge of the gospel or the plan of salvation, as would appear by the 27th verse of the 9th chapter of Second Nephi: "But wo unto him that has the law given; yea, that has all the commandments of God, like unto us, and that transgresseth them, and that wasteth the days of his probation, for awful is his state!"

Now, it is evident that such as these have no chance for redemption, no matter what may be done for them in hope or by faith, for they will have sinned against light and knowledge, and are, therefore, worthy of damnation. It is nowhere revealed that such as these will ever be forgiven, although we are informed that all of God's judgments are not given unto men. As in Alma, the prophet is speaking of the world as it should be found at the coming of Christ; the people at that time were all without a knowledge of Christ, and the plan of redemption, and Christ is to take upon him the transgressions only of those who believe on his name, and believing, of course, repent and do the works that he commands. "And these are they that shall have eternal life, and salvation cometh to none else." Now, this means that there is no other means of salvation revealed or given to the children of men, except that offered by the Son of God, and those who reject this, whether before or after they have received it in part, can not be saved, because they rejected the means of their redemption and concerning those for whom the work shall be done, so that we may not work by chance, or by faith alone, without knowledge, but with the actual knowledge revealed unto us. It stands to reason that, while the Gospel may be preached unto all, the good and the bad, or rather those who would repent and those who would not repent in the spirit world, the same as it is here, redemption will only come to those who repent and obey. There is, no doubt, great leniency given to people who are anxious to do the work for their dead; and, in some instances, very unworthy people may have the work done for them; it does not follow, however, that they will receive any benefit therefrom, and the correct thing is to do the work only for those of whom we have the testimony that they will receive it. However, we are disposed to give the benefit of the doubt to the dead, as it is better to do the work for many who are unworthy than to neglect one who is worthy. Now, we know in part, and see in part, but we steadfastly look forward to the time when that which is perfect will come. We are left largely to our own agency here, to exercise our own intelligence, and to receive all the light that is revealed, so far as we are capable of receiving it; and only those who seek the light, and desire it, are likely to find it.

With reference to John 5: 25, the word "hear" implies more than the simple meaning of the word; "and they who hear shall live," that evidently means, they who hear and obey, and not those who simply hear; this, of course, stands to reason.

JOSEPH F. SMITH.

EVILS OF MORTGAGING.

What a blessed condition would result in Zion if the evil of going into debt, of mortgaging the home, could be made very clear to every Latter-day Saint, young and old! Well, indeed, would it be if some of the burdens of the mortgage and its accompanying sorrows, could be felt and understood by every man who has in contemplation the pawning of his home and land for money—that he might comprehend its slavery and terror—as thoroughly prior

The New Presidency's First Official Statement (November 1901)

The new First Presidency, with the support of the Council of the Twelve, called a special general conference for 10 November to give Church members an opportunity to sustain the new authorities of the Church. The *Deseret Evening News* announced:

"OFFICIAL ANNOUNCEMENT to the Officers and Members of the Church of Jesus Christ of Latter-day Saints: Dear Brethren and Sisters: Agreeable with the decision of the Council of Apostles at their regular meeting Thursday, October 17, we hereby call a general conference of the Church of Jesus Christ of Latter-day Saints to be held in the Tabernacle, Salt Lake City, on Sunday, the 10th of November, next, at 10 o'clock a.m. for the purpose of voting upon the Church authorities."[14]

While President Joseph F. and counselors desired that the Saints have the opportunity to sustain their officers, they recognized the difficulty involved in having the Saints come back for the second general conference within five weeks. In a letter sent to stake presidents, the new First Presidency proposed that where attendance at the forthcoming general conference in Salt Lake City was not feasible because of "distance and expense," local stake leaders should call a special stake conference for 3 November. The "'authorities of the Church as they were sustained by the Council of Apostles on the 17th inst.' were to be sustained in these special Stake Conferences and a certified copy be sent to the General Conference convening on November 10th."[15]

They wrote: "As you will have learned through the columns of the Deseret News, we have called a special general conference of the church to be held on the 10th of November next, for the purpose of voting upon the authorities of the church as they were sustained by the Council of Apostles on the 17th inst., and officially announced in the Deseret News of the same date; and being desirous that as full a representation as possible of the stakes of Zion may be had upon that occasion, and fearing that distance and expense may prevent many of your people from attending, we therefore advise that you call and hold a special conference of your stake on Sunday, the 3rd prox., for the purpose of voting on the same question; and that the sense of said conference be expressed by resolution, and a certified copy thereof be sent either by mail or special representative to be read at the forthcoming conference in this city."[16]

Local Stake Conference (November 1901)

In Provo, the Utah County Stake gathered at the Provo Tabernacle, as directed by Church leaders in Salt Lake City, for a special conference to sustain new Church leaders on 3 November 1901. President David John noted in his diary: "It was attended by large congregations and an excellent spirit was manifested."[17] During his address, the *Deseret News* reported, President John "felt to say with his whole soul, 'Thank God for our new president, Joseph F. Smith, who was born to be a shepherd to the flock of Israel and would be preserved for many years to give strength and encouragement to the people and lead them onward and upward causing greater union and an increase in the love of the Gospel and in the spiritual advancement of the Saints.'"[18] Capturing the significance of the moment, he added that "a new era had come to the Church."[19]

The proposal to sustain the new First Presidency and the Council of the Twelve was brought forward to the local Saints and was "unanimously adopted."[20] After reviewing the history of President Joseph F.'s Church experiences, especially his service as a counselor in the First Presidency for twenty-one years, President John noted: "This is a good record."[21]

Special Conference at Salt Lake City (November 1901)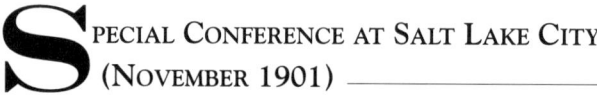

At the special conference in Salt Lake City on 10 November 1901, President Joseph F. was sustained as the sixth President of the Church. Emmeline B. Wells noted in her diary: "Prepared to go to the Special Conference was there in good time and saw the impressive services of voting by quorums of the Priesthood."[22] Joseph F. told the Saints assembled in the historic Tabernacle:

"I desire to make another remark or two before we close our conference. I will call your attention to the fact that the Lord in the beginning of this work revealed that there should be three High Priests to preside over the High Priesthood of His Church and over the whole Church (Doc. and Cov. 107:22, 64, 65, 66, 67, 91, and 92). He conferred upon them all the authority necessary to preside over all the affairs of the Church. They hold the keys of the house of God, and of the ordinances of the Gospel, and of every blessing which has been restored to the earth in this dispensation. This authority is vested in a Presidency of three High Priests. They are three Presidents. The Lord

himself so calls them. (D. & C., sec. 107:29.) But there is one presiding President, and his counselors are Presidents also. I propose that my counselors and fellow Presidents in the First Presidency shall share with me in the responsibility of every act which I shall perform in this capacity. I do not propose to take the reins in my own hands to do as I please; but I propose to do as my brethren and I agree upon and as the Spirit of the Lord manifests to us. I have always held, and do hold, and trust I always shall hold, that it is wrong for one man to exercise all the authority and power of presidency in the Church of Jesus Christ of Latter-day Saints. I dare not assume such a responsibility, and I will not, so long as I can have men like these [pointing to Presidents Winder and Lund] to stand by and counsel with me in the labors we have to perform and in doing all those things that shall tend to the peace, advancement and happiness of the people of God and the building up of Zion. If at any time my brethren of the Apostleship shall see in me a disposition to depart from this principle or a forgetfulness on my part of this covenant that I make today before this body of Priesthood, I ask them in the name of my Father, that they will come to me, as my brethren, as counselors in the Priesthood, as watchmen on the towers of Zion, and remind me of this covenant and promise which I make to the body of the Church in general conference assembled at this time. The Lord never did intend that one man should have all power, and for that reason He has placed in His Church Presidents, Apostles, High Priests, Seventies, Elders and the

various offices of the Lesser Priesthood, all of which are essential in their order and place according to the authority bestowed on them. The Lord never did anything that was not essential or that was superfluous. There is a use for every branch of the Priesthood that He has established in His Church. We want every man to learn his duty, and we expect every man will do his duty as faithfully as he knows how, and carry off his portion of the responsibility of building up Zion in the latter days.

"I felt like I wanted to say that much to these my brethren who bear the Holy Priesthood—men who wield influence for the salvation of souls, who set good examples before the people among whom they dwell, who teach them the right way, admonish them for sin, lead them in the path of duty, and enable them to stand firm and steadfast in the faith of the Gospel, wherewith they have been made free from sin and from the grasp of Satan. God bless all Israel, is my prayer in the name of Jesus, Amen."[23]

MITH FAMILY HOMES (1901–1918)

When U.S. President Benjamin Harrison granted Joseph F. amnesty in September 1891, Joseph F. was forced to decide whether he would abandon his plural wives and families as some opponents of the Church felt was necessary if he were going to comply completely with the terms of amnesty. Joseph F., along with many other Church members, believed they obeyed the law by not entering into new plural marriages.

Loyalty to family and his personal affection for them made the decision whether to continue emotional and financial support rather natural. However, he nevertheless was forced to disperse each family, "placing each wife in a different home."[24] He hoped this action would eliminate any further intrusion into his personal affairs.

He found most of his wives homes in Salt Lake City in the early 1890s. However, Mary Taylor Schwartz Smith was sent to Franklin, Idaho, for a time. Later, she returned to Salt Lake City and for a while lived on South Ninth East before moving to a home located on North Temple between Main and State Streets (now the site of the LDS Church Office Building). Julina Lambson Smith and children remained in the original Smith home at 333 West First North until after President Joseph F. became President of the Church.

Local city directories in the last two decades of the nineteenth century and the first two decades of the twentieth century provide Joseph F.'s main residential address. Beginning in the 1880s and into the 1900s, the Salt Lake City directories indicate that Joseph F. resided at 333 West First North.[25] For the next several years, the address remained the same, except that a telephone listing, "93," was added in 1900.[26]

The new 1905 directory indicated that President Joseph F.'s primary residence was now the "Bee Hive House," located on the corner of present-day State Street and South Temple.[27] The telephone number was listed as "207."[28] The Beehive House remained President Joseph F.'s personal residence until his death in November 1918.

The Shipler photographic firm in Salt Lake City preserved beautiful black-and-white images of the Smith family homes in a series of previously unpublished photographs. Taken from the original glass-plate negatives preserved at the Utah State Historical Society in Salt Lake City, these rare images provide another view of President Joseph F.'s world.

PLATE 65
JOSEPH F. AND ALICE ANN KIMBALL SMITH HOME, 25 SEPTEMBER 1906
MODERN PRINT FROM ORIGINAL GLASS-PLATE NEGATIVE, SHIPLER PHOTOGRAPHERS, USHS (PHOTO #28573). LOCATED AT 127 NORTH 300 WEST, SALT LAKE CITY.

PLATE 66
JOSEPH F. AND MARY TAYLOR SCHWARTZ SMITH HOME, 25 SEPTEMBER 1906
MODERN PRINT FROM ORIGINAL GLASS-PLATE NEGATIVE, SHIPLER PHOTOGRAPHERS, USHS (PHOTO #28574). LOCATED AT 56 EAST NORTH TEMPLE, SALT LAKE CITY.

PLATE 67
JOSEPH F. AND EDNA LAMBSON SMITH HOME, 25 SEPTEMBER 1906
MODERN PRINT FROM ORIGINAL GLASS-PLATE NEGATIVE, SHIPLER PHOTOGRAPHERS, USHS (PHOTO #28575). LOCATED AT 143 NORTH 300 WEST, SALT LAKE CITY.

PLATE 68
JOSEPH F. AND SARA ELLEN RICHARDS SMITH HOME, 25 SEPTEMBER 1906
MODERN PRINT FROM ORIGINAL GLASS-PLATE NEGATIVE, SHIPLER PHOTOGRAPHERS, USHS (PHOTO #28576). LOCATED AT 157 NORTH 300 WEST, SALT LAKE CITY.

Church Headquarters (1901–1918)

About the time Joseph F. was sustained as the sixth President of the Church, its headquarters still reflected the earlier pioneer frontier period. Although it is true that the Tabernacle and temple, located in Salt Lake City, were beautiful and imposing, the other administrative buildings did not reflect the growth and development of the Church, which now had more than 250,000 members.

In 1901, the First Presidency's office was located in the small, four-room annex of the Beehive House, where it had been since 1860. The Presiding Bishop's Office and the *Deseret News* facility shared the location on the corner of South Temple and Main Street. The Historian's Office and the recently established Genealogical Society of Utah were located on the south side of South Temple Street, opposite the Beehive House. The LDS College and the Deseret Sunday School Union were located in the Templeton Building, located west of the Historian's Office. Other Church officers, including the General Authorities, had their offices in their homes or businesses.

It was during President Joseph F.'s presidency and shortly thereafter that changes occurred when ten major buildings at Church headquarters were constructed to meet the increased growth. The first were the LDS College (1901), Barratt Hall (1902), Brigham Young Memorial Building (1902), Deseret News Building (1902), Bureau of Information (1902), Bishops' Building (1910), Deseret Gymnasium (1910), Hotel Utah (1911), Church Administration Building (1917), and Joseph F. Smith Memorial Building (1919).

Of particular note was the completion on 2 October 1917 of the Church Administration Building, which housed the First Presidency, Quorum of the Twelve, First Council of Seventy, Church historian, and the Genealogical Society offices. Throughout the rest of the twentieth century, it was the heart of the Church.

PLATE 69
PRESIDENT'S HOME (BEEHIVE HOUSE) AND PRESIDENT'S OFFICE, CA. 1914

C. R. SAVAGE & COMPANY, LDSCA. THE PRESIDENT'S OFFICE WAS LOCATED IN THE WING BETWEEN THE BEEHIVE HOUSE AND LION HOUSE, UNTIL THE COMPLETION OF THE NEW CHURCH ADMINISTRATION OFFICE IN 1917.

PLATE 70
CHURCH ADMINISTRATION OFFICE IN SALT LAKE CITY, CA. 1917

LDSCA. THIS FIVE-STORY GRANITE BUILDING, LOCATED AT 47 EAST SOUTH TEMPLE, HAS BEEN THE HEADQUARTERS FOR THE CHURCH SINCE IT WAS COMPLETED IN 1917. FOR THE FIRST TIME, THE FIRST PRESIDENCY AND THE COUNCIL OF THE TWELVE HAD OFFICES TOGETHER. ADDITIONALLY, THE HISTORIAN'S OFFICE AND THE GENEALOGICAL SOCIETY OF UTAH WERE HOUSED IN THE UPPER THREE FLOORS OF THE BUILDING.

First Presidency's Christmas Message (1901)

At the end of the year, 1901, President Joseph F. and his counselors issued their annual Christmas message, which included "Reminiscences by the First Presidency," dated 21 December 1901.[29]

"By special request of the 'Deseret News,' the First Presidency of the Church has prepared the following sketches, which will be of deep interest to the Latter-day Saints, and will furnish valuable information to the general readers of this Christmas edition."[30]

President Joseph F. chose to write about his early missions. Entitled, "My Missions," he recalled:

"Among the most precious memories in the life of an Elder of the Church of Jesus Christ of Latter-day Saints, are the periods spent by him upon missions, laboring for the salvation of mankind. The nature of the service expected of such men, and in most cases faithfully performed by them, is the best explanation of the almost universal verdict rendered by our returned missionaries, that their experiences in the mission field, despite the hardships and persecutions they encounter, are among the happiest, if not the very happiest of their lives. It is easily deductible from the teachings of the Savior, that the secret of true happiness is found in unselfishness, in devoting one's mind, heart and soul to the work of glorifying God by benefitting and saving mankind; and these teachings are amply confirmed by the experiences of the Elders of Israel in modern times.

"I have chosen as the subject of the Christmas communication you have requested, those periods of my life when I have been absent from home, preaching the Gospel or otherwise subserving the sacred cause with which we are identified."[31]

PLATE 71
JOSEPH F. SMITH ATTENDING THE SALT LAKE 20TH WARD, CA. 1901 TO 1902
USHS (PHOTO #9694).

President Joseph F. ended his recollections with a message of gratitude and holiday greeting:

"Grateful to the Lord for my present good health, peace and prosperity, from the summit of my sixty-three years I look back upon a life in which joy and sorrow, pleasure and pain, are intermingled, but with the former greatly predominating. No man that I know of has been more bounteously blessed by the Almighty than I have been; and no one, I believe, is more willing to acknowledge the Lord's hand in His blessings, or is more anxious to merit them and to make a good, wise use of them. And with these sentiments in my heart and with feelings of kindness and good-will for the entire Church of God and for mankind everywhere, I wish all a Merry Christmas and a Happy New Year."[32]

Plate 72
LDS Church First Presidency, ca. 1902
Heber Harris Thomas, LDSCA.
From left: John R. Winder, Joseph F. Smith (standing), and Anthon H. Lund.

Plate 73
Missionary Certificate, dated 4 August 1903, signed by First Presidency
LDSCA. Mischa Markow served several missions for the Church, including one in the Middle East.

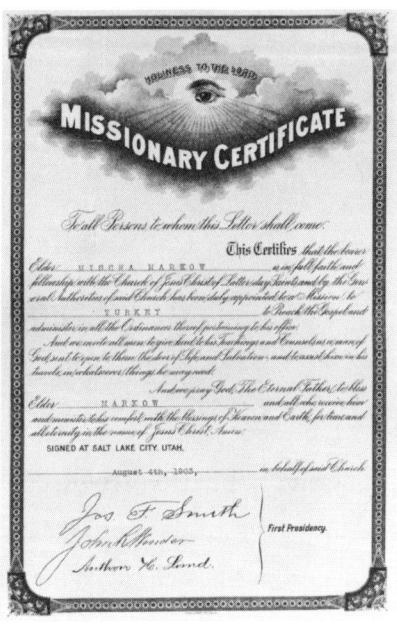

Plate 74
Montefiore Jewish Congregation, ca. 1947
USHS (Photo #21448).
President Joseph F. Smith was invited to speak at the cornerstone-laying services for the new Jewish Synagogue in Salt Lake City on 9 August 1903.

Reaching out to Others (August 1903)

During this period of turmoil and misrepresentation, President Joseph F. attempted to reach out to others beyond the Latter-day Saint community in many goodwill gestures. On 9 August 1903, he joined the Jewish community in Salt Lake City for an important beginning. The *Deseret Evening News* reported on the following day:

"The laying of the corner stone of the new synagogue being directed by the Congregation Montefiore on Third East between Third and Fourth South streets, occurred yesterday afternoon with impressive ceremony. The services took place under a canopy of American flags and were presided over by Mr. Levy, chairman of the building committee, who was presented by the master builder with a beautiful silver trowel, with which the mortar for the stone was spread."[33]

Among local dignitaries invited to attend were President Joseph F. and Elder John Henry Smith. President Joseph F. addressed the group:

"In his remarks President Smith offered congratulations upon the success which had attended the efforts of the congregation in building another house of worship. He spoke of their being the direct descendants of Abraham, the father of the faithful, and said the Latter-day Saints were firm believers in the prophecies contained in the Holy Bible concerning the destiny of the Jewish people. 'We believe,' he continued, 'that the Jews will be restored to their heritage more speedily than many anticipate. We feel that we can well afford to extend the hand of fellowship, for peace and good will should prevail among all descendants of the twelve tribes of Israel. You are descended from Judah; many of us are descended from Joseph through the loins of Ephraim. We therefore consider you our brethren and we ought to be friends. Peace be with you. God bless you in your efforts to do good.'"[34]

Later, the Church donated $650 toward the erection of the Montefiore congregation's synagogue.

The Prophet and the Automobile

Although President Lorenzo Snow was the first President of the Church to have the opportunity to ride in an automobile, President Joseph F. was the first to own the newest invention. The Clawson Film Company preserved some of the earliest views of President Smith in a moving automobile, including one scene of him and Charles W. Nibley alighting from a Studebaker touring car driven by E. Wesley Smith at Santa Monica, California, and another of President Joseph F. in a white automobile touring coat with other family members and Church leaders on the front steps of the Church Administration Building, moving toward the curb where he got into a Packard touring car with David A. Smith at the wheel and then moved away, giving his characteristic wave.

President Joseph F. was fully aware of the advantages of the development of the automobile. Additionally, he also knew of the dangers. In a letter to George Albert Smith, President Joseph F. made mention of a strange accident involving the death of a friend, William Grosebeck. The *Deseret Evening News* reported: "William Grosebeck, aged 65 years . . . a man prominent in mining and real estate circles and well known in this city for many years . . . [was] instantly killed at 7:37 o'clock this morning by Denver & Rio Grande passenger train No. 3, third section, at Fourteenth South where the road crosses the tracks on a slight grade."[35]

Apparently, the auto was heading for the crossing about the time the train approached the crossing. Grosebeck and another gentleman became frightened and jumped from the vehicle to avoid what they assumed would be a collision. However, they both jumped into the path of the train and were killed instantly. Joseph F. noted, "The death

PLATE 75
JOSEPH F. SMITH AND PARTY, CA. 1902 TO 1903

NEBEKER COLLECTION. JOSEPH F. SMITH RIDES IN AN AUTOMOBILE NEAR THE BEEHIVE HOUSE AT THE CORNER OF SOUTH TEMPLE AND STATE STREET IN SALT LAKE CITY. FRONT FROM LEFT: LEROI SNOW AND JOSEPH F. SMITH. BACK FROM LEFT: UNIDENTIFIED WOMAN, EMILY SMITH, AND UNIDENTIFIED WOMAN.

---

of Wm. Grosebeck is something horrible."[36] He then added: "Moral—never jump out of an auto going 30 miles an hour! One might as well be killed in it, but to jump right on to the R. R. Track!"[37]

BEFORE THE U.S. SENATE (MARCH 1904)

One historian notes that the hearings on whether Reed Smoot should retain his seat in the United States Senate began "what may have been the longest and most thorough investigation of any religious body in the history of the United States."[38] It was during these hearings in Washington from 1904 through 1907 that, for the first time, a President of the Church was asked to appear before a governmental body in the nation's capital.

PLATE 76
JOSEPH F. SMITH, 26 MAY 1903
FOX AND SYMONS, MLUU (P0036 #132).

PLATE 77 (LEFT)
POLITICAL CARTOON FROM THE CHICAGO JOURNAL, 9 MARCH 1904

BUNKER COLLECTION. THE CAPTION READS: "UP-TO-DATE FATHER GOOSE."
THE RHYME PUBLISHED WITH THIS CARICATURE READ: "THERE WAS AN OLD MAN WHO LIVED IN A SHOE—HE HAD SO MANY CHILDREN HE DIDN'T KNOW WHAT TO DO. HE COULDN'T KEEP COUNT—THEY JUST GREW AND GREW—AND BEFORE HE HARDLY KNEW IT, HE HAD FORTY-TWO."

PLATE 78 (RIGHT)
POLITICAL CARTOON FROM THE SATURDAY GLOBE, 12 MARCH 1904

BUNKER COLLECTION. THE CAPTION READS: "THE MORMON DEFIANCE—WHAT ARE YOU GOING TO DO ABOUT IT?"

PLATE 79 (RIGHT)
POLITICAL CARTOON, 12 MARCH 1904

BUNKER COLLECTION. THE CAPTION READS: "A MAN IS KNOWN BY THE COMPANY HE KEEPS."

PLATE 80 (ABOVE)
POLITICAL CARTOON FROM LIFE MAGAZINE, 31 MARCH 1904

BUNKER COLLECTION. THE CAPTION READS: "JOSEPH SMITH COMES TO WASHINGTON."

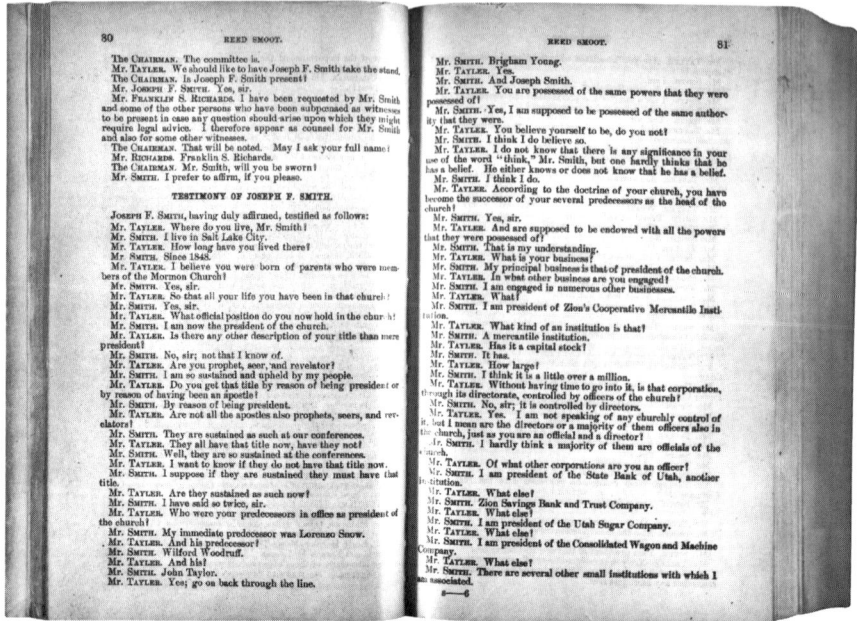

PLATE 81
PRINTED TESTIMONY OF JOSEPH F. SMITH FROM THE SENATE RECORD

THIS IMAGE REPRESENTS TWO OF THE TWO HUNDRED PAGES OF TESTIMONY OF PRESIDENT JOSEPH F. BEFORE THE SENATE COMMITTEE HEARINGS ON THE SEATING OF SENATOR REED SMOOT. PRESIDENT JOSEPH F. WAS THE FIRST CHURCH PRESIDENT TO APPEAR BEFORE THE UNITED STATES SENATE.

In 1904, President Joseph F. appeared before the "Committee on Privileges and Elections of the United States Senate" in Washington, D.C., beginning on 2 March and concluding on 9 March. President Joseph F.'s testimony, covering over two hundred pages in the official report, was published by the U.S. government.[39]

Topics addressed by President Joseph F. included the mundane and the technical aspects of Church history and doctrine. In many cases, he provided helpful insights to his life, his labors, and his interpretation of policies and procedures.

Senator Smoot's assistant, Carl Badger, provided George Albert Smith his own assessment of President Joseph F.'s testimony:

"I believe that President Smith, who has been on the stand for two days, has made a very good impression upon the committee. While his testimony has touched many delicate points, I might say the very vital points of controversy . . . I believe on the whole, that his testimony could not have been given more favorable than it has been and the general impression produced upon the members of the Committee who were open to favorable impression, has been entirely good."[40]

Others were impressed, including Senator Smoot's attorney, A. S. Worthington, who called President Joseph F. the "Grand Old Man" during one of the evening gatherings following a day before the Senate.[41]

The Second Manifesto (April 1904)

During the Smoot hearings, President Joseph F. was challenged by government leaders to take a more active role in disciplining members who continued to enter into new plural marriages. At the April Church conference, President Joseph F. responded:

"I am going to present a matter to you that is unusual and I do it because of a conviction which I feel that it is a proper thing for me to do. I have taken the liberty of having written down what I wish to present, in order that I may say to you the exact words which I would like to have conveyed to your ears, that I may not be misunderstood or misquoted. I present this to the conference for your action."[42]

He then presented an "Official Statement," which has become known as the "Second Manifesto." The document stated:

"Inasmuch as there are numerous reports in circulation that plural marriages have been entered into contrary to the official declaration of President Woodruff, of September 26, 1890, commonly called the Manifesto, which was issued by President Woodruff and adopted by the Church at its general conference, October 6, 1890, which forbade any marriages violative of the law of the land; I, Joseph F. Smith, President

PLATE 82
JOSEPH F. SMITH'S FAMILY, 13 NOVEMBER 1904
LDSCA. JOSEPH F. SMITH HAD FORTY-EIGHT CHILDREN, INCLUDING FIVE ADOPTED CHILDREN, WITH FIVE WIVES. THIS PHOTOGRAPH OF JOSEPH F. SMITH AND HIS FAMILY WAS TAKEN ON THE ANNIVERSARY OF HIS BIRTH. HE WAS SIXTY-SIX YEARS OLD IN 1904.

of the Church of Jesus Christ of Latter-day Saints, hereby affirm and declare that no such marriages have been solemnized with the sanction, consent or knowledge of the Church of Jesus Christ of Latter-day Saints, and I hereby announce that all such marriages are prohibited, and if any officer or member of the Church shall assume to solemnize or enter into any such marriage he will be deemed in transgression against the Church and will be liable to be dealt with, according to the rules and regulations thereof, and excommunicated therefrom. JOSEPH F. SMITH, President of the Church of Jesus Christ of Latter-day Saints."[43]

Time of Trial and Struggle

The previous year had provided President Joseph F. an opportunity to answer charges against himself, the Church, and the citizens of Utah. And while the enemies of the Church were busy fighting against it, President Joseph F. was stunned and hurt by the accusations of former members. In a meeting in the temple on New Year's Day, he vented his emotions and asked those present to pray for relief from the false tongues of traitors. Emmeline B. Wells attended the meeting and wrote: "President Joseph F. Smith spoke in seething terms of traitors. It was very solemn and impressive, no one who heard him can ever forget it, he said it was not a time for mirth or light-mindedness but for prayer and humility. He wept with emotion that could not be mistaken in spirit and fervency."[44]

PLATE 83 (ABOVE)
W. H. GROVES LATTER-DAY SAINT HOSPITAL, CA. 1905
LDSCA. INCORPORATED IN 1903, THE W. H. GROVES LATTER-DAY SAINT HOSPITAL IN SALT LAKE CITY OPENED IN JANUARY 1905 AS THE FIRST IN THE CHURCH'S HOSPITAL SYSTEM.

A NEW HOSPITAL SYSTEM (JANUARY 1905)

In the midst of continued vilification in the local and national press, President Joseph F. continued his efforts to improve the lives of the Latter-day Saints and their neighbors when he dedicated the Groves Latter-day Saint Hospital. In what would become a major health-care network in the Intermountain West, the Church opened the hospital in 1905. The *Improvement Era* reported: "The Groves Latter-day Saint Hospital was dedicated Wednesday, January 4th. The

PLATE 84 (RIGHT)
JOSEPH F. SMITH, CA. 1905
FOX AND SYMONS, NEBEKER COLLECTION. JOSEPH F. SMITH WROTE ON THE BACK OF THE PHOTOGRAPH: "YOURS TRULY. JOSEPH F. SMITH. MARCH 20TH 1905."

opening remarks were made by Hon. Franklin S. Richards and Bishop Robert T. Burton, and the dedicatory prayer was offered by President Joseph F. Smith. The new hospital, which is one of the best in the world, was opened for the reception of patients Monday, January 9th."[45]

Honoring Another Saint (May 1905)

In May 1905, President Joseph F. traveled to Provo to honor another Latter-day Saint, Bathsheba Wilson Smith, the beloved wife of George A. Smith and, at the time, the general president of the Relief Society. In honor of her eighty-third birthday, special ceremonies were conducted at the Brigham Young Academy and at the Utah Stake Tabernacle. Emmeline B. Wells noted, "There has never been such an oration to any woman in this Church before, President Smith most of all paying homage to her as a mother in Israel and exemplary in life and character."[46]

PLATE 85

Joseph F. Smith at a Picnic, ca. 1905

LDSCA. President Joseph F. Smith and other General Authorities gather for a picnic at John McDonald's home located at 1258 Browning Avenue in Salt Lake City.

PLATE 86
MONUMENT DEDICATION INVITATION

MLUU. IN ANTICIPATION OF THE ONE HUNDREDTH ANNIVERSARY OF THE PROPHET JOSEPH SMITH'S BIRTH, PRESIDENT JOSEPH F. DIRECTED THAT THE FARM IN VERMONT WHERE THE PROPHET HAD BEEN BORN BE PURCHASED AND A SUITABLE MONUMENT ERECTED. HE DEDICATED THE GRANITE SHAFT THERE ON 23 DECEMBER 1905.

JOSEPH SMITH MEMORIAL (DECEMBER 1905)

In the spring of 1905, the First Presidency sent Junius F. Wells to Sharon, Windsor County, Vermont, to pinpoint the site of the Joseph Smith Sr. farm and to buy the land as agent for the Church. On 21 May, the first of four pieces of land of the Mack homestead in Sharon township was purchased. Soon thereafter, a decision was made to erect a monument and memorial cottage at the site on the one hundredth anniversary of the Prophet's birth.

As the date of dedication drew closer, the First Presidency sent an invitation to several people to attend the services:

"The First Presidency of the Church of Jesus Christ of Latter Day Saints request the pleasure of your presence at the dedicatory services to be held on the occasion of the unveiling of the Monument of Joseph Smith the Prophet erected in his honor and to commemorate

PLATE 87 (ABOVE)
JOSEPH F. SMITH AND PARTY AT THE JOSEPH SMITH MONUMENT DEDICATION IN SHARON, VERMONT, 23 DECEMBER 1905

LDSCA. TOP FROM LEFT: JOHN SMITH, UNIDENTIFIED MAN, UNIDENTIFIED WOMAN, UNIDENTIFIED WOMAN, JOSEPH F. SMITH, UNIDENTIFIED WOMAN, JOSEPH FIELDING SMITH. BOTTOM FROM LEFT: UNIDENTIFIED MAN, UNIDENTIFIED WOMAN, GEORGE ALBERT SMITH, JOHN HENRY SMITH, UNIDENTIFIED MAN.

PLATE 88 (RIGHT)
JOSEPH F. SMITH AT THE SACRED GROVE, NEW YORK, DECEMBER 1905
LDSCA.

---

the One hundredth Anniversary of his birth on the morning of Saturday, the twenty-third of December One thousand, nine hundred and five at eleven o'clock at Sharon, Windsor County, Vermont.

Memorial services will be held on Sunday, the twenty-fourth of December, in all the Assemblies of the Latter Day Saints throughout the world. You are cordially invited to attend these services wherever most convenient to join in honoring the memory of one who was honored of God and is beloved by his people.

Owing to the Winter Season and limited accommodations, a personal response to this invitation is not expected by those living at a distance except in special cases."[47]

A company of twenty-five prominent Church officials, including President Joseph F., and members went by special car from Salt Lake City to attend the ceremonies of dedication in Vermont, leaving Salt Lake City on 18 December.

On 23 December, it was a special day when the group gathered in a small cottage erected at the site, over the hearthstone of what once had been the Joseph Smith Sr. home. The group sang "America" and "We Thank Thee, Oh God, for a Prophet."

President Joseph F. Smith dedicated the monument "with hearts full of gratitude to Thee for the light and truth of Thy Gospel, the authority of the Holy Priesthood, and the ordinances of salvation for the living and for the dead, revealed through Thy servant Joseph Smith." The monument was dedicated "in loving remembrance of him."[48]

He closed the dedication meeting: "Peace be with you, and unto this place, unto this monument, and unto all who come to visit it with feelings of respect in their hearts; and those who come without feelings of respect, may it have the effect of softening their hearts, opening their eyes, and causing them to reflect soberly upon this great problem of human life and redemption that has been opened up to the world through the instrumentality of the Prophet Joseph Smith."[49]

Following the dedication, the party made a pilgrimage to Church history sites, including those in New York and Ohio, eventually arriving in Salt Lake City on 1 January 1906, just about twelve noon.

PLATE 89
CERTIFICATE FOR JOSEPH F. SMITH AS DIRECTOR AND PRESIDENT OF THE SALTAIR BEACH COMPANY, DATED 9 JANUARY 1906
ASHWORTH COLLECTION.
DURING HIS LIFETIME, JOSEPH F. SMITH SERVED ON BOARDS AND/OR WAS PRESIDENT OF SCORES OF BUSINESSES.

PLATE 90
LDS GENERAL CONFERENCE, APRIL 1906
CHARLES ELLIS JOHNSON, USHS (PHOTO #22242).

The Church Debt Retired (1906)

As a result of several converging factors, including economic recessions during the period, droughts in Utah, prosecution and persecution of members of the Church in the 1880s by the federal government, Church commitments to temple building, missionary activity, immigration, and other enterprises, President Lorenzo Snow decided to take immediate steps to relieve the Church's debt. He did so by emphasizing tithing, withdrawing from many business enterprises that drained the Church of resources, and issuing "Salt Lake Temple Bonds" on 1 January 1899 in the amount of $1 million bearing interest at the rate of 6 percent per annum.

One of President Joseph F.'s major efforts was to free the Church from the debt. Finally, in 1906, the debt was completely paid off. That day, President Joseph F. left his office adjoining the Beehive House, eagerly looking for his wife Julina. However, he met his daughter, Rachel. She recalled the occasion:

"One day when we were living in the Beehive house, I came home from school and entered the door and walked into the little hall. My father had been in the kitchen and met me in the little hall. And he said, 'Liddy, do you know where mother is? I've looked all over for her, and I've got some news I want to tell her.' And I said, 'No, sir.' He said, 'Do you think she is upstairs?' He said, 'I've been every place.' And I said, 'I don't know.' He asked me several questions and I answered, 'I don't know.' He said, 'Well, I wanted her to be the first one to hear this good news.' . . . And the thing you don't know—and . . . he gave a little smile. He said, 'I'll tell you, and I wanted mother to know.'

PLATE 91
TRUSTEE-IN-TRUST BOND CERTIFICATE
DATED 31 DECEMBER 1898

LDSCA. JOSEPH F. SMITH GAVE THIS CERTIFICATE TO HIS DAUGHTER AND WROTE ON THE FRONT: "THIS BOND HAS BEEN REDEEMED BY THE CHURCH AND IS [CANCELED] AND VOID AND IS RETAINED ONLY AS A SOUVENIR. JOSEPH F. SMITH. T. IN T." ON THE BACK IS WRITTEN: "RACHEL S. TAYLOR GIVEN TO ME BY MY FATHER, PRES. JOSEPH F. SMITH."

And he said, 'The Church is at last out of debt,' and he showed me his bonds."[50]

A few days later, she noted: "He came in and he handed me a [canceled] bond, which I have today. And he said, 'Seeing you were the first one to hear, I'm going to give you one of these [canceled] bonds.'"[51]

A Busy Time (July 1906)

The first week of July 1906 was filled with meetings and celebrations. The Journal History reported on 5 July: "The regular meeting of the First Presidency and Twelve Apostles was held this morning."[52] Later in the evening, the Royal Hawaiian Band, which was on its first tour of the continental United States, gave a concert at SaltAir Resort. Among the sixty band members were several members of the Church who recognized President Joseph F. among the nearly four thousand concert goers. The local paper noted:

"The Royal Hawaiian band, with its glee club, was rendering one of its noted 'Hulas.' Suddenly Kawa Lehai, one of the most expert mandolinists among the natives, nudged his nearest neighbor. At the same moment a trio of singers turned to each other, nodded, and smiled a smile of satisfaction. They bowed toward the audience—few knew why—and at the finish of the song one of them stepped forward to the conductor, Herr Berger, and whispered something into his ear. The number which followed had not been announced on the program, and it was not sung. And only one person in the audience realized that it was the beautiful melody to which the Hawaiians sing, 'O my Father,' the famous Mormon anthem. That one person was President Joseph F. Smith. As he entered he was recognized by members of the band who were long ago converts to the principles of the Latter-day Saints Church and he alone upon taking his seat, noticed the compliment. The respected leader sat in silence until the last of the plaintive notes had died away. Then he glanced significantly toward the musicians, and was greeted by a score or more of smiling faces; by the people who were familiar with his features, not from personal

The Twentieth-Century Prophet

PLATE 92
JOSEPH F. SMITH AND GRANDSON, CA. 1906

J. B. KING, LDSCA. A STEREO-VIEW, A POPULAR FORMAT DURING THE LAST QUARTER OF THE NINETEENTH CENTURY AND THE FIRST DECADES OF THE TWENTIETH CENTURY, FROM A SET OF VIEWS ON LDS CHURCH HISTORY PUBLISHED BY A NON-LDS FIRM. THE CAPTION READS: "3374 JOSEPH F. SMITH AND GRANDSON, SALT LAKE CITY, UTAH. COPYRIGHT, 1906, BY J. B. KING." AS WAS SOMETIMES THE CASE, A FULLER DESCRIPTION IS PRINTED ON THE REVERSE SIDE OF THE STEREO-VIEW: "28.—PRESIDENT JOSEPH F. SMITH. THIS VIEW IS A REMARKABLY FINE AND REALISTIC LIKENESS OF JOSEPH F. SMITH, SIXTH PRESIDENT OF THE CHURCH OF JESUS CHRIST OF LATTER-DAY SAINTS, AND SON OF THE MARTYRED PATRIARCH, HYRUM SMITH. THE LITTLE BOY ON HIS KNEE, DAVID SMITH, IS A GRANDSON OF PRESIDENT SMITH, AN EXCEPTIONALLY BRIGHT LAD 3 YEARS OF AGE. PRESIDENT SMITH WAS BORN AT FAR WEST, CALDWELL COUNTY, MISSOURI, NOV. 13, 1838. HE WAS ORDAINED AN APOSTLE JULY 1, 1866, AND ACTED AS SECOND COUNSELOR IN THE FIRST PRESIDENCY OF THE CHURCH DURING THE ADMINISTRATIONS OF PRESIDENT JOHN TAYLOR, WILFORD WOODRUFF AND LORENZO SNOW. PRESIDENT SMITH IS A MAN OF KEEN INSIGHT, DISCHARGING THE DUTIES OF HIS OFFICE WITH GREAT ABILITY AND ELABORATE CARE. HIS ENTIRE LIFE SINCE CHILDHOOD HAS BEEN ACTIVELY CONNECTED WITH THE CHURCH OF WHICH HE IS NOW (1906) THE PRESIDENT."

acquaintance, but from having seen his photographs, which are liberally exhibited in the Mormon chapels throughout the islands. Until the end of the concert President Smith was a deeply interested listener."[53]

PLATE 93
JOSEPH F. SMITH AND PARTY AT BRITISH MISSION HOME, 1906

LDSCA. BACK FROM LEFT: UNIDENTIFIED MAN, UNIDENTIFIED MAN, MARTHA D. GRANT BOYLE, EDNA L. SMITH, GEORGE CARLOS SMITH, EMILY HARRIS WELLS GRANT, ABINADI [?] TOLMAN, HEBER CHASE SMITH, WALTER E. GRANT, AND ROBERT PRICE. MIDDLE FROM LEFT: NAN NIBLEY, ALVIN F. SMITH, CHARLES W. NIBLEY, JOSEPH F. SMITH, AND HEBER J. GRANT. FRONT FROM LEFT: WILLIAM A. MORTON, ALICE NIBLEY, GRACE GRANT EVANS, AND UNIDENTIFIED MAN. LOCATED ON HOLLY ROAD IN LIVERPOOL, THE MISSION OFFICE WAS MOVED SHORTLY AFTER PRESIDENT JOSEPH F. SMITH'S VISIT. PART OF HIS LABORS DURING THIS TOUR WAS THE CLOSING OF THE NEGOTIATIONS TO PURCHASE A FINE THREE-STORY HOME AND LOT, SUITABLE FOR THE CONSTRUCTION OF A CHAPEL, AT 295 EDGE LANE IN LIVERPOOL, KNOWN AS DURHAM HOUSE.

A VISIT TO EUROPE (JULY–SEPTEMBER 1906)

President Joseph F. departed Salt Lake City on 21 July 1906 for a tour of Europe. While there, he visited missionaries and members in Holland, Germany, Switzerland, France, England, and Scotland. The tour was the first time a Church president visited Europe. Arriving in Antwerp, Belgium, on 5 August, the party proceeded to the Netherlands.

The Saints in the United States received this report about his visit:

"*Der Stern* of August 15, has an account of the visit of President Joseph F. Smith in the Netherlands, on the 7th and 8th of August, accompanied by President Heber J. Grant of the British Mission, and Elder Chas. Nibley, who journeyed with him from Utah. Meetings were held at Amsterdam and Rotterdam, at which cities President Smith and others addressed attentive and large congregations. They left the Netherlands for a further visit to the continent on the 10th of August, having visited the Hague on the 9th where Alvin F. Smith joined the party. The visit of President Joseph F. Smith and party is of unusual interest, as it is the first time that a President of the Church, during his presidency, has visited Europe, and it came also as a surprise to the Saints and elders."[54]

On his way home from his European tour, President Joseph F. stopped in Carthage, Hancock County, Illinois. The Church had purchased the jail where his father and uncle were murdered. This was his first and only visit to the site. The experience harrowed up emotional memories.

Address to the World (March 1907)

With the conclusion of the Smoot hearings in Washington, D.C., President Joseph F. and his counselors thought it important to provide the public, through a document entitled "An Address. The Church of Jesus Christ of Latter-day Saints to the World," their feelings about the Smoot hearings. Issued on 26 March 1907, it was later adopted by vote of the Church, in general conference, on 5 April 1907.

They began the letter:

"In the hope of correcting misrepresentation, and of establishing a more perfect understanding respecting ourselves and our religion, we, the officers and members of the Church of Jesus Christ of Latter-day Saints, in general conference assembled, issue this Declaration. Such an action seems imperative. Never were our principles or our purposes more widely misrepresented, more seriously misunderstood. Our doctrines are distorted, the sacred ordinances of our religion ridiculed, and Christianity questioned, our history falsified, our character traduced, and our course of conduct as a people reprobated and condemned."

They continued:

"We solemnly declare the truth to be: Our religion is founded on the revelations of God. The gospel we proclaim is the Gospel of Christ, restored to earth in this the dispensation of the fulness of times. The high claim of the Church is declared in its title—The Church of Jesus Christ of Latter-day Saints. Established by divine direction, its name was prescribed by him whose Church it is—Jesus the Christ. The religion of this people is pure Christianity. Its creed is expressive of the duties of practical life. Its theology is based on the doctrines of the Redeemer.

"If it be true Christianity to accept Jesus Christ in person and in mission as divine; to revere him as the Son of God, the crucified and risen Lord, through whom alone mankind can attain salvation; to accept his teachings as a guide, to adopt as a standard and observe as a law the ethical code he promulgated; to comply with the requirements prescribed by him as essential to membership in his Church, namely, faith, repentance, baptism by immersion for the remission of sins, and the laying on of hands for the gift of the Holy Ghost—if this be Christianity, then are we

Christians, and the Church of Jesus Christ of Latter-day Saints is a Christian church.

"The theology of our Church is the theology taught by Jesus Christ and his apostles, the theology of scripture and reason. It not only acknowledges the sacredness of ancient scripture and the binding force of divinely-inspired acts and utterances in ages past; but also declares that God now speaks to man in this final gospel dispensation.

"We believe in the Godhead, comprising the three individual personages, Father, Son, and Holy Ghost.

"We hold that man is verily the child of God, formed in his image, endowed with divine attributes, and possessing power to rise from the gross desires of earth to the ennobling aspirations of heaven.

"We believe in the pre-existence of man as a spirit, and in a future state of individual existence, in which every soul shall find its place, as determined by justice and mercy, with opportunities of endless progression, in the varied conditions of eternity.

"We believe in the free agency of man, and therefore in his individual responsibility.

"We believe that salvation is for no select few, but that all men may be saved through obedience to the laws and ordinances of the gospel.

"We affirm that to administer in the ordinances of the gospel, authority must be given of God; and that this authority is the power of the Holy Priesthood.

"We affirm that through the ministration of immortal personages, the

PLATE 94
JOSEPH F. AND ALICE ANN KIMBALL SMITH FAMILY, CA. 1907

C. E. JOHNSON, NICHOLS COLLECTION. FRONT FROM LEFT: SARAH SANT, FIELDING, ROBERT SANT JR., AND ALICE. MIDDLE FROM LEFT: MANON L., ALICE MAY SMITH SANT, JESSE, JOSEPH F., ALICE ANN KIMBALL, AND LILETH N. SMITH. BACK FROM LEFT: CHARLES COULSON, ANDREW, ROBERT SANT, LUCY, AND HEBER CHASE.

Brigham Young University Training School 1907

PLATE 95

Joseph F. Smith at the Brigham Young University Training School, ca. 1907

LDSCA. View of students on hillside forming large block "Y."
President Joseph F. Smith stands in the middle of the crowd.

Holy Priesthood has been conferred upon men in the present age, and that under this divine authority the Church of Christ has been organized.

"We proclaim the objects of this organization to be, the preaching of the gospel in all the world, the gathering of scattered Israel, and the preparation of a people for the coming of the Lord."⁵⁵

Another Visit to Hawaii (February–March 1909)

On 17 February, President Joseph F. went to Hawaii, accompanied by Julina and three daughters, Emily J., Rachel, and Edith. Emma, the daughter of President Joseph F. and Edna, also came along. Additional members of the Salt Lake group included Samuel G. Woolley, president of the Hawaiian Mission; A. W. McCune; Charles W. Nibley; and Rebecca Neibaur Nibley and two daughters, Nan and Alice. The main purpose was to provide President Joseph F. some time to gain some much-needed rest. According to a report, the party "sailed from San Francisco on February 20, on the ship *Alameda*, arriving in Honolulu six days later." In the voyage, they experienced only two days of bad weather. President Joseph F. noted: "Last night was one of the worst I remember to have passed at sea. My arms, shoulders & back are lame and sore by trying to keep from being thrown out of my berth."⁵⁶ The trip otherwise was very delightful from beginning to end. During a break from a constant flow of visitors and meetings in Salt Lake City, President Joseph F. took time to catch up on some reading: "Read more of Sir Francis Drake's voyages. Most thrilling!"⁵⁷ Everybody whom the party met treated them with the utmost consideration and courtesy. "At Honolulu the ship was met by the Royal Hawaiian Band, and a large number of people, who had gathered to greet the party, which was

PLATE 96
JOSEPH F. SMITH AND PARTY IN HAWAII, 1909

LDSCA. SOMETIMES IDENTIFIED AS BEING TAKEN DURING THE 1915 HAWAIIAN TRIP, THIS PHOTOGRAPH SHOWS JOSEPH F. SMITH (SEATED NEAR THE CENTER OF THE PHOTOGRAPH), JULINA LAMBSON SMITH, ELIAS WESLEY SMITH (SON OF JOSEPH F.), EDITH, EMILY, AND RACHEL SMITH (DAUGHTERS OF JOSEPH F.), CHARLES W. AND REBECCA NEIBAUR NIBLEY, ELIZABETH C. MCCUNE, SAMUEL E. WOOLLEY (MISSION PRESIDENT), FRANKLIN JOHN WOOLLEY (FIFTH PERSON TO THE RIGHT OF JOSEPH F. SMITH).

---

entirely unknown to the visitors beforehand, the whole reception being entirely unsolicited, and being arranged, the leader said, as an expression of appreciation for the kindness shown to the band while in Salt Lake City some two years ago. The native Saints who had gathered completely covered the members of the party, on landing, with wreaths of flowers. They were then conducted to the conference house, where a feast was spread and the visitors given of the bounties of the land."[58]

The report indicated: "President Smith particularly enjoyed the poi, as it reminded him of his old mission days . . . ; to have another taste of that particular dish was a keen delight."[59]

President Joseph F. visited members and friends and the famous Kilauea Volcano and enjoyed the Pacific rainstorms. Meetings were held at Laie and Honolulu on Oahu and Hilo on the Big Island (Hawaii). After two months on the island, he and the party returned to Salt Lake City on 1 April 1909, just in time for the annual conference. The report indicated that "the trip did President Smith much good and he returns refreshed and strengthened for his arduous labors."[60]

Upon his return home following the visit to Hawaii, President Joseph F. plunged back into his administrative duties. In spite of the tremendous pressure of his workload, President Joseph F. kept up a prodigious correspondence activity. He could often be found late in the evening at a desk writing letters of encouragement, counsel, and news to members of the Church, family members, and others.

One such example from this period is a letter written to George Albert Smith, who was struggling with his health at the time:

"My Dear George Albert—I was very sorry, on hearing, last evening, that you were not feeling so well again, but cheered on learning you felt better today. I do not want you to worry about anything, and I do not

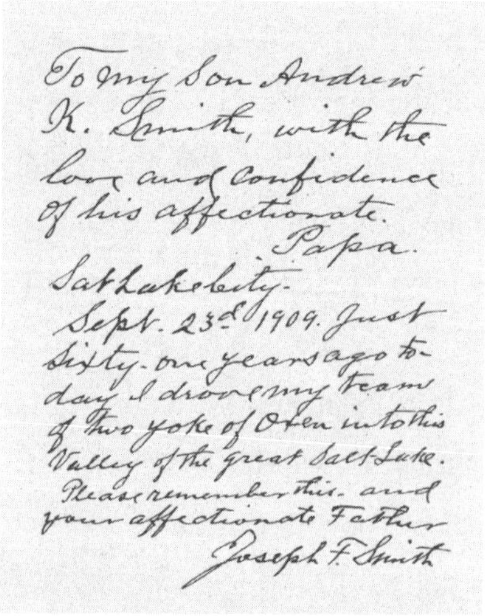

To my Son Andrew
K. Smith, with the
love and Confidence
of his affectionate.
Papa.
Salt Lake City.
Sept. 23rd 1909. Just
Sixty-one years ago to-
day I drove my team
of two yoke of Oxen into this
Valley of the great Salt Lake.
Please remember this. and
your affectionate Father
Joseph F. Smith

PLATE 97

JOSEPH F. SMITH INSCRIPTION, DATED 23 SEPTEMBER 1909

NEBEKER COLLECTION. IN A SHORT NOTE INSCRIBED IN A COPY OF THE RECENTLY PUBLISHED BOOK, *THE ORIGINS OF THE REORGANIZED CHURCH AND THE QUESTION OF SUCCESSION* (SALT LAKE CITY: DESERET NEWS, 1909) BY JOSEPH F. SMITH JR. (KNOWN TODAY AS JOSEPH FIELDING SMITH), JOSEPH F. SMITH WROTE: "TO MY SON ANDREW K. SMITH, WITH LOVE AND CONFIDENCE OF HIS AFFECTIONATE PAPA." HE ADDED A BRIEF NOTE RECALLING HIS ENTRANCE INTO THE GREAT BASIN ON THE SIXTY-FIRST ANNIVERSARY OF THE EVENT.

PLATE 98
JOSEPH F. SMITH
AT THE CORNERSTONE
LAYING OF THE KARL G.
MAESER BUILDING,
16 OCTOBER 1909
OLSON-HAFEN PHOTO, BYU. ONE OF SEVERAL PHOTOGRAPHS TAKEN ON THE OCCASION, THIS RARE IMAGE WAS TAKEN RIGHT AFTER THE LAYING OF THE CORNERSTONE (NOTE THE CRANE WITH THE AMERICAN FLAG DRAPED OVER IT IN FRONT OF JOSEPH F. SMITH) FOR THE FIRST BUILDING OF BRIGHAM YOUNG ACADEMY ERECTED ON "TEMPLE HILL," KNOWN AS UPPER CAMPUS.

want to worry you with a long letter. Please remember what the Lord said to his Apostles—'Take no thought of what ye shall eat etc.' I say this to you <u>The Lord will provide</u> for you, therefore don't worry. God bless you. I am affectionately your kinsman, Joseph F. Smith."⁶¹

Brigham Young Academy in Provo (October 1909)

President Joseph F. was an ardent supporter of education. One of his responsibilities in advancing education among the Latter-day Saints was his role as president of Brigham Young Academy, now known as Brigham Young University. The school made an important transition in 1909 when it constructed the first building on "Temple Hill," later known as Upper Campus. Eventually, Upper Campus displaced the lower campus as the heart of the school.

In October of that year, President Joseph F. traveled to Provo to preside over the cornerstone-laying ceremony of the Karl G. Maeser Building, the first building constructed on Temple Hill. The *Deseret Evening News* reported:

"President Joseph F. Smith declared that he was delighted with the progress of the building in honor of Dr. Maeser who was always true to the highest educational ideals, education of the mind and heart, education of the divine as well as the intellectual. . . . He said that he would contribute to the extent of his ability to the building fund. He remarked that he was not a Jesse Knight, a Gould, or Vanderbilt. . . . President Smith remarked that he was a very rich man, but that his greatest riches consisted of good wives and a large family of children with which he had been blessed. As soon as he returned home he said that he would send his check for $100."[62]

Following his brief remarks, he supervised the laying of the cornerstone and, eventually, dedicated it—beginning a new era for the school.

History of the Church by B. H. Roberts (October 1909)

In 1909, the Church took advantage of a wonderful opportunity to present its own history to the public. In an effort to support this prospect, President Joseph F. and his counselors sent a letter to all stake presidents in the Church, asking them to appoint an agent for the *Americana* magazine, which was currently publishing a "History of the Mormon Church" written by B. H. Roberts. Eventually, published in book form as the *Comprehensive History of the Church* in 1930, the installments were originally published serially from June 1909 until July 1915.

PLATE 99
JOSEPH F. SMITH'S COPY OF THE JUNE 1913 ISSUE OF AMERICANA
ASHWORTH COLLECTION.
B. H. ROBERTS' "HISTORY OF THE CHURCH" ARTICLES WERE SERIALIZED IN THE AMERICANA AND LATER PUBLISHED IN 1930 AS THE COMPREHENSIVE HISTORY OF THE CHURCH.

The First Presidency wrote: "We call your attention to 'Americana,' a monthly magazine published by the National Americana Society, New York, the magazine is devoted chiefly to Historical and Genealogical subjects, and cannot fail to be of very great interest to a community. . . . The magazine has opened its pages for the publication of a detailed, exhaustive 'History of the Mormon Church,' by Elder B. H. Roberts, to be illustrated with beautiful steel engravings and photogravures of the principal characters and places identified with the coming forth of the great latter-day work. . . . The opportunity afforded us by the publishers of Americana to tell in this adequate way our own story, is something of a new experience; for never before has such an opportunity been given to us to tell our own story of the rise, progress and present status of the Church to the world. . . .

"In view of the great good that will doubtless accrue to the Church by this proclamation of its message to the readers of 'Americana,' it has occurred to us that there would be some Latter-day Saints in all the Stakes of Zion who would be glad to subscribe for this magazine, both that they might have the history, because of its own intrinsic value as Mormon literature (together with the other very valuable reading matter in the magazine), as also to give encouragement to the publishers who have intrepidly afforded us this hearing before the world. . . .

"All this is in the interest of the Lord's work, and we pray that it may be blessed to the accomplishment of great good. Very truly your brethren, JOSEPH F. SMITH, JOHN R. WINDER, ANTHON H. LUND, First Presidency."[63]

PLATE 100
JOSEPH F. SMITH AND FAMILY AT THE SMITH HOMESTEAD IN SALT LAKE CITY, CA. 1910

LDSCA. JOSEPH F. WROTE ON THE BACK OF THIS PHOTOGRAPH, "THE OLD HOME OF MARY FIELDING SMITH, WIDOW OF HYRUM SMITH, WHERE SHE AND FAMILY SETTLED IN THE EARLY SPRING OF 1849: THEY HAVING ARRIVED IN SALT LAKE VALLEY SEPT. 23RD 1848. AND WINTERED ON MILL CREEK DURING THE WINTERS OF 1848–9. JOSEPH F. SMITH."

PLATE 101 (ABOVE)
JOSEPH F. SMITH AND PARTY CHANGING A TIRE
ON A ROAD TRIP, CA. 1910
MLUU (P0036 #145).

PLATE 102 (BELOW)
JOSEPH F. SMITH AND PARTY AT THE
GRAND CANYON, CA. 1910
MLUU (P0036 #3049). PRESIDENT ANTHON H. LUND AND BISHOP CHARLES W. NIBLEY
ARE PICTURED ALONG WITH PRESIDENT JOSEPH F. SMITH.

PLATE 103

LDS CHURCH FIRST PRESIDENCY, CA. 1910, THOMAS STUDIO

LDSCA. FROM LEFT: ANTHON H. LUND, JOSEPH F. SMITH, AND JOHN HENRY SMITH. ANTHON H. LUND WAS SUSTAINED AS FIRST COUNSELOR TO JOSEPH F. SMITH ON 7 APRIL 1910, FOLLOWING THE DEATH OF JOHN R. WINDER, FIRST COUNSELOR, IN MARCH 1910. JOHN HENRY SMITH WAS SUSTAINED AS SECOND COUNSELOR TO JOSEPH F. SMITH ON 7 APRIL 1910, REPLACING ANTHON H. LUND, WHO WAS SUSTAINED AS FIRST COUNSELOR IN THE FIRST PRESIDENCY ON THE SAME DAY.

Another Trip to Europe (Summer 1910)

Following the reorganization of the First Presidency in April 1910, President Joseph F. was on the move again. During the first week of July, he and his party, consisting of his wife Mary Taylor Schwartz Smith and others, made their way to New York on the first leg of a journey that would take him to Europe again.

The first stop in the tour was England and then on to Rotterdam, where some eleven hundred Latter-day Saints and friends gathered to hear President Joseph F. These gatherings were important aspects of the tours, and although he experienced frequent attacks of sciatica, his presence in Europe and England uplifted the local Saints and the missionaries who met him along the way. Future First Presidency member, Henry D. Moyle, was serving as a young missionary at the time. Following one of the meetings held during the tour, he wrote in his journal: "Pres. Smith then spoke to us again making his remarks along the line of things that we should do. He uttered a blessing on all assembled and you could feel in very deed that it was immediately answered."[64]

Andrew Jenson wrote about President Joseph F.'s visit to Scandinavia during his European tour:

"On July 27th the Scandinavian Mission was honored by the arrival in Copenhagen of the following brethren and sisters: President Joseph F. Smith and wife (Mary T. Smith), Franklin R. Smith, Charles W. Nibley (Presiding Bishop of the Church) with his wife Julia B. Nibley and two daughters. We took the visitors to the mission office in two automobiles and the president and his whole party soon found themselves at home with us. We conversed with our visitors until noon and then

PLATE 104
JOSEPH F. SMITH, ANDREW JENSON, AND OLUF ANDERSON, 2 AUGUST 1910

EMIL CLAUSEN, LDSCA. TAKEN IN COPENHAGEN, DENMARK, DURING PRESIDENT JOSEPH F. SMITH'S HISTORIC TOUR OF EUROPE, THIS PHOTOGRAPH SHOWS ANDREW JENSON (SCANDINAVIAN MISSION PRESIDENT) AND OLUF ANDERSON (EDITOR OF THE CHURCH'S SCANDINAVIAN PERIODICAL, *SKANDINAVIENS STJERNE*) WITH PRESIDENT JOSEPH F. SMITH

took the whole party out sightseeing. In the evening we held a meeting in our hall, which had been beautifully decorated for the occasion by our local sisters with flowers and a 'Velkommen' streamer hung between the two pillars in the lower end of the hall. Pres. Smith delivered the first speech in the meeting. . . . We had a splendid meeting in Copenhagen, although the parties were somewhat tired after their long journey from England."[65]

On the following day, 28 July, President Joseph F. and party traveled to Christiana, Norway, "where an enthusiastic reception was given us by the elders and local saints. The time was spent in meetings and sightseeing."[66]

Jenson continued his travel narrative: "On the 30th our party traveled to Stockholm, Sweden, where we were made welcome by Elder Peter Sundwall, president of the Swedish Mission. In Stockholm, on Sunday, President Smith and Bishop Nibley gave some excellent advise and bore powerful testimony."[67] On Monday, President Joseph F. attended the International Peace Conference being held in Stockholm at the time. In the afternoon, he and his party departed for Malmö, and as the "train pulled out the saints sang: 'We thank Thee, O God, for a Prophet.'"[68]

The party arrived in Copenhagen the next morning. Time was given to more sightseeing and a visit to the photographic studio of Emil Clausen, "where a number of pictures were taken."[69] In the evening, the Saints, with fifty-one missionaries, gathered to hear President Smith. Jenson noted, "President Smith was powerful in his utterances."[70]

Jenson provided more detail in a special report to the *Deseret Evening News*: "Peter Sundwall and Andrew Jenson, President Joseph F. Smith and Charles W. Nibley were admitted as special representatives from America. . . . After the regular session, we met with the American delegation under the chairmanship of Doctor Benj. F. Trueblood of Boston, who is secretary of the American Peace society."[71]

President Joseph F. and party left Denmark on 3 August, departing for Berlin, Germany, continuing their European tour before heading home to Salt Lake City.

Changes in the First Presidency and Council of the Twelve (1910–1911)

On 27 March 1910, John R. Winder, first counselor to President Joseph F., died at the age of eighty-nine. On 7 April, President Anthon H. Lund, second counselor in the First Presidency, was sustained as the first counselor, replacing President Winder. President Joseph F.

called John Henry Smith, a member of the Council of the Twelve, to become the second counselor in the First Presidency at the same time. At sixty-one years of age, President John Henry Smith served briefly until his death on 13 October 1911. Charles W. Penrose, a member of the Council of the Twelve, was sustained to succeed President John Henry Smith on 11 December 1911. Presidents Lund and Penrose served as counselors to President Joseph F. until his death in 1918.

PLATE 105
HOTEL UTAH, CA. 1912
C. R. SAVAGE & COMPANY, LDSCA. ONE OF THE IMPORTANT INDICATIONS OF THE CHURCH'S GROWTH AT THE BEGINNING OF THE TWENTIETH CENTURY WAS THE CONSTRUCTION OF THE HOTEL UTAH ON THE CORNER OF SOUTH TEMPLE AND MAIN STREET IN 1911. IT WAS, AT THE TIME, ONE OF THE CHURCH'S LARGEST INVESTMENTS AND WAS CONSTRUCTED TO FULFILL AT LEAST TWO GOALS: FIRST, AN INVESTMENT TO HELP FINANCE THE CHURCH'S EFFORTS TO PREACH THE GOSPEL TO THE LIVING AND REDEEM THE DEAD. SECOND, TO PROVIDE A PLACE FOR THE "WEARY TRAVELERS" WHERE THEY COULD "CONTEMPLATE THE GLORY OF ZION," AS WAS THE GOAL FOR THE NAUVOO HOUSE, WHICH THE LORD COMMANDED THE SAINTS TO BUILD ON THE BANKS OF THE MISSISSIPPI RIVER IN 1841 (SEE DOCTRINE AND COVENANTS 124:23).

On 8 December 1911, President Joseph F. ordained James E. Talmage an apostle and set him apart as a member of the Council of the Twelve:

"Dear Brother James E. Talmage, as your fellow servants and as Apostles of the Lord Jesus Christ in the authority of the Holy Priesthood, which is after the order of the Son of God, we lay our hands upon your head, and ordain you an Apostle in the Church of Jesus Christ of Latter-day Saints, and also set you apart to be one of the Quorum of the Twelve Apostles, and confer upon you all the keys, rights, privileges, blessings, and authority."[72]

Following the sacred and solemn ordination, George F. Gibbs, secretary to the First Presidency, noted, "This being done President Smith and all the brethren present congratulated Brother Talmage, and extended to him the right hand of fellowship."[73]

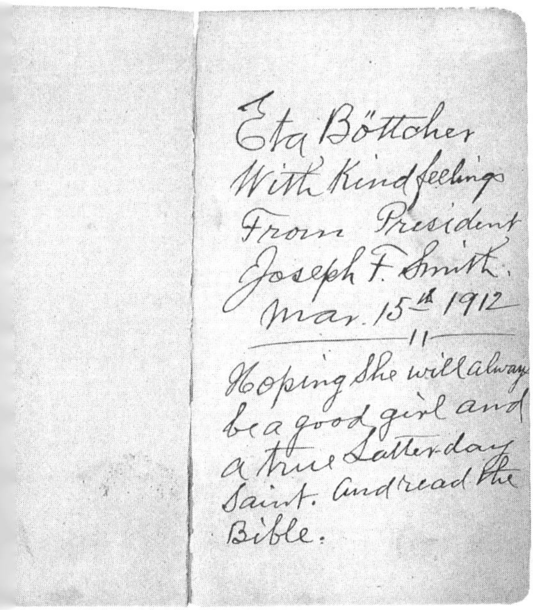

PLATE 106

JOSEPH F. SMITH INSCRIPTION IN BIBLE, DATED 15 MARCH 1912

ASHWORTH COLLECTION. PRESIDENT JOSEPH F. SMITH WROTE: "ETA BÖTTCHER WITH KIND FEELINGS FROM PRESIDENT JOSEPH F. SMITH MAR. 15TH 1912. HOPING SHE WILL ALWAYS BE A GOOD GIRL AND A TRUE LATTER-DAY SAINT. AND READ THE BIBLE."

FIRST PRESIDENCY, CA. 1911–12

Thomas Studio, LDSCA. From left: Anthon H. Lund, Joseph F. Smith, and Charles W. Penrose.

PLATE 108
JOSEPH F. SMITH AND FAMILY AT OCEAN PARK, CALIFORNIA, CA. JULY–AUGUST 1912
LDSCA. LOCATED ON HART DRIVE, THE SMALL BUNGALOW WAS ONLY STEPS AWAY FROM THE BEACH.

EXTENDED TRAVEL BY TRAIN (1901–1918)

President Joseph F. and other Church leaders spent hours, days, and sometimes weeks on the various train lines while traveling among the Saints. Usually, President Joseph F. had access to a private car, making these trips a little more comfortable for the venerated leader. On one such trip, a very extended excursion to Florida, President Joseph F. was accompanied by his wife Julina Lambson Smith and his daughter Emily Jane. She recalled:

"Moma & Papa at the rear of the train. Pres. Smith usually had his own car as they traveled on the railroad. He usually had one of his wives and some children accompany him. His wives took their turns as did the children. President Smith invited the railroad porters into his car to kneel and have family prayer with his family. They loved

PLATE 109
JOSEPH F. SMITH, CA. 1914
MLUU (P0036 #146). WHILE IN SOUTHERN CALIFORNIA, PRESIDENT JOSEPH F. SMITH TOOK ADVANTAGE OF THE CLIMATE AND PARTICIPATED IN MANY OF THE RECREATIONAL ACTIVITIES THAT WERE PART OF THE SOUTHERN CALIFORNIA LIFESTYLE, INCLUDING SWIMMING.

Pres. Smith. He admonished them to live their religion and some day, probably not in their life time or his, but some day those who lived worthily would receive the priesthood."[74]

A Retreat in Southern California (1913–1914)

Church leaders increased their visits to southern California following the completion of the direct rail line between Salt Lake City and Los Angeles in 1905. Soon, southern California became a place of refuge and relaxation for them. Therefore, in 1913, President Joseph F.

began to consider purchasing a home in southern California. He wrote to George Albert Smith: "My family is large—as you know, and my necessities seem to increase. . . . Suit my folks for a <u>rest</u> place, for a short time each, near the Sea Shore. And where <u>I</u> might <u>retire</u> for a week or so, occasionally 'all by my own self' as the children say. I cannot and therefore <u>never</u> expect to be '<u>alone</u>.'"[75]

In the spring of 1914, he apparently purchased a home in California to meet his needs. The home, known as "Deseret," was located in Santa Monica and provided an important refuge for President Joseph F. and others.

Among the activities President Joseph F. enjoyed while in southern California was golf. For those gathered at the grave-side funeral of President Joseph F. in 1918, Bishop Charles W. Nibley recalled one story about a day in Santa Monica:

"He got so that he could play a very good game, excellent indeed for a man of his years. But on one occasion . . . when we were playing, we were up within about one hundred feet of the flag at the hole we were making for. A light stroke should have driven the ball nearer the flag, but the inclination to look up as one tries to hit the ball got the best of him, and the consequence was he topped the ball and it rolled only a couple of feet or so. He bent over for the next stroke, and the one thing which all golfers most fear, and the hardest to overcome, is the habit of looking up or taking the eye off the ball just as you go to strike. This he did, the second time, when he topped it again and it moved but a few feet further. The third time he went up to it and hit it a whack that sent it rolling one hundred feet beyond the flag. His son, Wesley, who was playing with us, called out, 'Why, papa, what did you do that for? You knew it would roll away down there in the ditch!' The President straightened up and said, with a smile, 'Well, I was mad at it!'"[76]

PLATE 110
JOSEPH F. SMITH AND PARTY, CA. 1917

WALKER COLLECTION. PRESIDENT JOSEPH F. AS HE PREPARES TO LEAVE OR HAS ARRIVED IN A PRIVATE CAR PROVIDED BY THE RAILROAD COMPANY, MOST LIKELY IN SOUTHERN CALIFORNIA.

PLATE 111
JOSEPH F. SMITH'S RAIL PASS, DATED 21 JUNE 1917

SHUPE COLLECTION. THIS IS ONE OF THE MANY RAILROAD PASSES JOSEPH F. SMITH USED DURING HIS EXTENSIVE TRAVELS AMONG THE SAINTS IN THE UNITED STATES AND CANADA. THIS PARTICULAR PASS WAS ISSUED BY THE SALT LAKE, GARFIELD & WESTERN RAILWAY, OF WHICH JOSEPH F. SMITH WAS A DIRECTOR.

The Twentieth-Century Prophet

PLATE 112
Joseph F. Smith and Family on Porch of Church Home at Santa Monica, ca. 1917
Walker Collection.

PLATE 113
Joseph F. Smith at the Beneficial Life Convention, 6–7 June 1913

Utah Photo Materials Co., LDSCA. Front center from left: Charles W. Penrose (Rudger Clawson has his right hand on Penrose's shoulder), Anthon H. Lund, and Francis M. Lyman (Joseph F. Smith stands behind and between Anthon H. Lund and Francis M. Lyman). Taken on the steps of Barratt Hall at the Latter-day Saint University in Salt Lake City, Utah.

Temple Site Dedication in Canada (July 1913)

As early as 1901, President Joseph F. foresaw "the necessity arising for other temples or places consecrated to the Lord [beyond those constructed in Utah] for the performance of the ordinances of God's house, so that the people may have the benefits of the house of the Lord without having to travel hundreds of miles for that purpose."[77]

Nevertheless, when he announced to priesthood leaders during a Friday evening priesthood meeting in the Tabernacle in October 1912 that the Church would soon build a temple in Alberta, Canada, the congregation was astounded. Alberta Stake President Edward J. Wood, who was in attendance, records in his diary on this occasion: "Pres[ident] Smith . . . to the surprise of us all . . . announced that the Church would build a Temple in Canada and took a vote on it which received the especial support of all present."[78]

Later, President Heber J. Grant recalled the effect the announcement of the temple by President Smith made on him:

"I remember, as well as I remember anything that ever happened in my life, the thrill that went through my very being, the joy and satisfaction I experienced, as President Smith stood up in the Tabernacle and announced that a temple was to be erected in Canada. There are times in our lives when something comes into our souls in the nature, we might say, almost of an electric shock, that thrills our beings, and when we are thrilled by the Spirit of the living God, as I feel sure that audience was at the time of the announcement of the prospective erection of this building, we have not the language with which to express to God our gratitude for His blessings to us on such occasions."[79]

In July 1913, an estimated fifteen hundred to twenty-five hundred

PLATE 114
JOSEPH F. SMITH SPEAKING IN THE CARDSTON ALBERTA STAKE TABERNACLE, 27 JULY 1913
HENSON PHOTO, LDSCA.

persons gathered in Cardston to witness the site dedication by President Joseph F. President Wood provides a record of his feelings on the occasion in an important diary entry: "The Great Day for Canada—the greatest day in our history. The day our Temple site was dedicated."[80]

He continues: "We all went to the Temple site and never did I attend an out door meeting like it. We formed a hollow square [and] sang 'We Thank Thee Oh God for a Prophet.' George Albert Smith offered [the] prayer. We sang 'O Ye Mountain High' and Pres. Smith offered the dedicatory prayer, which was inspired indeed. Bishop [Charles W.] Nibley spoke well and took a vote from the hundreds present. We sang 'Our God We Raise to Thee' and closing prayer offered by Pres. Penrose."[81]

The Journal History of the Church provides the text of President Joseph F.'s prayer of dedication.[82] After beginning the prayer, President Smith turned attention to the occasion for which the Saints had gathered in Cardston: "We have met here this afternoon on this ground, which we have designated, to set it apart as a suitable place upon which to erect a temple to thy holy name, a place in which holy ordinances may be performed for the living and . . . the dead."[83] President Smith added a special plea:

"We pray, Holy Father, that we may be able to carry out thy plans, and fulfill thy laws and requirements in building this, another house unto thee, wherein thy Holy Spirit may dwell, also, the power of thy presence may be felt by those who administer and by those administered unto: that all things may be done according to thy requirements; and that all who enter may have in their hearts the love of God, the

PLATE 115
JOSEPH F. SMITH AND PARTY AT THE ALBERTA TEMPLE SITE DEDICATION, 27 JULY 1913

HENSON PHOTO, LDSCA. FROM LEFT: JOSEPH F. SMITH (HOLDING HIS SON ROYAL GRANT SMITH), MARY TAYLOR SCHWARTZ SMITH, CHARLES W. NIBLEY (ALBERTA STAKE PRESIDENT EDWARD J. WOOD STANDS BEHIND), GEORGE ALBERT SMITH, AND ZINA YOUNG CARD. THE SITE WAS THE FIRST TEMPLE SITE DEDICATED OUTSIDE THE UNITED STATES, SIGNALING THE BEGINNING OF THE EFFORT TO ESTABLISH ALL THE CHURCH'S PROGRAMS AND BLESSINGS BEYOND THE GREAT BASIN.

PLATE 116
JOSEPH F. SMITH AND PARTY, 28 JULY 1913
INTERNATIONAL SECURITIES COMPANY, LTD., MLUU (PH 0036/157).
JOSEPH F. SMITH VISITED THE LDS CHURCH RANCH, MORMON SETTLEMENTS, AND THE FAMOUS WATERTON LAKES PARK THE DAY FOLLOWING THE DEDICATION OF THE TEMPLE SITE IN CARDSTON.

love of neighbor, and of mankind, and that they may be instrumental in thy hands for the redemption of the dead and the saving of souls from sin and death."[84]

President Joseph F. concluded:

"And now, Holy Father, we have designated this piece of ground on which to build another temple unto thy name, for the benefit of thy people, and those who have departed this life who are in need, and shall prove worthy of the privileges and blessings of the gospel; sanctify—O Father, this plot of ground, and make it holy before thee. Fill those who walk upon it with the Spirit of Divine love. May they feel that they are walking on holy ground. . . . Holy Father, hear us, we pray, for we now set apart this ground, and dedicate it, and all that pertains to it, unto thee for the purpose of building thereon a House which shall be called the House of God, for the sole use and good of thy people, both living and dead. And we do it in the name of thy Son Jesus Christ, and by virtue and authority of the holy priesthood. Therefore, accept of this dedication, sanctify this ground, the work which shall be performed, and the building that shall be reared hereon, we ask it in the name of Jesus Christ. Amen."[85]

After the services, several photographs were taken of President Smith and groups of people. Apparently, at this point, many of the local Saints took the opportunity to shake the hand of President Smith. Alma C. Hanson recalled: "Lots of people shook his hand. I shook his hand."[86]

And while President Joseph F. did not live to see the completion of the first temple constructed in Canada, his "visit was indeed a red letter day for the Church in Canada" when he dedicated the site for the "only L.D.S. Temple in the British Empire."[87]

Another Birthday Celebration (November 1913)

President Joseph F. worked and celebrated on his birthday in November 1913. He attended the regular First Presidency and Council of the Twelve meeting in the Salt Lake Temple.

Sometime before evening, President Joseph F. posed in front of the camera of H. H. Thomas for a formal portrait on his seventy-fifth birthday. Photographs were sent out to family and friends—highlighting this special day in the life of President Joseph F. One of the poses

PLATE 117
JOSEPH F. SMITH, 13 NOVEMBER 1913
H. H. THOMAS, MLUU (P0036 #135). PRESIDENT JOSEPH F. WROTE ON THE BOTTOM OF THIS PHOTOGRAPH: "YOUR AFFECTIONATE COUSIN. JOSEPH F. SMITH AT 75. NOV 13TH 1838. NOV. 13TH 1913."

appeared in the *Improvement Era* a few months later for the general membership.⁸⁸

The *Deseret Evening News* reported to its readers the festivities held during the evening:

"The birthday party given in honor of President Joseph F. Smith's seventy-fifth anniversary by members of his family at the Bishop's building last night was a most enjoyable affair. About 120 persons were present, including 30 of President Smith's children and 50 grandchildren; and near relatives of the guest of honor made up the remainder of the party, including President Smith's sister, Mrs. Martha N. Harris. Two sons were unavoidably absent: Hyrum M., who is in England, in charge of the British mission, and Andrew K., who is doing missionary labor in Germany. The program was wholly informal and consisted of miscellaneous numbers, songs, piano selections, duets, etc., a feature being a vocal sextet by six of President Smith's daughters. Prominent in the exercises of the evening was the showing of motion pictures under the direction of E. Wesley Smith. The reels shown included pictures of the mission field in the Sandwich Islands, views of the general conference in this city two years ago, and comedy pictures. Informal chats and reminiscences added to the pleasure of the occasion."⁸⁹

PLATE 118
JOSEPH F. AND MARY TAYLOR SCHWARTZ, CA. 1914
KING COLLECTION.

PLATE 119
JOSEPH FIELDING SMITH AND JOSEPH F. SMITH, 5 JANUARY 1914

LDSCA. President Smith wrote at the bottom: "Joseph F. Smith Jr., and Joseph F. Smith Taken Jan. 5th 1914."

PLATE 120
EDNA LAMBSON AND JOSEPH F. SMITH, CA. 1914
LDSCA.

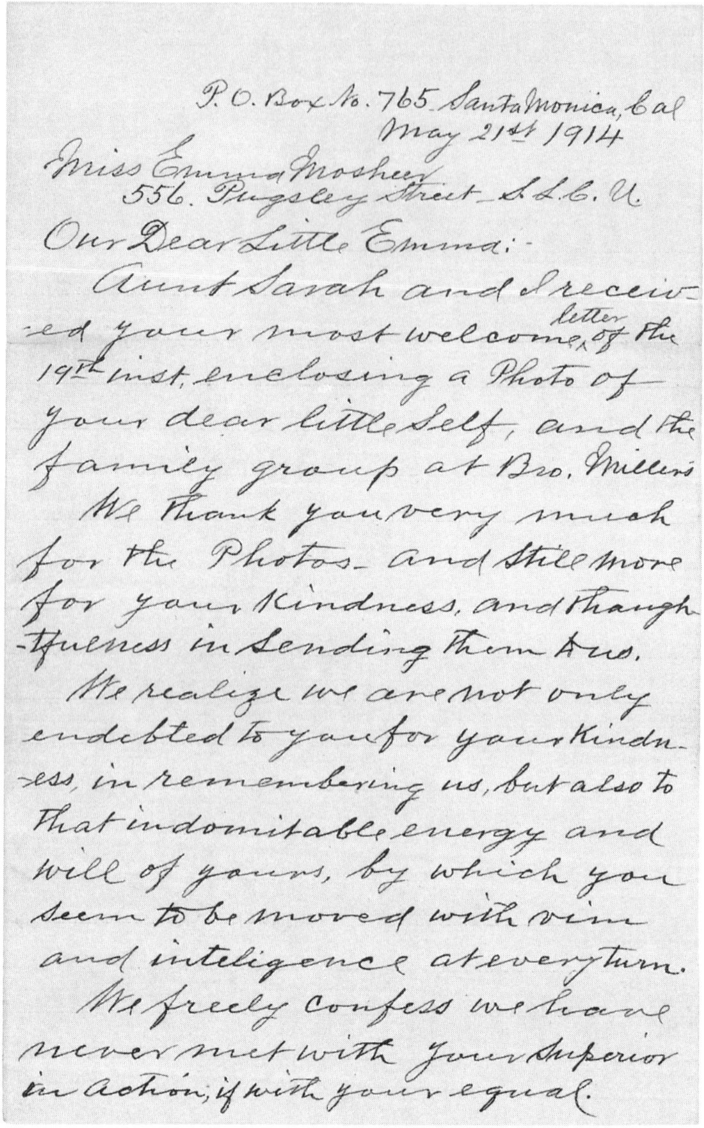

> P. O. Box No. 765. Santa Monica, Cal
> May 21st 1914
>
> Miss Emma Mosheer
> 556. Pugsley Street S. L. C. U.
>
> Our Dear Little Emma:—
>
> Aunt Sarah and I received your most welcome letter of the 19th inst, enclosing a Photo of your dear little Self, and the family group at Bro. Miller's
>
> We Thank you very much for the Photos— and Still more for your Kindness, and thoughtfulness in Sending them to us.
>
> We realize we are not only endebted to you for your Kindness, in remembering us, but also to That indomitable energy and will of yours, by which you seem to be moved with vim and inteligence at every turn.
>
> We freely confess we have never met with your Superior in Action; if with your equal.

PLATE 121
JOSEPH F. AND SARAH E. SMITH LETTER TO EMMA MOSHEER (PAGE ONE), DATED 21 MAY 1914
ASHWORTH COLLECTION. A DELIGHTFUL LETTER TO A NIECE, PROVIDING INSIGHTS TO JOSEPH F. SMITH'S PERSONALITY AND ABILITY TO COMMUNICATE TO CHILDREN.

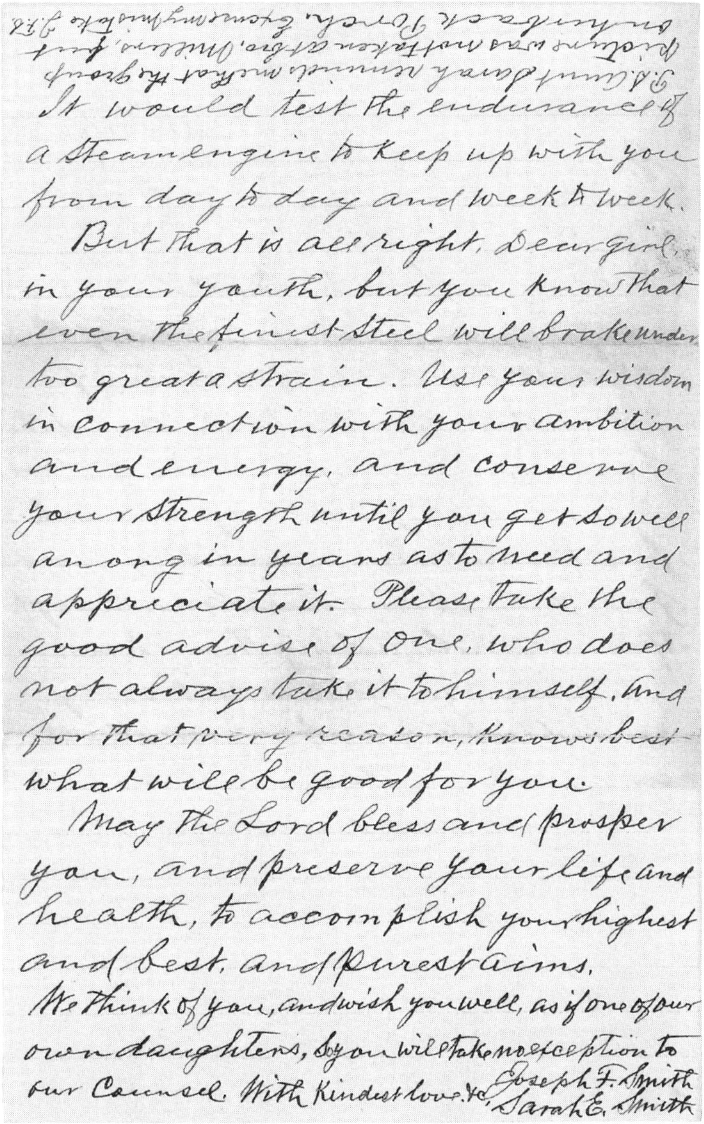

P.S. Aunt Sarah reminds me that the group picture was not taken at Bro. Millens, but on her back Porch. Excuse my mistake J. F. S.

It would test the endurance of a Steamengine to keep up with you from day to day and week to week.

But that is all right, Dear girl, in your youth, but you know that even the finest steel will brake under too great a strain. Use your wisdom in connection with your ambition and energy, and conserve your strength until you get so well anong in years as to need and appreciate it. Please take the good advise of One, who does not always take it to himself. And for that very reason, knows best what will be good for you.

May the Lord bless and prosper you, and preserve your life and health, to accomplish your highest and best, and purest aims.

We think of you, and wish you well, as if one of our own daughters, so you will take no exception to our Counsel. With kindest love &c,

Joseph F. Smith
Sarah E. Smith

PLATE 122

JOSEPH F. AND SARAH E. SMITH LETTER TO EMMA MOSHEER (PAGE TWO), DATED 21 MAY 1914

ASHWORTH COLLECTION. NOTE POSTSCRIPT: "P.S. AUNT SARAH REMINDS ME THAT THE GROUP PICTURE WAS NOT TAKEN AT BRO. MILLENS, BUT ON HER BACK PORCH. EXCUSE MY MISTAKE J. F. S."

PLATE 123
JOSEPH F. SMITH POSTCARD, DATED 5 DECEMBER 1914

BYU (MSS SCP-2219 #162). A POSTCARD PHOTOGRAPH SENT TO HIS DAUGHTER LUCY MACK SMITH, WHO WAS AT THE TIME AT THE CHURCH HOME, KNOWN AS "DESERET," IN SANTA MONICA, CALIFORNIA.

PLATE 124
JOSEPH F. SMITH POSTCARD, DATED 5 DECEMBER 1914

BYU (MSS SCP-2219 #162). THE REVERSE SIDE OF A POSTCARD PHOTOGRAPH INSCRIBED BY JOSEPH F. SMITH TO HIS DAUGHTER: "JUST TO REMIND HER OF HER VERY OWN TRUE AND LOVING PAPA."

PLATE 125
JOSEPH F. SMITH AND PARTY ON THEIR WAY TO HAWAII, 21 MAY 1915

WALKER COLLECTION. FROM LEFT: JULINA LAMBSON SMITH, JOSEPH F. SMITH, REBECCA NEIBAUR NIBLEY, AND CHARLES W. NIBLEY. TAKEN ON THE DAY THEY BOARDED THE SHIP FOR HAWAII, THIS VIEW SHOWS PRESIDENT JOSEPH F. AS HE BEGAN A HISTORIC VISIT TO HAWAII.

Dedicating Hawaii for a Temple (June 1915)

During a visit to Hawaii, President Joseph F. selected a site at Laie for a temple. On this occasion, he dedicated it, the second site dedicated for a temple during his presidency. He said at the time:

"I feel impressed to dedicate this ground for the erection of a Temple to God, for a place where the peoples of the Pacific Isles can come and do their temple work. I have not presented this to the Council of the Twelve or to my counselors; but if you think there would be no objection to it, I think now is the time to dedicate the ground."

"Never in my life," Elder Reed Smoot recalled, "did I hear such a prayer. The very ground seemed to be sacred, and he seemed as if he were talking face to face with the Father. I cannot and never will forget it if I live a thousand years."[90]

Upon his return to Utah, President Joseph F. announced to the Saints in the October conference the plans to build a temple in Hawaii. Just as with the Alberta Temple in Canada, President Joseph F. did not live to see the temple in Hawaii completed.

PLATE 126
JOSEPH F. SMITH AND PARTY, 1 JUNE 1915
LDSCA.

PLATE 127
JOSEPH F. SMITH AND PARTY AT THE INTERNATIONAL CONGRESS OF GENEALOGY IN SAN FRANCISCO, CALIFORNIA, JULY 1915

P. CARDINELL VINCENT CO., LDSCA. FRONT FROM LEFT: ROMANIA B. PENROSE, CHARLES W. PENROSE, ANTHON H. LUND, JOSEPH F. SMITH, MARY TAYLOR SCHWARTZ SMITH, EMMELINE B. WELLS. MIDDLE FROM LEFT: SUSA YOUNG GATES, HEBER J. GRANT, AUGUSTA WINTERS GRANT, CHARLES W. NIBLEY, JENETTE A. HYDE, ELIZABETH C. MCCUNE. BACK FROM LEFT: JAMES BLAKE, JOSEPH FIELDING SMITH, ANNIE WELLS CANNON, MARK AUSTIN, LEWIS ANDERSON.

INTERNATIONAL CONGRESS OF GENEALOGY (JULY 1915)

Identified as the "highlight of the decade for the Church genealogical program," the International Congress of Genealogy, held in conjunction with the World's Fair in San Francisco in July 1915, followed President Joseph F.'s visit to Hawaii.[91] Some 250 Latter-day Saints attended the meeting, including President Joseph F. and Mary Taylor Schwartz Smith. The Genealogical Society of Utah hosted a full-day session for delegates, representing forty-six organizations. The Church's increasing role in genealogical work was recognized when President Joseph F.'s son Joseph Fielding Smith and Susa Young Gates were appointed to several permanent assignments for the group. Additionally, the proceedings of the event were published in the *Utah Genealogical and Historical Magazine* in October 1915 and January 1916.

THE TWENTIETH-CENTURY PROPHET

PLATE 128 (LEFT)
JOSEPH F. SMITH PORTRAIT, OIL ON CANVAS, 1915
ALBERT SALZBRENNER, MCHA. THE 2 OCTOBER 1915 EDITION OF THE *DESERET EVENING NEWS* INDICATES: "MR. SALZBRENNER THE ARTIST . . . CAME FROM DRESDEN, GERMANY, STUDIED MANY YEARS UNDER THE NOTED ARTIST HOFFMAN AND ALSO UNDER THE SCULPTOR SCHILLING. THIS IS THE SECOND PORTRAIT HE HAS PAINTED OF PRES. SMITH."

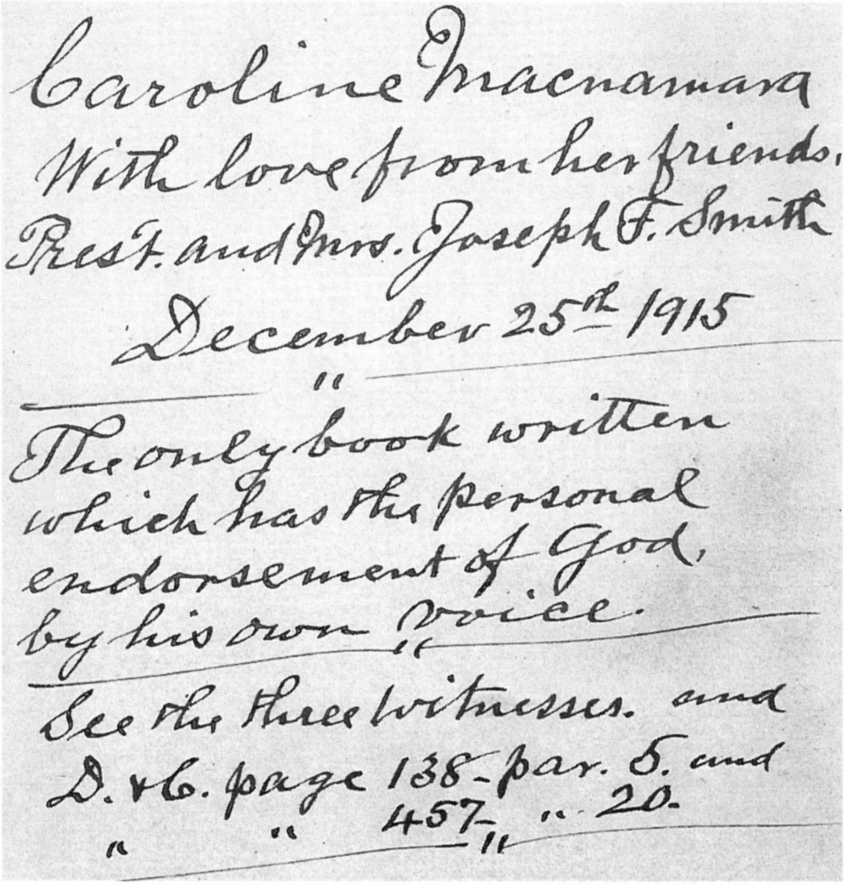

> Caroline Macnamara
> With love from her friends,
> Pres't. and Mrs. Joseph F. Smith
> December 25th 1915
> "
> "The only book written which has the personal endorsement of God, by his own voice."
> See the three witnesses. and
> D. &. C. page 138 - par. 5. and
> "   "   457 - " 20.
> "   "

PLATE 129 (ABOVE)
JOSEPH F. SMITH INSCRIPTION IN A BOOK OF MORMON, DATED 25 DECEMBER 1915
ASHWORTH COLLECTION. PART OF THE INSCRIPTION READS: "THE ONLY BOOK WRITTEN WHICH HAS THE PERSONAL ENDORSEMENT OF GOD, BY HIS OWN VOICE."

PLATE 130
JOSEPH F. SMITH AND MIA SUPERINTENDENCY, CA. 1915

CLAWSON FILM COMPANY, J. F. MCCONKIE COLLECTION. FROM LEFT: B. H. ROBERTS, JOSEPH F. SMITH, AND HEBER J. GRANT. THIS IS ONE OF FOUR IMAGES TAKEN FROM A BLACK-AND-WHITE FILM BY SHIRLEY Y. AND CHESTER CLAWSON IN THE FRONT OF THE SALT LAKE TEMPLE SHOWING PRESIDENT JOSEPH F. SMITH STROKING HIS BEARD AS HE WAS KNOWN TO DO. MORE CANDID THAN GENERAL PORTRAITS FROM THIS PERIOD, THIS IMAGE PROVIDES A MORE LIFELIKE VIEW OF HIM.

PLATE 131
JOSEPH F. SMITH AND MIA SUPERINTENDENCY, CA. 1915
CLAWSON FILM COMPANY, J. F. MCCONKIE COLLECTION. SEE PREVIOUS CAPTION.

PLATE 132
JOSEPH F. SMITH AND MIA SUPERINTENDENCY, CA. 1915
CLAWSON FILM COMPANY, J. F. MCCONKIE COLLECTION. SEE CAPTION, PLATE 130.

PLATE 133
JOSEPH F. SMITH AND MIA SUPERINTENDENCY, CA. 1915
CLAWSON FILM COMPANY, J. F. MCCONKIE COLLECTION. SEE CAPTION, PLATE 130.

PLATE 134
JOSEPH F. SMITH, CA. 1915

CLAWSON FILM COMPANY, BYU (P-148–173). ONE OF TWO IMAGES TAKEN FROM A BLACK-AND-WHITE FILM BY SHIRLEY Y. AND CHESTER CLAWSON SHOWING PRESIDENT JOSEPH F. SMITH (CLOSE-UP) IN FRONT OF THE TEMPLE. THE FILM SEGMENT SHOWS PRESIDENT SMITH TALKING, THEN REMOVING HIS HAT, AND THEN REMOVING HIS GLASSES. THESE IMAGES FROM THE FILM PROVIDE A CANDID AND LIFELIKE VIEW OF THE PROPHET.

PLATE 135
JOSEPH F. SMITH, CA. 1915

CLAWSON FILM COMPANY, BYU (P-148–174). SEE PREVIOUS CAPTION.

Golden Wedding Anniversary (May 1916)

In May 1916, President Joseph F. celebrated a fifty-year anniversary—his marriage to Julina Lambson. In what was reported to be the largest event held in the Beehive House for some time, President Smith's family gathered to honor the couple on Friday evening, 5 May. Some three hundred relatives and personal friends honored the couple in the beautifully decorated official residence of the President between 8 and 11 P.M. At least three beautiful photographs were taken during the event by the respected Thomas Photographic Studio of Salt Lake City.

A local newspaper reported: "Mrs. Smith was attired in a handsome

PLATE 136
JOSEPH F. AND JULINA SMITH GOLDEN WEDDING ANNIVERSARY, 5 MAY 1916
THOMAS STUDIO, LDSCA.

PLATE 137
JOSEPH F. AND JULINA SMITH GOLDEN WEDDING ANNIVERSARY, 5 MAY 1916
THOMAS STUDIO, LDSCA.

gown of white soiree silk combined with georgette crepe and gold lace."[92] The paper continued: "The affair in accordance with the wishes of President and Mrs. Smith was very simple and devoid of any ostentation. But from the time the guests exchanged words of congratulation with the president and his wife until the last had departed they commented upon the genial hospitality and interest of the occasion."[93]

Apparently, earlier in the day, President Joseph F. and Julina met with children and grandchildren in the Beehive House. The activities for the family gathering included games, refreshments, and motion-picture opportunities. Now lost, the film footage taken on this day included views of the Beehive House and President Joseph F.'s grandchildren posed on its historic grounds.

New Church Buildings (May 1916)

Within a few weeks of his golden wedding anniversary, President Joseph F. traveled to southern California to dedicate a new meetinghouse in San Diego. At the beginning of the meeting, President Joseph F. addressed the Saints in attendance. A reporter noted:

"In his introductory remarks [he] called attention very feelingly to the attendance of little children and welcomed them to the meeting, which, by-the-by, was so crowded that many were compelled to stand. He said, as reported in part by President Stephen [Bjorson], that he would prefer to stand during the entire service rather than see one of the little children turned away from the church. The Latter-day Saints build their churches with a view to care for the needs of children."[94]

PLATE 138

JOSEPH SMITH AND PARTY AT THE DEDICATION OF THE SAN DIEGO CHAPEL IN SOUTHERN CALIFORNIA, 21 MAY 1916

PUBLISHED IN THE IMPROVEMENT ERA 19 (JULY 1916): 842.

PLATE 139
JOSEPH F. SMITH'S INSCRIPTION IN THE BOOK ADDED UPON, DATED 11 JULY 1916
ASHWORTH COLLECTION.

PLATE 140—SAME AS COVER
JOSEPH F. SMITH PORTRAIT, OIL ON CANVAS, 1916
JOHN W. CLAWSON, MCHA. PRESIDENT JOSEPH F. GENERALLY HAD SOME TREATS IN HIS POCKET. ONE OF HIS GRANDCHILDREN REMEMBERS ANOTHER YOUNG GRANDCHILD STANDING BEFORE THIS PORTRAIT, HOLDING OUT HER HAND AND ASKING HER GRANDFATHER FOR A TREAT.

PLATE 141
LDS FIRST PRESIDENCY, CA. 1916

THOMAS STUDIO, WALKER COLLECTION. FROM LEFT: ANTHON H. LUND,
JOSEPH F. SMITH, AND CHARLES W. PENROSE.

PLATE 142
JOSEPH F. SMITH AND PARTY, CA. 1917
BRIGHAM YOUNG UNIVERSITY.

PLATE 143
Joseph F. Smith at Kimball Family Reunion, 14 June 1917
RUFUS DAVID JOHNSON, LDSCA. TAKEN AT MILL CREEK IN BOUNTIFUL, DAVIS COUNTY, UTAH, THIS IMAGE IS CROPPED TO FOCUS ON THE GROUP IN THE MIDDLE OF THIS UNUSUALLY LONG PHOTOGRAPH, FOCUSING ON JOSEPH F. SMITH.

Kimball Family Reunion (June 1917)

More than a hundred descendants of Heber C. Kimball gathered for a family reunion on 14 June 1917, the 116th anniversary of Heber's birthday. The *Deseret Evening News* reported: "The ruins of the old [Heber C. Kimball] mill formed a picturesque setting for the picnic and social. . . . Wild flowers have always been found in abundance about the old building and it has always been a favorite spot for trapping wild game, wolves and bears not being infrequent visitors."[95] Several photographs were taken on the occasion by Rufus D. Johnson, including one preserved in the LDS Church Archives. This beautiful black-and-white image is an extra-long photograph showing the group posed at the stream near the old grist mill.

A Journey to Southern Utah (September 1917)

President Joseph F. inspected the Mormon settlements in central and southern Utah for the last time in September 1917. He left Salt Lake City on a ten-day tour in company with Church leaders and officers, including Anthon H. Lund, Heber J. Grant, Hyrum M. Smith, Joseph F. Smith Jr., Joseph W. McMurrin, Charles W. Nibley, David A. Smith, Stephen L Richards, and Andrew Jenson. The party also consisted of several of his own family members, including one of his wives and three daughters-in-law, who accompanied their husbands (Hyrum M., Joseph F. Jr., and David A. Smith).

This trip provided the Latter-day Saints in central and southern Utah one last opportunity to meet President Joseph F., receive counsel, and show their affection for the aged leader. It also allowed President Joseph F. to reciprocate and demonstrate his feelings for the Latter-day Saints, for whom he had been a faithful servant. A participant in the tour observed: "He is one of the people—not apart from them; and, like the apostles of old, he mingles with them on terms of equality and fellowship. The humblest member may stand up like a man and greet him as his brother."[96]

In each of the more than thirty communities visited during this swing through central and southern Utah, the Saints gathered to see, touch, hear, and honor their prophet. "Before reaching Holden an escort of automobiles appeared, and in the town a number of people had assembled, bearing flags and flowers; the occupants of each car receiving a beautiful bouquet."[97] At Cedar City, some seven hundred children gathered to present flowers to President Joseph F., and at Monroe, "hundreds of children and adults lined both sides of the street, waving flags and singing 'America' as the cars passed."[98] The people of Leeds provided "baskets of the most delicious fruits."[99] The young people of Richfield "threw flowers into the cars as they passed," and at Aurora, President Joseph F. "shook hands with those assembled."[100]

A tearful departure occurred at Redmond when a young women's choir began singing "God Be with You Till We Meet Again" as the motorcade began leaving the community. In Centerfield, a number of "little girls clothed in white" presented each member of the party a bouquet of flowers.[101]

When the President's party entered Manti, they discovered the streets were "decorated with flags and bunting, and a large 'Welcome' banner across the main street, where a procession was formed, a brass band in the lead, with hundreds of children marching on each side of the automobile party, from the city limits to the main business center, where the procession halted, and the assembled host sang, 'We thank thee, O God, for a Prophet.'"[102] Farther along the journey, while the "guests marched to the place of meeting [in Mount Pleasant] their pathway was literally strewn with flowers."[103] And finally, at Fairview, the party was greeted by those assembled, including "a surprising number of children," singing "We Thank Thee, O God, for a Prophet." The crowd swarmed around "the cars to greet the President and his associates." The Prophet arose and spoke briefly, "commending the children and inquiring, 'Where in the world do you all come from?' and venturing the assertion that they have some of the best fathers and mothers in the world. Referring to the C. R. Savage picture, 'Utah's Best Crop' [a montage of the faces of numerous children] the President declared: 'I see before me in reality almost a duplicate of that wonderful photograph.'"[104]

During the entire journey, children reached out to shake President Joseph F.'s hand, and others wept for joy as they greeted the Prophet. For most, this was the last opportunity to do so with their beloved leader who had served as a General Authority for nearly forty years.

The photographic images surviving from the trip provide a documentary view of President Joseph F.'s "journey to the south" and, in an unexplainable way, a sense of being an observer of the outpouring of love shown President Joseph F. by the Saints and his own joy as he moved among those he loved and served so faithfully.

PLATE 144
JOSEPH F. SMITH AND PARTY AT COVE FORT, 11 SEPTEMBER 1917

(CURRENTLY A CHURCH HISTORIC SITE AND VISITOR CENTER IN CENTRAL UTAH.) IMPROVEMENT ERA 21 (DECEMBER 1917): 101. IN THE TRADITION ESTABLISHED BY BRIGHAM YOUNG, PRESIDENT JOSEPH F. MADE FREQUENT TRIPS THROUGHOUT THE MORMON SETTLEMENTS IN THE WEST. IN WHAT WOULD BE ONE OF HIS LAST, PRESIDENT JOSEPH F. LEFT SALT LAKE CITY ON 11 SEPTEMBER 1917. THE FOLLOWING IMAGES, THOUGH NOT CLEAR, ARE RARE IMAGES OF HIS VISITS AMONG THE SAINTS DURING THIS LAST YEAR OF HIS LIFE.

PLATE 145
LATTER-DAY SAINTS AT MANTI, UTAH, GREETING PRESIDENT JOSEPH F. SMITH'S PARTY, 19 SEPTEMBER 1917
IMPROVEMENT ERA 21 (DECEMBER 1917): 108.

PLATE 146
JOSEPH F. SMITH'S PARTY RECEIVING BOUQUETS OF FLOWERS, 19–20 SEPTEMBER 1917
IMPROVEMENT ERA 21 (DECEMBER 1917): 107. FROM LEFT: HEBER J. GRANT, ANTHON H. LUND, AND JOSEPH F. SMITH.

PLATE 147

JOSEPH F. SMITH'S PARTY AT THE STEPS OF THE MANTI TEMPLE

19–20 SEPTEMBER 1917; IMPROVEMENT ERA 21 (DECEMBER 1917): 154.

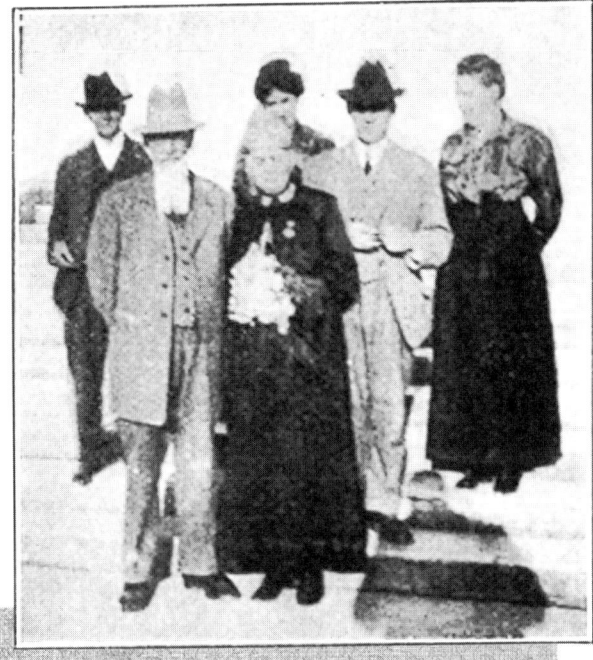

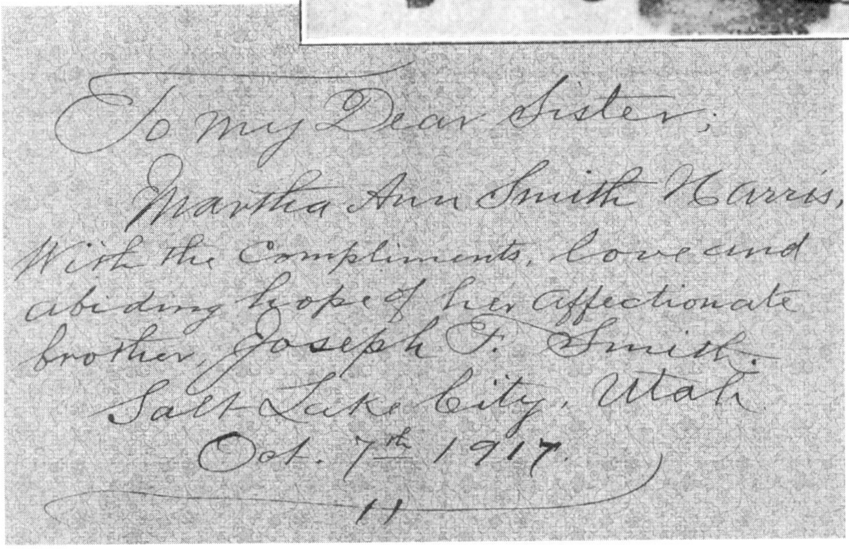

To my Dear Sister;
Martha Ann Smith Harris,
With the Compliments, Love and
abiding hope of her affectionate
brother, Joseph F. Smith.
Salt Lake City, Utah
Oct. 7th 1917.

PLATE 148

JOSEPH F. SMITH'S INSCRIPTION

DATED 7 OCTOBER 1917, KING COLLECTION. THE INSCRIPTION IS FOUND IN JAMES T. JAKEMAN, *ALBUM: "DAUGHTERS OF THE UTAH PIONEERS AND THEIR MOTHERS,"* (SALT LAKE CITY: WESTERN ALBUM PUBLISHING COMPANY, [1916]). THE BEAUTIFUL BOOK WAS PRESENTED TO PRESIDENT JOSEPH F. SMITH'S YOUNGER SISTER, MARTHA ANN SMITH HARRIS. FROM THE TIME OF THEIR MOTHER'S DEATH IN 1852 UNTIL HIS OWN DEATH IN 1918, JOSEPH F. SMITH WROTE MANY LETTERS TO HIS SISTER. MORE THAN A HUNDRED LETTERS WRITTEN BETWEEN 1854, WHEN HE WENT ON HIS FIRST MISSION, AND 1916, NEAR THE TIME OF HIS DEATH, SURVIVE IN FAMILY HANDS. THEY REVEAL A DEEP LOVE AND CONCERN FOR MARTHA ANN FOLLOWING THE DEATH OF THEIR MOTHER IN 1852.

The Death of Hyrum M. Smith (January 1918)

In January 1918, Elder Hyrum M. Smith died of peritonitis following an operation. The *Deseret Evening News* noted: "In the death of Elder Hyrum M. Smith the Church loses a stalwart official and the community loses a valued citizen."[105] President Anthon H. Lund provides a poignant word-picture of President Joseph F.'s final farewell to his beloved son: "Prest. Smith broke down and groaned when he came in to take the last look of his son, witnessed a very sad scene."[106] His son's death was a severe trial to the aged prophet and is part of the tapestry of the background of the Vision of the Redemption of the Dead he witnessed in October 1918.

A Declaration of Divine Authority (April 1918)

President Joseph F. issued an official document entitled "An Authoritative Declaration," stating that the divine authority resting in The Church of Jesus Christ of Latter-day Saints was sanctioned by God. President Joseph F. stated:

"The Church of Jesus Christ of Latter-day Saints is no partisan Church. It is not a sect. It is THE CHURCH OF JESUS CHRIST OF LATTER-DAY SAINTS. It is the only one today existing in the world that can and does legitimately bear the name of Jesus Christ and His divine authority. I make this declaration in all simplicity and honesty before you and before all the world, bitter as the truth may seem to those who are opposed and who have no reason for that opposition. It is nevertheless true and will remain true until He who has a right to rule among the nations of the earth and among the individual children

PLATE 149
FIRST PRESIDENCY AND GENERAL AUTHORITIES, 6 APRIL 1918
SALT LAKE CITY; IMPROVEMENT ERA 21 (1918): 638. TAKEN DURING GENERAL CONFERENCE, THIS IS THE ONLY KNOWN PHOTOGRAPH TAKEN DURING JOSEPH F. SMITH'S ADMINISTRATION OF THE FIRST PRESIDENCY AND OTHER GENERAL AUTHORITIES, INCLUDING THE TWELVE AND THE CHURCH PATRIARCH, JOHN SMITH.

---

of God throughout the world shall come and take the reins of government and receive the bride that shall be prepared for the coming of the Bridegroom.

"Many of our great writers have recently been querying and wondering where the divine authority exists today to command in the name of the Father and of the Son and of the Holy Ghost, so that it will be in effect and acceptable at the throne of the Eternal Father. I will announce here and now, presumptuous as it may seem to be to those who know not the truth, that the divine authority of Almighty God, to speak in the name of the Father and of the Son, is here in the midst of these everlasting hills, in the midst of this intermountain region, and it will abide and will continue, for God is its source, and God is the power by which it has been maintained against all opposition in the world up to the present, and by which it will continue to progress and grow and increase on the earth until it shall cover the earth from sea to sea. This is my testimony to you, my brethren and sisters, and I have a fulness of joy and of satisfaction in being able to declare this without regard to, or fear of, all the adversaries of the truth.

"The above declaration was made at the morning service of the annual conference on the 88th anniversary of the organization of The Church of Jesus Christ of Latter-day Saints, 6 April 1918."[107]

Honoring His Father (June 1918)

Junius F. Wells assisted President Joseph F. in erecting monuments to the Prophet Joseph Smith in 1905 and to Oliver Cowdery in 1911. Again, in 1918, Wells helped honor another early Saint—Hyrum Smith, the Patriarch—by erecting a monument in the Salt Lake City Cemetery.

On the anniversary of the martyrdom of the Prophet Joseph Smith and Patriarch Hyrum Smith, President Joseph F. gathered with family, friends, and a special group of people, "old Saints from Nauvoo." Seated under a canopy of trees on the southern part of the Smith family burial plot, near the Sixth Avenue entrance to the City Cemetery, the services began at 4 P.M.

Several people spoke on the occasion, including Bishop David A.

PLATE 150
JOSEPH F. SMITH AND FAMILY AT HYRUM SMITH MONUMENT DEDICATION, 27 JUNE 1918
IMPROVEMENT ERA 21 (AUGUST 1918): 864. A COPY-PRINT, THIS RARE IMAGE IS ONE OF THE LAST PHOTOGRAPHS TAKEN OF PRESIDENT SMITH BEFORE HIS PASSING IN NOVEMBER 1918. HE IS SEATED IN THE CENTER IN A BLACK SUIT SURROUNDED BY HIS GRANDCHILDREN.

Smith, Elder Heber J. Grant, and President Charles W. Penrose, who also offered the prayer of dedication. Those gathered on this anniversary also were privileged to hear some brief remarks from President Joseph F. The aged and weak family patriarch began:

"I scarcely know whether I shall have the strength that I feel I need, under the present conditions and circumstances, to express a few thoughts and a degree of the vast feeling of gratitude which we owe to Brother Junius F. Wells, to my counselors, to the Council of the Twelve apostles and the Presiding Bishopric, who have moved in the matter of building this monument to the name and honor of my father."[108]

He added: "I am blessed today with thirty-five children living, all of whom, so far as I know, have a standing in the Church of Jesus Christ of Latter-day Saints, and I believe their hearts are in the work of the Lord. I am proud of my children. I have today over eighty-six grandchildren, some of whom have reached nearly the stage of manhood and womanhood, and those who have reached the years of accountability are members of the Church in good standing. I trust the time will never be when a descendant of Hyrum Smith will be other than a faithful member of the Church of Jesus Christ of Latter-day Saints, for which Joseph the Prophet, and his elder brother Hyrum were willing to shed their blood."

As he prepared to close his remarks at this extraordinary gathering, President Joseph F. asserted:

"I am rich; the Lord has given me great riches in children and in children's children; and in the fact that my children have, so far, honored me and their grandfather and their mothers and the Church of Jesus Christ of Latter-day Saints. O! there is nothing in all the world, between now and . . . eternity, equal to the Cause of Truth that Joseph Smith, the boy-prophet, was instrumental in the hands of God of revealing and re-establishing upon the face of the earth. . . .

"I trust and pray that all my children and my children's children, to the latest generation, will abide in the truth. I want you to just take a look here at [the] little flock of my grandchildren—right here, every one of them. I love them. I know them all. I never meet them but what I kiss them, just as I do my own children. I don't care how dirty their faces are, if I can only have the privilege of meeting with my grandchildren and kissing them and letting them know that I love them just as I love my own children. Then I shall be satisfied, and I expect to continue it as long as I can."[109]

Before the close of the ceremonies, those who had seen the Prophet Joseph Smith and Patriarch Hyrum Smith were invited to stand. Amazingly, eight individuals besides President Joseph F. stood to be honored on this historic occasion.

The Last Conference (October 1918)

The Church general conference began promptly at ten o'clock on Friday morning, 4 October 1918. Because President Joseph F. had been very ill for several months, the members of the Church did not anticipate his attendance at any of the sessions. It was "a complete surprise to the large congregation" when President Joseph F. "entered through the door at the stand."[110] As he did, the great Tabernacle organ "peeled forth a chord and the vast audience arose spontaneously and stood in affectionate reverence until he acknowledged with a wave of the hand the beautiful and sincere tribute of love and respect which the Church and congregation so beautifully exhibited towards their beloved leader. . . . He was visibly affected when he arose to make his opening speech which was listened to with profound silence."[111]

General Relief Society President Emmeline B. Wells noted in her diary: "Pres. Smith came to the conference and made the opening remarks much to everyone's surprise."[112] Elder James E. Talmage of the Council of the Twelve wrote: "<u>Oct. 4, Fri.</u>: The 89th Semi-annual Conference of the Church opened in the Tabernacle at 10 A.M. To the surprise and joy of the people President Joseph F. Smith was present."[113]

President Joseph F. stated to those in attendance on this historic gathering:

"As most of you, I suppose, are aware, I have been undergoing a siege of very serious illness for the last five months. It would be impossible for me, on this occasion, to occupy sufficient time to express the desires of my heart and my feelings, as I would desire to express them to you, but I felt that it was my duty, if possible, to be present and take some little part this morning in the opening session of this eighty-ninth Semi-annual Conference of the Church of Jesus Christ of Latter-day Saints."[114]

In a reflective comment, President Joseph F. recalled:

"For more than seventy years I have been a worker in this cause with you and your fathers and progenitors, pioneers who broke the way into these valleys of the mountains; and my heart is just as firmly set with you today as it ever has been. Although somewhat weakened in body, my mind is clear with reference to my duty, and with reference to the duties and responsibilities that rest upon the Latter-day Saints; and I am ever anxious for the progress of the work of the Lord, for the prosperity of the people of the Church of Jesus Christ of Latter-day Saints throughout the world. I am as anxious as I ever have been, and as earnest in my desires that Zion shall prosper, and that the Lord shall favor his people and magnify them in his sight, and in the knowledge and understanding of the intelligent people of all the world."[115]

As he closed his opening address during the morning session of the conference on 4 October, President Joseph F. said: "I bless you in the name of the Lord Jesus Christ, and invoke his favor and blessing and protection upon you now and forever. Amen."[116] Edward H. Anderson, clerk of the conference, noted that "at the close of President Smith's remarks the organist struck a chord of 'We thank thee, O God, for a prophet.' The congregation arose in unison, and without announcement, and under strong emotion, sang that sacred song so dear to the Saints."[117] The occasion was a fitting tribute for one who had diligently served the Lord and the Saints for so many years.

Two days later, President Joseph F. spoke to the Saints for the last time during the closing session of the conference: "I have only one regret, and that is that this day could not be lengthened out some six or eight or twelve hours longer, so that we could hear from the rest of the brethren who are full of the spirit of their missions and of the Lord, and that you, one and all of you, would be delighted to hear. But the time will not permit."[118]

Just a day before the beginning of conference, President Joseph F. received an important vision. During the conference, he briefly alluded to the spiritual prompting he had received, but only later would the Saints discover the significance of those remarks (see discussion in "Chapter Five, A Doctrinal Legacy").

The Last Days (November 1918)

Elder George Albert Smith noted on 17 November 1918: "The Presidency and Quorum of Twelve fasted and prayed in the temple for the President. He was seized with pleurisy and suffered much pain."[119] On the following day, Elder James E. Talmage noted with due concern: "We cannot be oblivious to the fact that the condition of President Joseph F. Smith grows more serious and alarming every day. I have called daily of late and sometimes several times in a day, and each time I see him I realize that he is weaker than before."[120]

Joseph Fielding Smith provided a glimpse of the last days of the Prophet in his biography of his father:

"On the anniversary of the day he was sustained as President of the Church, November 10, 1918, his children assembled to pay him honor and to receive from his lips such counsel as he felt to give. It was the Sabbath day and but three days preceding his birthday anniversary. The children came fasting and in the spirit of prayer. On that occasion he delivered a short address to his children. . . . This was the last time in mortal life that he beheld the gathering of his family, and this was his last address. His family, all who were present, will always remember this eventful occasion. One week later, Sunday, November 17th, he was taken with an attack of pleurisy which continued to grow in intensity, finally developing into pleuro-pneumonia, and he passed away Tuesday morning, November 19, 1918."[121]

EATH OF PRESIDENT JOSEPH F. (NOVEMBER 1918)

President Joseph F. died in the Beehive House on 19 November 1918 at eighty years of age. Word quickly spread beyond Utah of his passing. On Capitol Hill in Washington, D.C., Utah Republican Senator and LDS Apostle Reed Smoot was in conference when an Associated Press reporter informed him of the event.

Reed Smoot recorded in his diary later in the day:

"I sent a telegram to [President of the Twelve] Heber J. Grant as follows: 'Wire me date of President Smith's funeral. Have wired family through David [Smith].' At 8:45 p.m. I received a telegram from Presidents [Anthon H.] Lund and [Charles R.] Penrose as follows: 'President Smith died this morning four fifty oclock. No funeral.' I sent the following telegram to Bp. David A. Smith [Presiding Bishopric]: 'Evening papers announce the death of your father, President Smith. He was an ideal citizen, father, husband and servant of God. Please convey to the family the heartfelt sympathies of myself and family. We sorrow with all Israel today. How we all loved and honored him. God bless his loved ones forever.' His death will be regretted by Mormon, Jew and Gentile. It will make a mighty change in the affairs of the church and Utah. I considered him my dearest friend on earth."[122]

Emmeline B. Wells was "very much affected" when she heard the news that President Joseph F. was failing. She recorded rather morosely: "The Pres. Died at 4:50 this morning. Clarissa & I went up to the Bee Hive House but Julina was resting and we did not see her. We went in however and saw the president. I am greatly grieved."[123]

On the same day, Elder James E. Talmage noted: "I called at the Beehive House about 7:30 and looked again upon the beloved but not lifeless countenance. Except for the emaciation due to his long and weakening illness the face expressed no suggestion of suffering. He lay as one of the Lord's mighty patriarchs in repose."[124]

On the following day, Emmeline B. Wells wrote: "I went up to the Bee Hive house to day to see the President. He looks very grand and beautiful in his lovely robes."[125]

Presidents Lund and Penrose of the First Presidency informed the Saints:

"At a meeting of the general authorities of the Church and representatives of the family this morning, it was unanimously decided that in view of existing health conditions in the community, it would be improper to hold public funeral services for the late President Joseph F.

Smith. This decision, though regretfully adopted, is a measure of prudence which will meet with general approval, we feel sure. Such services as shall be held at the time of interment in the city cemetery will therefore be brief. At a later date, however, announcement of which will be duly made, memorial services will be held throughout the whole Church for the beloved leader whose loss we so sincerely, but perforce silently, mourn."[126]

In the Beehive House (November 1918)

President Joseph F.'s body was placed in the Beehive House "in [a] metal casket in the large room on the southeast corner."[127] One observer noted, "The ever-present smile so characteristic in life was still on his lips."[128] His granddaughter, Amelia Smith McConkie, who was two and a half years old at the time, recalled:

"I was so very young. I remember looking at the floral pattern of the carpet. It was beautiful! I was tracing it with my finger. I also remember the black boots of the men and shoes of the women. I could only see at that level. There was a big box in the room. I remember people going over to the box and crying. Then they would move away. Eventually my father picked me up in his arms and asked me, 'Do you want to see your Grandfather?' So he lifted me up and walked over to the box so I could look in. There was a glass over the top of the box. My Grandfather was laying. I thought he was sound asleep. He was laying there so peaceful. He was dressed in white and it was so vivid because everyone else was dressed in black. I did not know he was dead at the time."[129]

Church leaders announced to the public that there would be no viewing, as had been the case for those who preceded President Joseph F. as the leader of the Latter-day Saints. However, "there were so many called and all seemed to have some especial reason for wishing to look on his face that generally everybody who wished to was permitted to pass through." The report continued: "The room was literally filled with flowers, beautiful emblems of love and respect, artistic designs and simple pieces. All morning they came and room was made for more until the last hour by taking away the pieces that came earlier."[130]

James E. Talmage reported in his diary:

"A day of sad and solemn duty. Funeral services over the remains of President Joseph F. Smith were conducted today under the unusual circumstances entailed by the ban placed upon public assemblies through order of the State Board of Health. While it was impossible to hold services indoors, multitudes of people gathered on South Temple Street for blocks both east and west of the Beehive House. I shall not attempt to record here details respecting the cortege nor give any extended account of the brief but impressive services held by the open grave. . . . Shortly before the hour set for the start toward the cemetery the Apostles and the Patriarch went in a body from the Church Office Building to the Beehive, where we looked for the last time upon the mortal remains of the man of God who has so nobly finished his work and who has now so deservedly gone to his reward. . . . A spirit of solemn sadness mingled with resignation was manifest throughout."[131]

Members of the leading councils left the Church Office Building and gathered at the Beehive House, along with family members. Pallbearers were selected from the General Authorities and included David O. McKay, Anthony W. Ivins, James E. Talmage, Stephen L

Richards, and Richard R. Lyman. Their movement from the Beehive House to the waiting hearse is captured in a rare motion-picture segment taken at the time. Other General Authorities following this group included Heber J. Grant, Anthon H. Lund, Charles W. Penrose, Rudger Clawson, George Albert Smith, Hyrum G. Smith, and Joseph F. Smith Jr.

Funeral Procession (November 1918)

The *Deseret Evening News* headline for 22 November 1918 read: "Prest. Joseph F. Smith Followed to Grave by Magnificent Cortege."[132] As noted above, Church leaders decided it was not prudent to hold a public funeral because of the threat of the worldwide influenza epidemic. Nevertheless, the citizens of Utah and members of the Church wanted to pay their last respects to President Joseph F. Smith.

Church leaders met together and "each member had an opportunity to express himself. Splendid eulogies were pronounced on the life of President Joseph F. Smith. Great sorrow at the parting was manifest."[133]

First, "the wheels of industry stood silent and mute" throughout the state. Second, "at the moment that the casket was being conveyed from his home to the hearse in waiting, the great bell in the tower of the Cathedral of the Madeleine sounded a paean of reverence and respect." Third, "throngs on South Temple Street in front of the Bee Hive House stood with bared and bowed heads." Fourth, "flags were at half mast and crepe hung from the doors of all Church offices and the various places of business with which the beloved Church leader had been associated."[134]

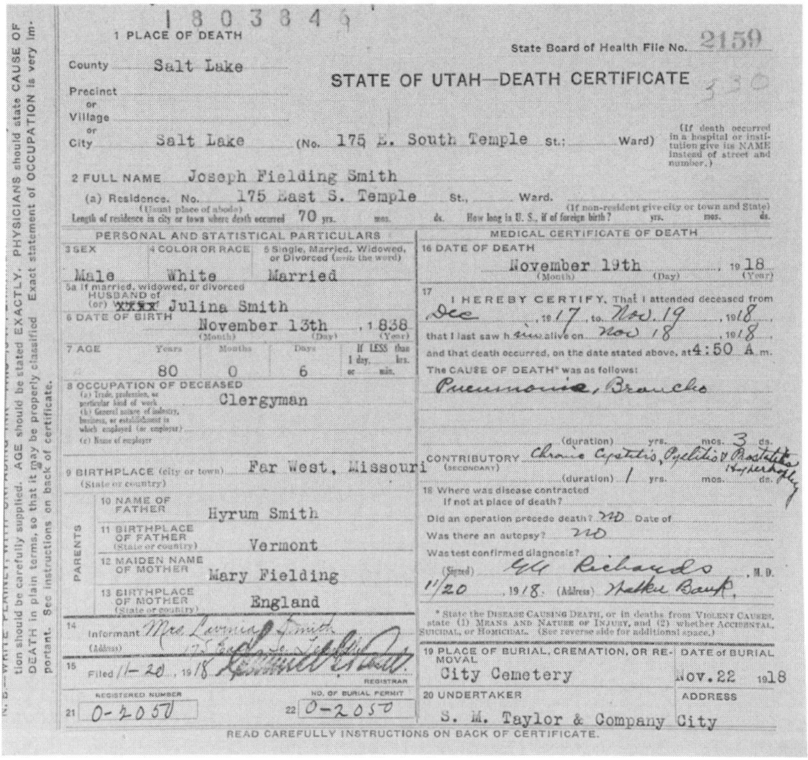
1803346

1 PLACE OF DEATH

State Board of Health File No. 2159

County Salt Lake

Precinct or Village or City Salt Lake (No. 175 E. South Temple St.; Ward)

STATE OF UTAH—DEATH CERTIFICATE

(If death occurred in a hospital or institution give its NAME instead of street and number.)

2 FULL NAME Joseph Fielding Smith

(a) Residence. No. 175 East S. Temple St., Ward. (Usual place of abode) (If non-resident give city or town and State)

Length of residence in city or town where death occurred 70 yrs. mos. ds. How long in U. S., if of foreign birth? yrs. mos. ds.

PERSONAL AND STATISTICAL PARTICULARS

3 SEX Male

4 COLOR OR RACE White

5 Single, Married, Widowed, or Divorced (write the word) Married

5a If married, widowed, or divorced HUSBAND of (or) XXXX Julina Smith

6 DATE OF BIRTH November 13th, 1838 (Month) (Day) (Year)

7 AGE 80 Years 0 Months 6 Days. If LESS than 1 day, hrs. or min.

8 OCCUPATION OF DECEASED (a) Trade, profession, or particular kind of work Clergyman (b) General nature of industry, business, or establishment in which employed (or employer) (c) Name of employer

9 BIRTHPLACE (city or town) (State or country) Far West, Missouri

PARENTS

10 NAME OF FATHER Hyrum Smith

11 BIRTHPLACE OF FATHER (State or country) Vermont

12 MAIDEN NAME OF MOTHER Mary Fielding

13 BIRTHPLACE OF MOTHER (State or country) England

14 Informant Mrs Levira Smith (Address) 175 E. So. Temple

15 Filed 11-20, 1918 REGISTRAR

REGISTERED NUMBER 21 0-2050

NO. OF BURIAL PERMIT 22 0-2050

MEDICAL CERTIFICATE OF DEATH

16 DATE OF DEATH November 19th, 1918 (Month) (Day) (Year)

17 I HEREBY CERTIFY, That I attended deceased from Dec 17, 1917, to Nov. 19, 1918, that I last saw him alive on Nov 18, 1918, and that death occurred, on the date stated above, at 4:50 A.m.

The CAUSE OF DEATH* was as follows: Pneumonia, Broncho

(duration) yrs. mos. 3 ds.

CONTRIBUTORY (SECONDARY) Chronic Cystitis, Pyelitis & Prostatitis Hypertrophy (duration) 1 yrs. mos. ds.

18 Where was disease contracted if not at place of death?

Did an operation precede death? no Date of

Was there an autopsy? no

Was test confirmed diagnosis?

(Signed) G. G. Richards, M. D.

11/20, 1918. (Address) Walker Bank.

*State the DISEASE CAUSING DEATH, or in deaths from VIOLENT CAUSES, state (1) MEANS AND NATURE OF INJURY, and (2) whether ACCIDENTAL, SUICIDAL, or HOMICIDAL. (See reverse side for additional space.)

19 PLACE OF BURIAL, CREMATION, OR REMOVAL City Cemetery

DATE of BURIAL Nov. 22, 1918

20 UNDERTAKER S. M. Taylor & Company

ADDRESS City

READ CAREFULLY INSTRUCTIONS ON BACK OF CERTIFICATE.

N. B.—WRITE PLAINLY, WITH UNFADING INK—THIS IS A PERMANENT RECORD. Every item of information should be carefully supplied. AGE should be stated EXACTLY. PHYSICIANS should state CAUSE OF DEATH in plain terms, so that it may be properly classified. Exact statement of OCCUPATION is very important. See instructions on back of certificate.

PLATE 151

Joseph F. Smith's "State of Utah Death Certificate"

DATED 20 NOVEMBER 1988, USA.

The report continued: "On the street in front of the house people gathered in throngs but all was reverence and silence and there was naught to mar the peacefulness of the occasion nor to make the dead regret if he could have known all that took place."[135] The city police "roped off the sidewalk in front of the Beehive House, and the street from the monument at Main and South Temple to far east of the Eagle Gate was filled with automobiles waiting to fall into the procession. Each took its turn and the long cortege was formed in perfect order. Other traffic was suspended to make way for the cortege and one by one the automobiles moved up the street until the procession was

PLATE 152
JOSEPH F. SMITH'S FUNERAL, 22 NOVEMBER 1918
CLAWSON FILM COMPANY, J. F. McCONKIE COLLECTION. FROM THE BLACK-AND-WHITE FILM BY SHIRLEY Y. AND CHESTER CLAWSON, TAKEN ON THE DAY OF PRESIDENT JOSEPH F. SMITH'S BURIAL. THE FIRST VIEW SHOWS CHURCH LEADERS TAKING PRESIDENT JOSEPH F. SMITH'S CASKET FROM THE BEEHIVE HOUSE.

PLATE 153
JOSEPH F. SMITH'S FUNERAL, 22 NOVEMBER 1918
CLAWSON FILM COMPANY, J. F. McCONKIE COLLECTION. FROM THE BLACK-AND-WHITE FILM BY SHIRLEY Y. AND CHESTER CLAWSON, TAKEN ON THE DAY OF PRESIDENT JOSEPH F. SMITH'S BURIAL. THIS VIEW SHOWS CHURCH LEADERS PLACING PRESIDENT JOSEPH F. SMITH'S CASKET INTO A WHITE HEARSE.

complete. When the word was given the long line moved to the cemetery, where President Joseph F. Smith shall take his place in the great tomb of mankind 'with patriarchs of the infant world—with kings, the powerful of the earth—the wise, the good, fair forms, and hoary seers of ages past all in one mighty sepulcher.'"[136]

At the Cemetery (November 1918)

A group gathered for a brief graveside service, which was presided over by President Anthon H. Lund. A small group from the Mormon Tabernacle Choir, under the direction of Professor A. Lund, sang, "I Know That My Redeemer Lives." A quartet, composed of George D. Pyper, John D. Spencer, H. G. Whitney, and Hugh W. Dougall, sang "What Voice Salutes the Startled Ear." An invocation by Elder George Albert Smith was then offered.

A Hawaiian quartet sang "Aloha Oe," followed by Bishop Charles W. Nibley, who provided a fitting tribute to his friend of more than forty years. President Heber J. Grant spoke next. A small portion of his address was captured on film, which shows him at the pulpit that had been erected at the grave. "This was draped in white with an American flag covering the front and Hawaiian leis hanging from the corners."[137] In the rare film footage taken during the services, floral arrangements are seen flanking the casket.

Elder George Albert Smith provides a word-picture of the proceedings at the cemetery: "At grave, a service of an hour was held. . . . It was a time of general mourning."[138] Emmeline B. Wells gave another view of the experience: "This morning was wet & stormy and very depressing for the people on this solemn occasion. The funeral of Pres. Smith. I rode in the carriage with Sister Penrose, Clarissa, Ida. I did not get out at the cemetery because of the cold. . . . The funeral was not at all satisfactory but the flowers were wonderful. And many people came."[139] The photographs and motion pictures taken at the time attest to the beautiful floral tributes for President Smith.

Elder George Albert Smith added one last reflection to his diary entry following the funeral service: "Personally I feel that I have lost

PLATE 154
JOSEPH F. SMITH'S INTERMENT, 22 NOVEMBER 1918
DESERET EVENING NEWS, 23 NOVEMBER 1918. ONE OF THREE PHOTOGRAPHIC IMAGES PUBLISHED IN THE SATURDAY EDITION OF THE *DESERET EVENING NEWS* UNDER THE HEADING "SCENES DURING OBSEQUIES OF PREST. JOSEPH F. SMITH." BECAUSE NO PUBLIC FUNERAL WAS HELD, THESE RARE PHOTOGRAPHS PROVIDED READERS A VIEW OF THE SMALL GRAVESIDE SERVICE HELD IN THE SALT LAKE CITY CEMETERY IN HIS HONOR.

PLATE 155
MEMORIAL SERVICE FOR JOSEPH F. SMITH
CA. 1918–19, LDSCA. CHURCH LEADERS IN SALT LAKE CITY, UNABLE TO HOLD A PUBLIC FUNERAL, INDICATED THAT MEMORIAL SERVICES FOR PRESIDENT JOSEPH F. SMITH COULD BE HELD AT A LATER DATE THROUGHOUT THE CHURCH. THIS MEMORIAL SERVICE WAS HELD IN HAWAII SOMETIME AFTER HIS DEATH IN UTAH.

---

another father [his own father, John Henry Smith, died in 1911]. He has always been very kind to me and I love him and his memory most sincerely."[140]

The Church at the End of the Year (December 1918)

There were nearly half a million Latter-day Saints around the world (495,962), living in 75 stakes, 839 wards, and 22 missions at the end of the year 1918. Following more than fifty-two years of service as a General Authority of the Church, seventeen of which he was the Prophet, Seer, and Revelator, President Joseph F. finally joined his father, mother, and loved ones in what must have been a joyful occasion.

The word-pictures and visual images of his world and life, preserved in so many wonderful essays and books, provide an opportunity to become familiar with a genuinely humble, warm, faithful, and fearless disciple of the Lord Jesus Christ. He said on 16 March 1902, shortly after becoming President of the Church, "Now, my brethren and sisters, I know that my Redeemer lives. I feel it in every fiber of my being. I am just as satisfied of it as I am of my own existence. I cannot feel more sure of my own being than I do that my Redeemer lives, and that my God lives, the Father of my Savior. I feel it in my soul; I am converted to it in my whole being. I bear testimony to you that this is the doctrine of Christ, the gospel of Jesus, which is the power of God unto salvation. It is 'Mormonism.'"[141]

Not only was President Joseph F. a bridge from the nineteenth-century Church to the modern Church but also, as President Harold B. Lee noted, "he . . . presided during the stormy days when an antagonistic press maligned the Church, but his was the steady arm by the Lord's appointment to carry off the Church triumphantly."[142]

NOTES

1. As cited in D. Michael Quinn, *The Mormon Hierarchy: Extensions of Power* (Salt Lake City: Signature Books, 1997), 804. An extensive search through the journals of stake presidents from this period failed to locate the original source citation.

2. John Henry Smith Diary, 17 October 1901, John Henry Smith Papers, 1875–1911, MLUU; as cited in Jean Bickmore White, ed., *Church, State, and Politics: The Diaries of John Henry Smith* (Salt Lake City: Signature Books, 1990), 496.

3. Rudger Clawson Diary, 17 October 1901, Rudger Clawson Papers, 1898–1905, MLUU; as cited in Stan Larson, ed., *A Ministry of Meetings: The Apostolic Diaries of Rudger Clawson* (Salt Lake City: Signature Books, 1993), 339.

4. Abraham O. Woodruff Journal, 17 October 1901, BYU.

5. Clawson Diary, 17 October 1901; as cited in Larson, *A Ministry of Meetings*, 339.

6. J. H. Smith Diary, 17 October 1901; as cited in White, *Church, State, and Politics*, 496.

7. Clawson Diary, 17 October 1901; as cited in Larson, *A Ministry of Meetings*, 339.

8. Wilford Woodruff Journal, 23 January 1881; LDSCA; as cited in Scott G. Kenney, ed., *Wilford Woodruff's Journal, 1833–1898*, 9 vols. (Midvale, Utah: Signature Books, 1983–85), 8:8.

9. J. H. Smith Diary, 23 December 1905; as cited in White, *Church, State, and Politics*, 496.

10. L. John Nuttall Diary, 17 October 1901, typescript, BYU.

11. David John Diary, 16 October 1901, BYU.

12. Emmeline B. Wells Journal, 3 November 1901, typescript, BYU.

13. Edward H. Anderson, "Joseph Fielding Smith: Sixth President of the Church of Jesus Christ of Latter-day Saints," *Improvement Era* 5 (December 1901): 138.

14. "Official Announcement," *Deseret Evening News*, 8 November 1901, 4.

15. James R. Clark, comp., *Messages of the First Presidency of The Church of Jesus Christ of Latter-day Saints*, 6 vols. (Salt Lake City: Bookcraft, Inc., 1965–75); hereafter cited as *MFP*, 4:2.

16. Ibid.

17. John Diary, 3 November 1901.

18. "Utah Stake Conference," *Deseret Evening News*, 4 November 1901, 7.

19. Ibid.

20. John Diary, 3 November 1901.

21. John Diary, 10 November 1901.

22. Wells Journal, 10 November 1901.

23. *MFP*, 4:5–6.

24. Joseph Fielding Smith Jr. and John Stewart, *The Life of Joseph Fielding Smith: Tenth President of The Church of Jesus Christ of Latter-day Saints* (Salt Lake City: Deseret Book, 1972), 61.

25. *R. L. Polk & Co.'s Salt Lake City Directory, 1894–5* (Salt Lake City: R. L. Polk & Co., 1894), 675.

26. Ibid., 660.

27. Ibid., 869.

28. Ibid.

29. Joseph F. Smith, "My Missions," *Deseret Evening News*, 21 December 1901, 57; MFP, 4:18.

30. Ibid; MFP, 4:18.

31. Ibid; MFP, 4:18.

32. Ibid; MFP, 4:23.

33. "Jewish People Congratulated," *Deseret Evening News*, 10 August 1903, 2.

34. Ibid.

35. "Two Leap from Auto to Shocking Death," *Deseret Evening News*, 16 August 1912, 1.

36. Joseph F. Smith to George Albert Smith, 18 August 1912, George Albert Smith Papers, Ms. #36, MLUU.

37. Ibid.

38. Thomas G. Alexander, *Mormonism in Transition: A History of the Latter-day Saints, 1890–1930* (Urbana and Chicago: University of Illinois Press, 1986), 19.

39. *Proceedings Before the Committee on Privileges and Elections of the United States Senate in the Matter of the Protests against the Right of Hon. Reed Smoot, a Senator from the State of Utah, to Hold His Seat* (Washington: Government Printing Office, 1904), 1:79–91.

40. Carl A. Badger to George Albert Smith, 4 March 1904, George Albert Smith Papers, Ms. #36, MLUU.

41. Ibid.

42. In CR, April 1904, 75.

43. Ibid.

44. Wells Journal, 1 January 1905.

45. See "The New Latter-day Saints Hospital," *Improvement Era* 8 (February 1905): 317.

46. Wells Journal, 1 May 1905.

47. "Invitation," LDSCA.

48. *Proceedings at the Dedication of the Joseph Smith Memorial Monument* (Salt Lake City: The Church of Jesus Christ of Latter-day Saints, Salt Lake City, n.d.), 22.

49. Ibid., 26.

50. "Interview [Salt Lake City, Utah] January 1974," Rachel Smith Taylor, 1890–1986, LDSCA.

51. Ibid.

52. Journal History of The Church of Jesus Christ of Latter-day Saints, Historical Department Archives; hereafter cited as JH, 5 July 1906, 7.

53. "Hawaiian Musicians Recognize Prest. Smith," *Deseret Evening News*, 7 July 1906, 5.

54. "Messages from the Missions," *Improvement Era* 9 (October 1906): 975.

55. "An Address. The Church of Jesus Christ of Latter-day Saints to the World," *Improvement Era* 10 (May 1907): 481–83.

56. Joseph F. Smith Diary, 21 February 1909, Joseph F. Smith Papers, 1856–1918, LDSCA; as cited in typescript extracts, Scott G. Kenney Collection, BYU.

57. Ibid, 24 February 1909.

58. "Trip of President Smith and Company to Hawaii," *Improvement Era* 12 (May 1909): 581, 583.

59. Ibid., 583.

60. Ibid.

61. Joseph F. Smith to George Albert Smith, 7 September 1909, George Albert Smith Papers, Ms. #36, MLUU.

62. "Corner Stone Laid at B.Y.U.," *Deseret Evening News*, 16 October 1909, 2.

63. MFP, 4:197–99.

64. Henry D. Moyle Journal, 25 July 1910, LDSCA. This excerpt was provided by a staff member of the Historical Department of the Church.

65. Andrew Jenson, *Autobiography of Andrew Jenson* (Salt Lake City: Deseret News Press, 1938), 469.

66. Ibid.

67. Ibid., 469–70.

68. Ibid., 470.

69. Ibid.

70. Ibid.

71. "President Joseph F. Smith at Stockholm," *Deseret Evening News*, 20 August 1910, 4.

72. James E. Talmage Journal, 8 December 1911, BYU.

73. As cited in Talmage Journal, 8 December 1911.

74. Emily Jane Smith Walker, "'Mama & Papa' at the rear of the train," Julina Lambson Smith Family Photograph Album, Mary Lou Walker, Salt Lake City, Utah.

75. Joseph F. Smith to George Albert Smith, 27 May 1913, George Albert

Smith Papers, Ms. #36, MLUU.

76. Joseph F. Smith, *Gospel Doctrine: Selections from the Sermons and Writings of Joseph F. Smith, Sixth President of The Church of Jesus Christ of Latter-day Saints* (Salt Lake City: Deseret Book, 1966); hereafter cited as GD, 520–21.

77. See Conference Reports of The Church of Jesus Christ of Latter-day Saints; hereafter cited as CR, April 1901, 69.

78. Edward J. Wood Diary, [4] October 1912, Edward J. Wood Papers, LDSCA.

79. As cited in V. A. Wood, *The Alberta Temple: Centre and Symbol of Faith* (Calgary: Detselig Enterprises Ltd., 1989), 28.

80. Wood Diary, 27 July 1913.

81. Ibid.

82. JH, 27 July 1913, 3–4.

83. Ibid., 3.

84. Ibid.

85. Ibid., 3–4.

86. Alma C. Hanson Interview by Jeni Broberg Holzapfel and Richard Neitzel Holzapfel, August 1999, in possession of authors.

87. Edward J. Wood, "Years Together, 1892–1952," Edward J. Wood Papers, LDSCA.

88. See *Improvement Era* 17 (February 1914): 282.

89. "Prest. Smith's Family Observe His Birthday," *Deseret Evening News*, 14 November 1913, 20.

90. As cited in R. Lanier Britsch, *Unto the Islands of the Sea: A History of the Latter-day Saints in the Pacific* (Salt Lake City: Deseret Book, 1986), 153.

91. James B. Allen, Jessie L. Embry, and Kahlile B. Mehr, *Hearts Turned to the Fathers: A History of the Genealogical Society of Utah, 1894–1994* (Provo: BYU Studies, Brigham Young University, 1995), 79.

92. "Golden Wedding of Prest. and Mrs. Smith is Celebrated," *Deseret Evening News*, 6 May 1916, 16.

93. Ibid.

94. "President Smith at San Diego," *Improvement Era* 19 (July 1914): 841.

95. "Members of Kimball Family Celebrate Pioneer's Birthday," *Deseret Evening News*, 16 June 1917, Section 2, 9.

96. F. W. Otterstrom, "A Journey to the South," *Improvement Era* 21 (December 1917): 100.

97. Ibid., 108.
98. Ibid., 109.
99. Ibid.
100. Ibid., 110.
101. Ibid.
102. Ibid., 110–11.
103. Ibid., 111.
104. Ibid.
105. "Elder Hyrum M. Smith Dies of Peritonitis Following Operation," *Deseret Evening News*, 24 January 1918, 1.
106. Anthon H. Lund Diary, 27 January 1918, Anthon H. Lund Papers 1860–1921, LDSCA, as cited in typescript extracts, Scott G. Kenney Collection, BYU.
107. MFP, 5:98–99.
108. "The Hyrum Smith Monument," *Improvement Era* 21 (August 1918): 859.
109. Ibid., 860–62.
110. "'I have Dwelt in the Spirit of Prayer,'" *Improvement Era* 22 (November 1918): 80.
111. Ibid.
112. Wells Journal, 4 October 1918.
113. Talmage Journal, 4 October 1918.
114. In CR, October 1918, 2.
115. Ibid.
116. Ibid., 2–3.
117. Ibid., 3.
118. Ibid., 150–51.
119. George Albert Smith Journal, 17 November 1918, George Albert Smith Papers, Ms. #36, MLUU.
120. Talmage Journal, 15 November 1918.
121. Joseph Fielding Smith, comp., *Life of Joseph F. Smith: Sixth President of The Church of Jesus Christ of Latter-day Saints* (Salt Lake City: Deseret Book, 1938); hereafter cited as *LJFS*, 477–79.
122. Reed Smoot Diary, 19 November 1918, BYU; as cited in Harvard S. Heath, ed., *In the World: The Diaries of Reed Smoot* (Salt Lake City: Signature Books, 1997), 404.

123. Wells Journal, 18 November 1918.
124. Talmage Journal, 19 November 1918.
125. Wells Journal, 21 November 1918.
126. MFP, 5:113–14.
127. "Prest. Joseph F. Smith Followed to Grave by Magnificent Cortege," *Deseret Evening News*, 22 November 1918, 1.
128. Ibid.
129. Amelia Smith McConkie Interview, 18 August and 24 September 1999, by Richard Neitzel Holzapfel, in authors' possession.
130. "Prest. Joseph F. Smith Followed to Grave by Magnificent Cortege," 1.
131. Talmage Journal, 22 November 1918.
132. "Prest. Joseph F. Smith Followed to Grave by Magnificent Cortege," 1.
133. George Albert Smith Diary, 21 November 1918.
134. "Prest. Joseph F. Smith Followed to Grave by Magnificent Cortege," 1.
135. Ibid.
136. Ibid.
137. Ibid.
138. George Albert Smith Diary, [22] November 1918.
139. Wells Journal, 22 November 1918.
140. George Albert Smith Diary, [22] November 1918.
141. GD, 69.
142. In CR, October 1972, 18.

CHAPTER FIVE

A Doctrinal Legacy

President Joseph F. was a powerful preacher of righteousness. One finds countless comments about the effects of his sermons and talks from those who heard him speak during his lifetime.

One of the earliest observations comes from Wilford Woodruff in 1866, just weeks before Joseph F. was ordained an apostle by President Brigham Young. Joseph F. spoke in the Bowery, a shaded structure on the Temple Block, during the regular Sabbath-day meeting. Elder Woodruff observed, "Joseph F Smith spoke in the Afternoon 1 Hour 15 minutes & the power of God was upon him & he manifested the same spirit that was upon his Uncle Joseph Smith & his Father Hyram Smith."[1]

The *Deseret News* reported a brief synopsis of the discourse a few days later:

"Elder J. F. Smith treated on the nature and magnitude of the work which the Saints are engaged in to combat sin and overcome evil, and the importance of their being fully alive to their duties. He reviewed our condition today, urged that all our energies should be devoted to serving God and seeking to overcome iniquity; and strongly advised the young particularly, and all generally, to keep the company of those who are the friends of God and truth, and who are striving to walk in righteousness before the Lord."[2]

Later, after Joseph F. became President of the Church, Emmeline B.

Wells noted her impressions after listening to him in the Salt Lake Temple in November 1905: "At the Temple today Pres. Jos. F. smith made a most telling address, in which he gave his views on the subject of charity. Every one present must have felt its power."[3]

One of Joseph F.'s most significant and important talks, entitled "In the Presence of the Divine," was given in the April General Conference of the Church in 1916.

The Latter-day Saints gathered in the Tabernacle on Temple Square for the first time in many months because of repairs and enhancement of the world-famous organ. President Joseph F. told those present:

"Sometimes the Lord expands our vision from this point of view and this side of the veil, so that we feel and seem to realize that we can look beyond the thin veil which separates us from that other sphere. If we can see by the enlightening influence of the Spirit of God . . . beyond the veil that separates us from the spirit world, surely those who have passed beyond, can see more clearly through the veil back here to us than it is possible for us to see them from our sphere of action. I believe we move and have our being in the presence of heavenly messengers and of heavenly beings."[4]

Many of those listening felt the divine inspiration that accompanied the delivery of this remarkable sermon on 6 April 1916. The talk is one of the most important given during his presidency. President Joseph F. indicated that he needed "the assistance of the Good Spirit, and of the good feeling and faith and sympathy of my brethren and sisters this morning in an endeavor to speak to you for a short time."

He added: "I can not express my gratitude, with the language in my possession, which I feel this morning in being permitted, under the mercies of the Father of us all, to be present with you and behold the sight that I see in the assembled multitudes gathered here in the opening session of this conference, on the eighty-sixth anniversary of the organization of the Church of Jesus Christ of Latter-day Saints."

In a section identified as "Those Who Have Gone Before Rejoice With Us," President Smith indicated: "I feel sure that the Prophet Joseph Smith and his associates, who, under the guidance and inspiration of the Almighty, and by his power, began this latter-day work, would rejoice and do rejoice, if they are permitted to look down upon the scene that I behold in this tabernacle...."

He continued: "I thank God for the feeling that I possess and enjoy, and for the realization that I have, that I stand not only in the presence of Almighty God, my Maker and Father, but in the presence of his Only Begotten Son in the flesh, the Savior of the world; and I stand in the presence of Peter and James (and perhaps the eyes of John are also upon us and we know it not); and that I stand also in the presence of Joseph and Hyrum and Brigham and John, and Wilford, and Lorenzo, and those who have been valiant in the testimony of Jesus Christ and faithful to their mission in the world, who have gone before...."

At this point, President Smith was overcome by emotion and said:

"I hope you will forgive me for my emotion. You would have peculiar emotions, would you not? if you felt that you stood in the presence of your Father, in the very presence of Almighty God, in the very presence of the Son of God and of holy angels? You would feel rather emotional, rather sensitive. I feel it to the very depths of my soul this moment. So I hope you will forgive me, if I exhibit some of my real feelings, I am only a child...."

The Saints felt the power of his testimony as he continued his discourse:

"It is my duty to proclaim to my brethren, to the household of faith, as well as to the world, when opportunity presents, that I believe in the living God, the Father of our Lord and Savior Jesus Christ, who begot his Son, his Only Begotten in the flesh, and that Son grew from his birth unto his manhood, and developed into the very image and likeness of his Father. . . .

" . . . [T]his is the gospel of Jesus Christ, to know the only true and living God and his Son whom he has sent into the world, which knowledge comes through obedience to all his commandments, faith, repentance of sin, baptism by immersion for the remission of sins, the gift of the Holy Ghost by the laying on of hands by divine authority, and not by the will of man. This, then, is the gospel of Jesus Christ which is the power of God unto salvation: obedience to the truth, submission to the order that God has established in his house, for the house of God is a house of order and not a house of confusion. God has set in his Church apostles and prophets and evangelists, and pastors and teachers, whose duty it is to administer to the people, to teach, instruct, expound, exhort, admonish and lead in the path of righteousness. . . . "

He closed his remarks as he blessed the Saints: "God bless you and all the household of faith, and help us to be true and faithful to the end, realizing that the battle is not to the strong, nor the race to the swift, but to him that endures to the end. Amen."[5]

Shortly after Joseph F.'s death in 1918, his faithful counselor, Anthon H. Lund, stated:

"He was a great preacher of righteousness. How often have I sat listening to his voice and rejoiced in the truths that he put forth, the encouraging words he spoke and the words of warning he gave unto the people! Take a view of his life. God had given him a strong and abiding faith. He never wavered. . . . He loved the gospel. He loved to bear his testimony that Jesus was the Redeemer and Savior of the world. He bore testimony to the truth of the gospel, and to the divinity of the mission of Joseph Smith, and his testimony always strengthened the faith of those who listened to him."[6]

President Joseph F. left the Church a great legacy of gospel scholarship through his countless sermons and essays. Shortly after being called as the new President of the Church in 1972, President Harold B. Lee said: "When I want to seek for a more clear definition of doctrinal subjects, I have usually turned to the writings and sermons of President Joseph F. Smith."[7] It has been so for many before and since President Lee.

First Discourse Published

In February 1867, twenty-eight-year-old Joseph F. spoke in the Tabernacle in Salt Lake City. This talk was apparently the first complete talk of Joseph F. to be published. He began: "Very unexpectedly to me I have been asked to stand before you for a short time this afternoon; and although to me it is a great task to attempt to speak to so many, yet it is a pleasure to be able to express my feelings in relation to the truth. . . . "

Elder Smith added: "I desire so to live continually that my thoughts and feelings may be right before God, that my heart may be pure and open to the influences and dictations of the Holy Spirit, that I may be led wholly by the truth, and in the path that leads to eternal life. . . . "

He also stated: "This is a great and important work—one that we do not fully comprehend. When the Spirit of the Lord rests powerfully upon us, we realize it to some extent; but we do not always have that Spirit in such copious measure, and when we are left to ourselves we are weak, frail and liable to err. This shows to us that we should be more faithful than we have ever been, and that day and night, wherever we are and under whatever circumstances we may be placed, in order to enjoy the Spirit of the Gospel we must live to God by observing truth, honoring his law, and ever manifest a vigorous determination to accomplish the work he has assigned us."

He then said: "I thank the Lord that I have the privilege of being associated with this people; and, whatever men may say or do, I desire that the testimony of the truth may continue with me, that I may ever realize for myself that the Gospel has again been revealed to man on the earth. . . .

"I feel well and thankful to have the privilege of being a Saint; and I hope, brethren and sisters, that anything good that is said to us we will feel like carrying out in our lives. It is our duty, and we should never fail to do so.

"May God bless us and all Israel, and keep us in the paths of truth. . . .

" . . . May God grant it, and help us all to be faithful, that we may be numbered among those who obtain a crown and inheritance, is my prayer in the name of Jesus. Amen."[8]

This fully reported discourse became the first of a large and important body of teachings by Joseph F. to which members of the Church continue to turn to find counsel, wisdom, and admonitions.

First Presidency Doctrinal Statements

It is not only his discourses that form the basis of Joseph F.'s doctrinal legacy. During his presidency, several important documents signed by the First Presidency and/or the Twelve were issued that still serve as a touchstone of Latter-day Saint belief. One such document, *The Origin of Man: By the First Presidency*, was issued in 1909 during a time when evolution was gaining attention in the academic world.[9]

They wrote: "In presenting the statement that follows we are not conscious of putting forth anything essentially new; neither is it our desire so to do. Truth is what we wish to present, and truth—eternal truth—is fundamentally old. A restatement of the original attitude of the Church relative to this matter is all that will be attempted here. To tell the truth as God has revealed it, and commend it to the acceptance of those who need to conform their opinions thereto, is the sole purpose of this presentation.

"'God created man in his own image, in the image of God created he him; male and female created he them.' In these plain and pointed words the inspired author of the book of Genesis made known to the world the truth concerning the origin of the human family. . . ."[10]

They added: "The Church of Jesus Christ of Latter-day Saints, basing its belief on divine revelation, ancient and modern, proclaims man to be the direct and lineal offspring of Deity. God Himself is an exalted man, perfected, enthroned, and supreme. By His almighty power He organized the earth, and all that it contains, from spirit and element, which exist co-eternally with Himself. He formed every plant that grows, and every animal that breathes, each after its own kind, spiritually and temporally—'that which is spiritual being in the likeness of that which is temporal, and that which is temporal in the likeness of that which is spiritual.' He made the tadpole and the ape, the lion and the elephant but He did not make them in His own image, nor endow them with Godlike reason and intelligence. Nevertheless, the whole animal creation will be perfected and perpetuated in the Hereafter, each class in its 'distinct order or sphere,' and will enjoy 'eternal felicity.' . . .

"Man is the child of God, formed in the divine image and endowed with divine attributes, and even as the infant son of an earthly father and mother is capable in due time of becoming a man, so the undeveloped offspring of celestial parentage is capable, by experience through ages and aeons, of evolving into a God."[11]

Another important doctrinal statement issued during Joseph F.'s presidency was released on 30 June 1916 under the signatures of the First Presidency and the Quorum of the Twelve. Entitled "The Father and The Son; A Doctrinal Exposition by The First Presidency and The Twelve," it appeared in the *Improvement Era* in August 1916 and as a separate pamphlet about the same time.[12]

Outlining how the term "Father" is used in scriptures, they wrote: "The term 'Father' as applied to Deity occurs in sacred writ with plainly different meanings. Each of the four significations specified in the following treatment should be carefully segregated."

President Joseph F. and his counselors and members of the Twelve indicated that in some cases, the term "Father" is applied to God because He is our literal parent. Second, the term "Father" is applied to Jesus Christ because He is the Creator of heaven and earth, or "The Father of the heavens and of the earth." Third, the term "Father" is applied to Jesus Christ because those who accept His gospel become

His "sons and daughters" through spiritual rebirth. Finally, the term "Father" is applied to Jesus Christ by His "Divine Investiture of Authority" where He represents His "Father in power and authority."

These official statements released during Joseph F.'s presidency provided the Latter-day Saints with responses to important questions and remain, to this day, the basis of LDS doctrine on the subjects.

Teachings of Joseph F. Smith

The most comprehensive, single-volume collection of Joseph F.'s teachings is the book *Gospel Doctrine: Selections from the Sermons and Writings of Joseph F. Smith, Sixth President of The Church of Jesus Christ of Latter-day Saints*, originally published in 1919.[13] The contents include such sections as "Truth, the Foundation," "The Eternal Nature of the Church, the Priesthood, and Man," "Revelation," "Free Agency," "God and Man," "The Purpose and the Mission of the Church," "The First Principles of the Gospel," "The Church and the Man," "Priesthood," "Spiritual Gifts," "Obedience," "Prayer," "Tithing; the Poor; Industry," "Temperance; the Sabbath," "Many Duties of Man," "Auxiliary Organizations," "Political Government," "Eternal Life and Salvation," and "Joseph Smith, the Prophet."

The compilers added additional sections, including "Personal Testimonies and Blessing" and "President Joseph F. Smith." The latter contains an essay by Elder John A. Widtsoe written in 1914 entitled "An Appreciation"; "Reminiscences," by Charles W. Nibley, Presiding Bishop of the Church; "A Biographical Sketch," by Edward H. Anderson, originally published in 1901; and another brief essay by Anderson entitled "Last of the Old School of Veteran Leaders."

Reprinted numerous times, including as a two-volume manual released in 1970–71 and 1971–72 for a two-year course of study in the Melchizedek Priesthood quorums of the Church, this book is found in many homes and libraries throughout the Church.

So monumental is this book that Deseret Book released it as part of its "Classics in Mormon Literature Series" in October 1986. President Joseph F.'s great-grandson, Joseph Fielding McConkie, provided a new preface for this edition, highlighting the significance of President Smith's teachings and life.[14]

The goal in compiling the original collection of extracts was to get the "grist of his teachings without including the scaffolding."[15] To find the pearls of his teachings, the compilers searched through a number of sources including the *Journal of Discourses, Deseret News, Young Woman's Journal, Contributor, Millennial Star, Logan Journal, Relief Society Magazine, Women's Exponent, Juvenile Instructor, Genealogical Magazine*, and the Conference Reports.

The original preface, written by the compilers, provides the best justification for the compilation:

"President Joseph F. Smith was so long in the public service of the Church that his published sermons and writings would fill many volumes. The difficult problem of the compilers of this volume has been to make a collection of extracts that would do full justice to the man and that, at the same time, could be contained in a volume of moderate size. Every reader who knows Church literature will note the shortcomings of the work; and none more than the compilers. However, incomplete as it may be, this collection is well worth while, for it contains a wealth of gospel wisdom, to instruct, comfort, and inspire the Saints.

"The literature of the Church has been carefully and systematically searched to discover all of President Smith's public writings and sermons. Those of a historical nature have not been used in this collection, as they may well be made into another volume.

"The compilers give their thanks to the many who, with hearts full of love for President Smith, have helped in the work.

"The work has reaffirmed to us that prophets, speaking for God, are with us."[16]

The original introduction, written in May 1919 by the Committee on Courses of Study for the Priesthood, provides the background on how it came to be published in the first place: "President Joseph F. Smith incidentally stated on one occasion that when he should pass away, unlike many of his brethren, he would leave no written work, by which he might be remembered. It was his modest way of viewing his own ministry and literary labors, for President Smith would live in the hearts of the people even if he had said nothing for the printed page; but on the contrary, it was discovered that there are volumes in print, though at that time it had not been gathered and was therefore not so well known.

"One of the compilers of this volume, Dr. John A. Widtsoe, listening to his remark, thought to himself, 'certainly it cannot be true that he has left no written work.' He then decided to look into his published writings and sermons, conceived the idea of making extracts from them and arranging these extracts by subjects and in chapters, in the form of a book. The result is this splendid volume now presented to the public under the title GOSPEL DOCTRINE.

"Doctor John A. Widtsoe interested his brother, Prof. Osborne J. P. Widtsoe, also Albert E. Bowen, Doctor F. S. Harris, and Joseph

PLATE 156
JOSEPH F. SMITH WRITINGS
MCHA. FROM LEFT: "VISION OF THE REDEMPTION OF THE DEAD," PUBLISHED IN *IMPROVEMENT ERA* 22 (DECEMBER 1918): 166–70; *THE FATHER, THE SON: A DOCTRINAL EXPOSITION BY THE FIRST PRESIDENCY AND THE TWELVE*, PUBLISHED IN JUNE 1916; *GOSPEL DOCTRINE*, PUBLISHED IN 1919; AND JOSEPH F. SMITH TO JOHN MCCARTHY LETTER DATED 25 FEBRUARY 1896.

Quinney, in the work of compiling and classifying from the voluminous writings and sermons of President Smith, such extracts as would bear upon the subjects chosen for consideration—subjects covering a wide range in gospel doctrine and philosophy, as taught by the Latter-day Saints. Lorenzo N. Stohl generously paid the expenses of the work.

"Without price, and as a matter of love for the work in hand, these brethren proceeded with the compilation, had four typewritten copies prepared, nicely bound and titled, and were privileged, sometime before the death of the President, to offer him the first typewritten copy of the work, with their love and gratitude for his life, his example, and his inspired teachings, as well as for his gentle kindness and constant helpfulness to each of them.

"Needless to say, the presentation and the work were gladly accepted and gave President Smith great delight.

"The Committee on Study for the Priesthood Quorums, being apprised by the compilers of the work, conceived the idea, under the initiative of Elder David O. McKay, of the Council of the Twelve, of making it a text book for the Priesthood. The volume is now presented to the Melchizedek Priesthood Quorums of the Church for their study and consideration. To accompany it is 'A GUIDE' for the direction of teachers and students, and adopted for convenience in reference and study.

"The sermons and writings of President Joseph F. Smith teach, in wisdom and moderation, practically every essential doctrine of the Latter-day Saints concerning the present life and the life hereafter. Not only that, but they abound in helpful counsel and advice on everyday practices in right living, stated in simple and persuasive language. President Smith's sermons and writings breathe the true spirit of the Gospel, are sound as gold in tenet and precept, and express the will of the Master in every word. Gathered, classified, arranged, and printed as in this volume, they constitute a compendium of the doctrine and teachings of the Church that we believe will stand as a safe guide for its members for generations to come.

"In presenting this compilation to the public, we are confident that every reader will be fully repaid in its perusal, containing, as it does, rich and vital selections from the sayings, teachings and sermons of one of the foremost prophets of the Lord in the Dispensation of the Fulness of Times."[17]

Vision of the Redemption of the Dead

Of all the writings, sermons, and personal teachings, Joseph F.'s greatest doctrinal legacy is the vision he had shortly before his death. With decades of spiritual preparation, Joseph F. was given a vision in Salt Lake City, Utah, on 3 October 1918.

As he spoke to the Latter-day Saints, in what would be his last general conference in October 1918, President Joseph F. provided those gathered in the historic Tabernacle some insights about the events of the previous few months:

"I will not, I dare not, attempt to enter upon many things that are resting upon my mind this morning, and I shall postpone until some future time, the Lord being willing, my attempt to tell you some of the things that are in my mind, and that dwell in my heart. I have not lived alone these five months. I have dwelt in the spirit of prayer, of supplication, of faith and of determination; and I have had my communication with the Spirit of the Lord continuously; and I am glad to say to you, my brethren and sisters, that it is a happy meeting this morning for me to have the privilege of joining with you in the opening of this eighty-ninth Semi-annual Conference of the Church."[18]

Only later did the Saints discover that he had received an important vision, given just the day before on 3 October 1918. The vision, now contained in Doctrine and Covenants 138, is actually a series of visions and has become known as the "Vision of the Redemption of the Dead."

A Doctrinal Legacy

The introductory material to the Vision of the Redemption of the Dead provides a word-picture of the event as he sat in his room in the Beehive House:

"On the third of October, in the year nineteen hundred and eighteen, I sat in my room pondering over the scriptures; and reflecting upon the great atoning sacrifice that was made by the Son of God, for the redemption of the world; and the great and wonderful love made manifest by the Father and the Son in the coming of the Redeemer into the world; that through his atonement, and by obedience to the principles of the gospel, mankind might be saved.

"While I was thus engaged, my mind reverted to the writings of the apostle Peter, to the primitive saints scattered abroad throughout Pontus, Galatia, Cappadocia, and other parts of Asia, where the gospel had been preached after the crucifixion of the Lord. I opened the Bible and read the third and fourth chapters of the first epistle of Peter, and as I read I was greatly impressed, more than I had ever been before, with the following passages: 'For Christ also hath once suffered for sins, the just for the unjust, that he might bring us to God, being put to death in the flesh, but quickened by the Spirit: By which also he went and preached unto the spirits in prison; Which sometime were disobedient, when once the long-suffering of God waited in the days of Noah, while the ark was a preparing, wherein few, that is, eight souls were saved by water.' (1 Peter 3:18–20.)

"'For for this cause was the gospel preached also to them that are dead, that they might be judged according to men in the flesh, but live according to God in the spirit.' (1 Peter 4:6.) As I pondered over these things which are written, the eyes of my understanding were opened,

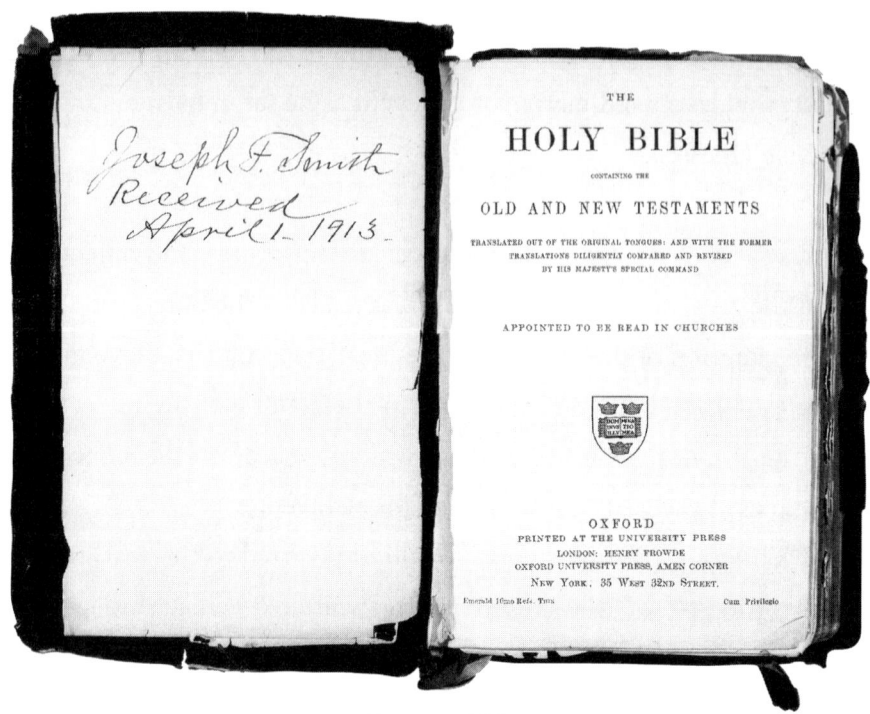

PLATE 157
JOSEPH F. SMITH'S BIBLE
JACKSON COLLECTION. JOSEPH F. SMITH OBTAINED THIS OXFORD UNIVERSITY PRESS KJV BIBLE ON 1 APRIL 1913. ACCORDING TO FAMILY TRADITION, THIS BIBLE WAS IN HIS POSSESSION AND THE ONE HE WAS PROBABLY READING DURING THE PERIOD WHEN THE VISION OF THE REDEMPTION OF THE DEAD WAS RECEIVED.

---

and the Spirit of the Lord rested upon me, and I saw the hosts of the dead, both small and great."[19]

Following a long description of what he beheld in the vision, President Joseph F. solemnly testified, "Thus was the vision of the redemption of the dead revealed to me, and I bear record, and I know that this record is true, through the blessing of our Lord and Savior, Jesus Christ, even so. Amen."[20]

Before the end of the month the written account was submitted to

PLATE 158
JOSEPH F. SMITH'S BIBLE

JACKSON COLLECTION. SHOWS JOSEPH F. SMITH'S BIBLE OPENED TO 1 PETER 3–4. HE NOT ONLY MARKED IN RED THE PASSAGE OF 1 PETER 3:18–21 BUT ALSO OUTLINED IT WITH A PENCIL MARK TO THE RIGHT. HE ALSO OUTLINED 1 PETER 4:6. THESE PASSAGES WERE THE ONES THAT ACTED AS A CATALYST FOR THE VISION RECEIVED ON 3 OCTOBER 1918, AS NOTED IN DOCTRINE AND COVENANTS 138:6–10.

---

the counselors in the First Presidency, the Council of the Twelve, and the Patriarch, and was unanimously accepted by them.

His son Joseph Fielding Smith, scribe and a member of the Quorum of the Twelve, recalled the event years later:

"Some of these manifestations [those that occurred between the April and October 1918 general conferences] which he declared at the conference he had received, he had mentioned to his son Joseph Fielding both before and following the general conference.... It was later, October 31, 1918, submitted to his counselors and the council of the Twelve and the Patriarch, and by them unanimously accepted. This manifestation reveals to us some new light in relation to the visitation of our Lord to the spirits of the dead, while his body was in the tomb."[21]

Elder James E. Talmage highlights the momentous occasion in a contemporary diary entry at the time of the meeting in the Salt Lake Temple:

"Attended meeting of the First Presidency and the Twelve. Today President Smith, who is still confined to his home by illness, sent to the Brethren the account of a vision through which, as he states, were revealed to him important facts relating to the work of the disembodied Savior in the realm of departed spirits, and of the missionary work in progress on the other side of the veil. By united action the Council of the Twelve, with the Counselors in the First Presidency, and the Presiding patriarch accepted and endorsed the revelation as the Word of the Lord. President Smith's signed statement will be published in the next issue (December) of the Improvement Era, which is the organ of the Priesthood quorums of the Church."[22]

Soon thereafter, the revelation was released to the Latter-day Saints through the official publications of the Church. Eventually, in 1976, the revelation was presented to the body of the Church and accepted as canonized scripture.[23]

 NEW CENTURY AND BEYOND

Beginning in January 2000 and for the next two years, Latter-day Saints across the world will study the teachings of President Joseph F. Smith in the priesthood and Relief Society organizations of the

A Doctrinal Legacy

Church. The Melchizedek Priesthood and Relief Society manual, *Teachings of Presidents of the Church: Joseph F. Smith*, provides an important collection from President Joseph F.'s teachings on a variety of timeless issues and fundamental doctrines of the restored gospel.[24]

Joseph F. left the Latter-day Saints a great doctrinal legacy. His successor, President Heber J. Grant, spoke of this legacy in the June 1919 Church conference, the first held since the passing of Joseph F.:

"I bear witness to you that from my early childhood days, when I could not thoroughly understand and comprehend the teachings of the gospel, that I have had my very being thrilled, and tears have rolled down my cheeks, under the inspiration of the living God, as I have listened to Joseph F. Smith when preaching the gospel. I believe that Joseph F. Smith and his son Hyrum M. Smith more than any other men to whom I have listened, who were born in the Church of Christ in our day, were the greatest preachers of righteousness. I know that whenever I heard that Joseph F. Smith was going to speak in one of the wards, that time and time again as a young man I have left my own ward and gone to listen to him, because he always filled my being and lifted me up as I listened to him proclaim the gospel of Jesus Christ. I bear witness that he was one of the greatest prophets of God that has ever lived; that God was with him from the day that he went forth as a little boy of fifteen years of age, to proclaim the gospel of Jesus Christ

MAY WE BE FAITHFUL TO THE END

in the Hawaiian Islands, until the day when, after giving sixty-five years of his life to the work of God, he closed his earthly career.

"May God bless each and all of us who have a knowledge of the divinity of the work in which we are engaged, and may we be faithful to the end as our prophet was, our beloved leader who has left us, Joseph F. Smith, is my prayer, and I ask it in the name of Jesus Christ. Amen."[25]

NOTES

1. Wilford Woodruff Journal, 24 June 1866, LDSCA; as cited in Scott G. Kenney, ed., *Wilford Woodruff's Journals, 1833–1898*, 9 vols. (Midvale, Utah: Signature Books, 1983–85), 6:289.

2. "Home Items," *Deseret News*, 28 June 1866, 236.

3. Emmeline B. Wells Journal, 5 November 1905, typescript, BYU.

4. In CR, April 1916, 2–3.

5. Joseph F. Smith, "In the Presence of the Divine," *Improvement Era* 19 (May 1916): 646–52.

6. In CR, June 1919, 17–18.

7. Ibid., October 1972, 18.

8. Journal of Discourses, 26 vols. (London: Latter-day Saints' Book Depot, 1854–1886); hereafter cited as *JD*, 11:305–6, 309, 313–14.

9. James R. Clark, comp., *Messages of the First Presidency of The Church of Jesus Christ of Latter-day Saints*, 6 vols. (Salt Lake City: Bookcraft, Inc., 1965–75): hereafter cited as *MFP*, 4:200.

10. Ibid., 4:201.

11. Ibid., 4:206.

12. "The Father and the Son: A Doctrinal Exposition by the First Presidency and the Twelve," *Improvement Era* 19 (August 1916): 934–42.

13. Joseph F. Smith, *Gospel Doctrine: Selections from the Sermons and Writings of Joseph F. Smith, Sixth President of The Church of Jesus Christ of Latter-day Saints* (Salt Lake City: Deseret News, 1919); hereafter cited as *GD*.

14. See Joseph Fielding McConkie, "Preface to Classics in Mormon Literature Edition," *Gospel Doctrine: Sermons and Writings of President Joseph F. Smith* (Salt Lake City: Deseret Book, 1986), vii–xii.

15. John A. Widtsoe to F. S. Harris, 31 August 1917, provided by Allan K. Parrish, Orem, Utah.

16. *GD*, Preface.

17. *GD*, Introduction.

18. CR, October 1918, 2.

19. Doctrine and Covenants 138:1–11.

20. Doctrine and Covenants 138:60.

21. Joseph Fielding Smith, comp., *Life of Joseph F. Smith: Sixth President of The Church of Jesus Christ of Latter-day Saints* (Salt Lake City: Deseret Book, 1938); hereafter cited as *LJFS*, 466.

22. Talmage Journal, 31 October 1918.

23. For a full discussion of the historical setting, doctrinal implications, and the history of the publication of the revelation, see Robert L. Millet, "The Vision of the Redemption of the Dead," *Hearken, O Ye People: Discourse on the Doctrine and Covenants, Sperry Symposium 1984* (Sandy, Utah: Randall Book Co., 1984), 251–69.

24. See *Teachings of Presidents of the Church: Joseph F. Smith* (Salt Lake City: The Church of Jesus Christ of Latter-day Saints, 1998).

25. In CR, June 1919, 13–14.

CONCLUSION

A Tribute to President Joseph F. Smith, June 1919

The annual conference of the Church, generally held in April, was postponed in 1919 because of the worldwide influenza epidemic that affected as much as one-fifth of the world's population, killing more than 21 million people in just four months. Finally, on 1 June 1919, conditions in Utah allowed the Saints to gather at Temple Square for the eighty-ninth annual conference of the Church, the first conference since the death of President Joseph F. Smith on 19 November 1918. Elder James E. Talmage noted: "<u>June 1, Sunday</u>: This day is marked by the opening of the 89th Annual Conference of the church, which has been deferred to this date from the usual time of gathering on account of the prevalence of influenza last April. It proved to be a day long to be remembered."[1]

The numbers in attendance at this historic conference precluded everyone from being accommodated in the Tabernacle itself. Heber J. Grant, the new President of the Church, stated: "We regret that all of the Saints cannot be present in one building to hear the remarks that may be made upon this occasion."[2] President Grant indicated that overflow meetings would be held so everyone could participate in the general conference. He also indicated that those speaking should "devote the time and their remarks to the memory of President Joseph F. Smith."[3]

These tributes by the General Authorities constitute one of the finest collections of stories and recollections about the life and ministry of a President of the Church ever presented in a general conference setting. In them, we hear the personal voices of those who labored with President Joseph F. Smith in the cause of the gospel and, in many cases, those who knew him best. They tell of hardships, trials, and tribulations. They also reveal Joseph F. Smith's spirituality, courage, dedication, love, and humility. All in all, they provide another window that allows insights into the heart, mind, and soul of this Prophet-Patriarch.

President Heber J. Grant's Tribute

President Grant was born in 1856 while Joseph F. was serving his first mission in Hawaii. Heber J. Grant was ordained an apostle in 1882, and thus began a long association with Joseph F., who was then serving as second counselor in the First Presidency with President John Taylor.

In the Tabernacle itself, President Grant spoke on the "courage of President Joseph F. Smith" during his opening remarks and provided the Saints a fitting tribute to the man who had led The Church of Jesus Christ of Latter-day Saints from October 1901 until his death in November 1918.[4]

Elder James E. Talmage provided his own assessment of the new President's talk:

"President Heber J. Grant delivered an impressive address lasting nearly an hour, and never before have I heard him speak with greater force, power and evidence of inspiration. He paid due tribute to his predecessors in the office of presidency, and devoted a large share of the time to testimony concerning the life work and ministry of the late

President Joseph F. Smith. According to action taken in our council meeting last Thursday, the services of this day were to be devoted largely as a memorial to President Joseph F. Smith. When he passed away on the 19th of November last and when he was buried on the 22nd of the month, the quarantine regulations forbade any general assembly within doors for funeral services or otherwise."[5]

During his talk, President Grant recalled the story of Joseph F.'s second mission to Hawaii in 1864:

"Lorenzo Snow was drowned in the harbor of Honolulu, in the Hawaiian Islands, and it took some hours to bring him to life again. At that particular time the Lord revealed to him the fact that the young man Joseph F. Smith, who had refused to get off the vessel that had carried them from San Francisco to Honolulu, and get into a small boat, would some day be the Prophet of God. Answering Lorenzo Snow who was in charge of the company, he said: 'If you by the authority of the Priesthood of God, which you hold, tell me to get into that boat and attempt to land, I will do so, but unless you command me in the authority of the Priesthood, I will not do so, because it is not safe to attempt to land in a small boat while this typhoon is raging.' They laughed at the young man Joseph F. Smith, but he said, 'The boat will capsize.' The others got into the boat, and it did capsize; and but for the blessings of the Lord in resuscitating Lorenzo Snow he would not have lived, because he was drowned upon that occasion. It was revealed to him, then and there, that the boy, with the courage of his convictions, with the iron will to be laughed at and scorned as lacking courage to go in that boat, and who stayed on that vessel, would yet be the Prophet of God. Lorenzo Snow told me this upon more than one occasion, long years before Joseph F. Smith came to the presidency of the Church."[6]

At this point of his opening address, the new Church President gave a heartfelt "eulogy" in memory of his predecessor:

"I now come to Joseph F. Smith. I apologize to his family for reading a personal letter of sympathy. I had no idea as I sat down and picked up my pen and poured out my heart in love and sympathy to the family, that I would ever read in public that letter; but I had failed to get my mind upon anything that I particularly desired to say upon this occasion, and last night I borrowed from one of his sons a copy of the letter; and although it may not be good ethics, I wish to read it, because therein are the sentiments of my heart, poured out in love to his family.

> 'At Home, November 20, 1918.
>
> *'To the family of President Joseph F. Smith.*
>
> *'My dearly beloved friends:* Language fails me to express to you my love for your dear departed father and husband. In dear Aunt Eliza R. Snow's words I can truthfully say, "He was beloved, beloved by all."

'For thirty-six years I have labored under his Presidency, while he was counselor to or the President of the Church. During all this time no man could possibly have inspired one over whom he presided with more love or confidence for him than President Smith did me. I have said many times that no man who ever lived, with whom I have been associated, had been beloved by me as much as your dear departed husband and father.

'I could not and did not in my heart bring myself to feel that he was going to leave us until the afternoon of the 18th, when I called and David said he wanted to see me. The President took my hand and pressed it with a power and strength that was far from what one could expect from a dying man, and he blessed me with power and the Spirit of the living God, and there was love in his eyes and a strong pressure of his hand, and with nearly every word he spoke his pressure of my hand thrilled my being, and tears of gratitude to God and love for His mouthpiece upon the earth filled my heart. His blessing was all that I could ask or expect had he been my own dear father.

'Sister Bowman entered and kissed and wept over her father, and I walked into the little front office and wept, feeling that the last words I would ever hear from his beloved lips had been spoken when he said to me, "The Lord bless you, my boy, the Lord bless you, you have a great responsibility. Always remember this is the Lord's work and not man's. The Lord is greater than any man. He knows whom He wants to lead His Church and never makes any mistakes. The Lord bless you."

'I returned to my office, but I did not even have the heart to mail some letters which I had written earlier in the day. I went home and after eating supper I again visited the President, whom I found in great pain, and he asked President Lund who was there to bless him and supplicate the Lord to release him, and call him home. We placed our hands upon his head and President Lund told the Lord how much we loved our President and of our gratitude for the joy and happiness we had had in laboring with him, but asked that he be called home if his life could not be spared to us.

'The next morning I awoke at one o'clock and was not able to get to sleep until after six-thirty, as my mind was with the President. I got the November *Era* and reread the President's talk at the October conference, and after doing so I wrote in my *Era* at the close of his talk:

'"Nov. 19/18. Re-read twice and wept as I think of how near death's door the President is.

'"It is 3:45 and I have been awake since one a.m.—*Heber J. Grant*."

'The President lived but one hour and five minutes after I had written that he was near death's door.

'The Lord has been very good to me in times of

UPHOLD THE RIGHT THOUGH FIERCE THE FIGHT

sorrow, and I hope and pray with all my heart that He will bless and comfort your sorrowing hearts, as you read of his goodness to me. I am enclosing a copy of a letter telling of the blessings given to me in times of affliction. There are two poems among those published with my letter to Brother and Sister Winters which have comforted and blessed me. "The Changed Cross," and "Providence is Over All."[7] Especially have I been blessed while reading Sister Woodmansee's inspiring words. I knew her from my earliest recollection until the day of her death, and my love of her poem was no doubt increased from the fact that she lived in perfect harmony with its teachings.

'I was once talking of the favorite poems of our Church leaders and I turned to President Smith and asked him which of our hymns was his favorite and he said he hardly knew, but he thought that perhaps his favorite was the splendid hymn, "Uphold the Right, Though Fierce the Fight," by that heroic little soul, Sister Emily Hill Woodmansee. I enclose a copy of this hymn with this letter.[8]

'I have never known the joy and comfort of a father's love, but Presidents Joseph F. Smith, Francis M. Lyman, John Henry Smith, and others of my near and dear associates have given me a father's love and filled the place in my affections as completely as men not one's father could possibly do.

'Never in my life have I listened to more inspiring words than those at the funeral of my dear departed mother and at the funeral of my dear brother, Joseph Hyrum, which were spoken by President Smith.

'I am thankful beyond any power to tell for the inspiration to do my full duty in the battle of life which has come to me from the example and loving teachings of your beloved father and husband.

'Flowers fade in a day, and so I shall send each of you for Gusta and myself in loving remembrance of your dear departed husband and father the book "Their Yesterdays." I send this book for the reason that when I read it, March 20th, 1914, I marked one of the passages which seemed to me at the time I read the book to be inspirational. It is on pages 228–9.[9] I wrote in my book the sentiments of my heart at the time regarding President Smith in connection with the words on those pages. What I wrote was as follows: "More than any man I have ever known, President Joseph F. Smith has done this. God bless him forever, and his posterity after him. The fact that he is the Prophet of God today is a great testimony to me of the divinity of 'Mormonism' so called."

'Little did I think when I wrote these words that he would have departed this life by now.

'One of the most sincere and earnest prayers of my heart has been that President Smith should live to celebrate the one hundredth anniversary of the birth of the Church. I prayed for this some months ago at the close of a Temple fast meeting, and the Lord so abundantly blessed me that I felt my prayer would be answered, and I sat down weeping for joy.

'I could go on writing for hours, but I will close by sending my assurance and that of Sister Grant of our profound sympathy, and our most earnest prayer for God to comfort and bless your sorrowing hearts. President Smith sealed us as husband and wife for time and all eternity, and Gusta shares in all the expressions of love for him and admiration of his character in this letter. Again, may God bless you and your loved ones now and forever.

'Your affectionate brother,

'(Signed) HEBER J. GRANT.'

"At the grave of President Joseph F. Smith I read a poem entitled

'A Real Man'[10] and I expressed there the hope that I might live to be like Joseph F. Smith. I read at the grave the poem by Eliza R. Snow, written for the Prophet Joseph Smith. 'He was beloved, beloved by all.' The prayer that I had in my heart, the desire that I had to follow in the footsteps of this man of God, who presided over us with so much inspiration, with so much devotion, with so much integrity to God and to his fellow-men, the desire that I might be like him, is still in my heart. I pray God to bless his memory. I pray God to bless his wives and his children, that they may emulate his most wonderful and splendid example. I bear witness to you that from my early childhood days, when I could not thoroughly understand and comprehend the teachings of the gospel, that I have had my very being thrilled, and tears have rolled down my cheeks, under the inspiration of the living God, as I have listened to Joseph F. Smith when preaching the gospel. I believe that Joseph F. Smith and his son Hyrum M. Smith, more than any other men to whom I have listened, who were born in the Church of Christ in our day, were the greatest preachers of righteousness. I know that whenever I heard that Joseph F. Smith was going to speak in one of the wards, that time and time again as a young man I have left my own ward and gone to listen to him, because he always filled my being and lifted me up as I listened to him proclaim the gospel of Jesus Christ. I bear witness that he was one of the greatest prophets of God that has ever lived; that God was with him from the day that he went forth as a little boy of fifteen years of age, to proclaim the gospel of Jesus Christ in the Hawaiian Islands, until the day when, after giving sixty-five years of his life to the work of God, he closed his earthly career.

"May God bless each and all of us who have a knowledge of the divinity of the work in which we are engaged, and may we be faithful to the end as our prophet was, our beloved leader who has left us, Joseph F. Smith, is my prayer, and I ask it in the name of Jesus Christ. Amen."[11]

President Anthon H. Lund's Tribute

Anthon H. Lund of the First Presidency followed President Grant and provided insights into the life and labors of Joseph F. President Lund was born in Denmark just weeks before Joseph F.'s father was murdered in Carthage Jail in 1844. President Lund was ordained an apostle in 1889, during the difficult days of the "underground," when Joseph F. was serving as Wilford Woodruff's second counselor in the recently constituted First Presidency. In 1901 he was called by President Joseph F. as a second counselor in the First Presidency when Joseph F. became President of the Church. In 1910, President Lund became President Joseph F.'s first counselor, serving there until Joseph F.'s death in 1918. He was a longtime friend, counselor, and confidant. He said on this important occasion:

JOSEPH F. SMITH
HIS LIFE WAS EXEMPLARY

"We have heard President Grant speak about Brother John Taylor, about Brother Woodruff, and Brother Lorenzo Snow, and we have for some time looked forward to a day on which speeches should be made in memory of the prophet Joseph F. Smith. He was indeed loved by all. He was a great man. He was a great preacher of righteousness. How often have I sat listening to his voice and rejoiced in the truths that he put forth, the encouraging words he spoke and the words of warning he gave unto the people! Take a view of his life. God had given him a strong and abiding faith. He never wavered. As early as fifteen years he was called to go to a land where much of the blood of Israel was found. The four years he spent there were not years perhaps like many of us would have liked, but he looked upon them with joy and thankfulness, for he loved the people among whom he labored. They loved him, and though they were poor and he was poor also, still those years were blessed years to him and to that people.

"President Smith was a dutiful child to his mother. He loved her with the greatest love. He often alluded to her and to the inestimable blessing that she had been to him. She taught him to read, she helped him in his studies, and her memory was ever kept by him in the deepest reverence. He liked to talk about her, and as he was a dutiful and loving child himself, when he had children he was a loving father and a loving husband. He loved the little ones, even those not belonging to his family, and I have noticed how little children would be drawn to him even if they were perfect strangers. There was an atmosphere about him that gave them confidence, so that they were not afraid to come and have him take them up in his arms.

"I have walked with him in the street and nearly every few steps he would meet acquaintances and have to stop and shake hands with them. He was loved by those who knew him. He never forgot his friends, even if he had not seen them for many years. His life was an exemplary one.

"Ever since I remember anything about him he was to me the type of a true Latter-day Saint; and when I got more intimately connected with him I saw, every day, more and more evidence of his being just what I had imagined him to be. He was a true Latter-day Saint. He loved the gospel. He loved to bear his testimony that Jesus was the Redeemer and Savior of the world. He bore testimony to the truth of the gospel, and to the divinity of the mission of Joseph Smith, and his testimony always strengthened the faith of those who listened to him.

"President Smith was a good manager of the affairs of the Church. When his administration began, the Church was owing nearly a million dollars of bonds. President Smith was a man that did not like to be in debt, and as he felt in this regard himself, so he felt for the Church, and he put forth all his energy that the Church might get out of the bondage of debt. It took about five years to do this, because so many other responsibilities had to be met, but I remember one day in the old office building how he rejoiced when we made a bon-fire of bonds that called for a million of dollars, for we felt, now is the Church free from debt.

"During the administration of President Smith there was an epoch of building meetinghouses and stake houses, ward tithing offices, academies and temples. More has been done during these years in this regard than ever before, not only at home, but abroad; meeting houses have been erected in the missions of the United States, England, Scandinavia, and on the islands of the sea, and the people rejoice in having places of their own where they can go and worship God. When we travel here, at home, we are pleased to see these beautiful meetinghouses that have been erected, and very few have been built without help by the Trustee-in-Trust. And the work of building meetinghouses continues.

"President Smith was a spiritual-minded man, and he was well versed in all things pertaining to the priesthood, to temple work and to the different activities of the Church. Before I came into the presidency I have often gone to him and asked for his advice and counsel, and I always found it to be the very best that could be given; and when I was called to be his counselor I felt indeed humble, and wondered how I could perform such an office to a man like him. During the seventeen years that we sat at the council table together, I admired the man more and more. I saw how true he was to his professions, how true he was to the interests of the Church, how true to his brethren and the Saints in general.

"When a case came before him to judge, he and his counselors would talk it over and give it their careful consideration until they came to the same conclusion. We felt indeed that he was a man of God, a man raised up to perform a wonderful work. We all miss Brother Joseph F. Smith. We loved him. We knew that he was a fearless man. When it came to anything pertaining to the Church, whatever he thought was for the best good of the work, he was not afraid to undertake it. In reflecting upon his life, we see many things that are faith-promoting, and showing that the Lord's hand was with him, protecting him and giving him success in his labors.

"May the Lord bless his families and his children, that they may emulate the noble example that he has set them, and may we all, brethren and sisters, remember what he has done, may his memory remain green in our minds, and may we carry out that which he worked for so earnestly all his life."[12]

Elder B. H. Roberts' Tribute

B. H. Roberts of the First Council of Seventy was the first to address an overflow meeting held in the Assembly Hall, just south of the Tabernacle on Temple Square. Joseph F. already had completed his first mission to Hawaii and was serving in the Utah militia as Johnston's army marched toward Utah when Elder Roberts was born in England in 1857. Later, B. H. Roberts was called as one of the First Seven Presidents of Seventy in 1888, when Joseph F. was serving in the Council of the Twelve following the death of President John Taylor, which released him as a member of the First Presidency. Elder Roberts noted on this special occasion:

"We stand at the point where one presidency leaves us, and another is inaugurated. I think it is fitting that we should not only have our minds drawn out towards the man who is taking on new responsibilities, viz., President Heber J. Grant, but that we should also remember in loving kindness the faithful labors of him who, so short a time ago, was the President, and very worthily the President of the Church of Jesus Christ of Latter-day Saints, viz., President Joseph F. Smith. Those of us who were in close association with him and who knew him and worked with him, cannot, I think, look upon this inauguration of a new president without calling to mind the devotion, the fidelity, and the splendid administrative abilities of Joseph F. Smith, son of Hyrum Smith, the Patriarch of the Church, the second presiding Patriarch of the Church, succeeding the father of the Prophet

Joseph, who was the first presiding Patriarch of the Church. This man Hyrum Smith was a man upon whom the Lord conferred very splendid and very great blessings, especially in regard to his posterity. Blessings and promises that had been previously pronounced upon the head of Oliver Cowdery were also gathered up and placed upon the head of Hyrum Smith and his posterity after him. And truly the blessing has been realized in the posterity of Hyrum Smith, for I think there is no other man in the Church from the beginning until now who has been more abundantly blessed in his posterity than has Hyrum Smith. He was blessed in his two sons, the late Patriarch John Smith, who for so many years was a prominent figure in our community, and known throughout the Church, many thousands of the Saints receiving patriarchal blessings under his hands. Hyrum Smith was likewise blessed, and splendidly blessed, in the person of his great son Joseph F. Smith, who for so many years devoted himself to the work of the ministry in the days of his youth, and finally was brought into the quorum of the Twelve Apostles, while yet a young man, which position he held for many years. At the inauguration of the administration of President John Taylor he became a counselor to President Taylor. He sustained the same position to President Wilford Woodruff, and then to President Lorenzo Snow; and finally he came to the presidency himself, and held that position for more than seventeen years. And under his administration the Church was truly and greatly blessed, blessed not only by the wisdom that was manifested in his counsels, but also blessed by the example of his righteous life. So that when he passed away he passed away in honor and much beloved by the people. The blessing pronounced upon the head of Hyrum Smith is not only

A Tribute to President Joseph F. Smith

MAN OF GREAT INTEGRITY

manifested in the person of John Smith, the Patriarch, and President Joseph F. Smith, but from the loins of President Smith there came forth men and women who were highly honored in the community, and who have found place for ministry in the Church. Two of his sons have been brought into the apostolate of the Church, faithful men. One of them, Elder Hyrum M. Smith, as you of course recall, passing away about a year or more ago; but he left a name and a fame that is honored in Israel. I am glad to say that President Smith is still honored by one of his sons being sustained this day as one of the Twelve Apostles. President Smith, then, was honored in his life; and worthily represented the second Presiding Patriarch in the Church; and this succession of righteous men in the family of Hyrum Smith shows that the blessings of the Lord pronounced upon the heads of his servants are not mere words, but represent substance, represent realities. So God has magnified this family in the Church, and has especially honored this branch of it as he promised to do in one of the revelations now extant in the Book of Doctrine and Covenants."[13]

Elder J. Golden Kimball's Tribute

J. Golden Kimball of the First Council of Seventy added his own tribute to those gathered in the Assembly Hall following B. H. Roberts' address. J. Golden Kimball was the son of Heber C. Kimball, one of the important father figures in Joseph F.'s life. Joseph F. was serving as second counselor in the First Presidency when J. Golden was sustained as one of the First Seven Presidents of Seventy in 1892. After more than twenty-three years of association as a General Authority, J. Golden provided this context to the life and ministry of the sixth President of the Church:

"I am proud of the fact that I am a natural born heir, and was given birth in this land of liberty and freedom. We are not called upon to cry out, 'All hail to the king.' I thank God, I belong to a Church which is the Church of Jesus Christ of Latter-day Saints. It does not belong to President Joseph F. Smith, and he made no such claim, but it belongs to God the Father, and to his Son, Jesus Christ. There are no such things as earthly kings in Christ's Church. There never will be any king-men in Christ's Church. For when his disciples came to him, he tried to teach them the great lesson: whosoever will be greatest among you, let him be servant of all; and when these same apostles asked the Savior, 'Who is the greatest in the kingdom of heaven?' he called a little child to him and said: 'Except ye be converted, and become as little children ye shall not enter into the kingdom of heaven.' Joseph F.

Smith was like that. He was a man of great integrity. Few men had greater integrity or greater faith. He loved God with all his heart, with all his soul, and with all his might and that is all a man can do."[14]

Elder Rulon S. Wells' Tribute

Rulon S. Wells of the First Council of Seventy followed Elder Kimball. Elder Wells was the son of President Daniel H. Wells, who worked closely with Joseph F. when they both served with President Brigham Young as counselors in the First Presidency and later in the Endowment House in Salt Lake City. Joseph F. was second counselor to Wilford Woodruff when Rulon S. Wells was sustained as one of the Seven Presidents of Seventy during the historic conference of April 1893—the time of the dedication of the Salt Lake Temple. He said this about Joseph F.:

"It is only natural that I should greatly love President Joseph F. Smith. I imbibed it from my father [Daniel H. Wells]. He was very closely associated with my father, and my father with him in the ministry, in laboring in the house of the Lord and otherwise in the building up of the Church and kingdom of God on the earth. From my earliest boyhood I have always loved Joseph F. Smith, and when his name was first presented no one voted more heartily than I did to sustain him as the prophet, seer and revelator of the Church and the president of it in all the world. And throughout my life I have been more or less familiar with his labors and ministry. But I will not undertake, my brethren and sisters, in the few moments that are allotted to me to speak of his great work among the children of men, but I think more of those particular labors that have had a direct influence and bearing upon me and upon my life, for I can truly say that there is no man in the Church that has exerted a greater and more powerful influence over me in my life than Joseph F. Smith. No man has so moved me from the bottom of my soul as he has done. Tears have welled up in my eyes, and my heart has been filled with joy and with the testimony of the truth under the influence of the Spirit of the Lord as it has been manifest in this great man. I have listened to him when it seemed to me that God was speaking to me direct, and the words he spoke sank so deeply into my heart that I have wondered why it was that all who heard him upon that occasion did not feel and know that the gospel is true, that they who heard it as it was proclaimed by this great man and restored from heaven through the instrumentality of his illustrious uncle, the Prophet Joseph Smith, were not thoroughly converted and convinced as to the truth of it. The occasion to which I now refer was a funeral service held in honor of a dearly loved sister of mine, Emma Wells, who died in the year, 1877. He was the speaker upon that occasion. He spoke forth the words of eternal life. He explained the gospel of the Lord Jesus Christ. There were many there, kindred and friends and outsiders, non-members of the Church, a goodly number; and I marveled that any one could go from that service without being convinced in their souls that he was a servant of God, and that he spoke the truth as it had been revealed from heaven. It was the plan of life and salvation, the gospel of the Lord Jesus Christ as it has been restored in its purity. Upon various occasions he has thus filled my soul with the testimony of the truth and has exerted a power and influence over me which I hope will always remain with me.

"When I think of the influence his ministry has had upon me and upon my life, and then contemplate his extensive labors in this community, I have wondered how many thousands have been thus filled with joy and with the testimony of the truth. And if it be true that when a man labors all his life and succeeds in saving but one soul, great will be his joy with that soul in the kingdom of our Father, then what must be in store for this great man as he goes back into the kingdom of his Father, having labored nearly all his life in the ministry and brought so many souls unto the knowledge of the truth. I praise God for having sent such a noble spirt into the world. I thank him for his noble life, for his worthy example in this community. I thank the Lord for his labors among the people, for great good has been the results. I honor his memory today and join my brethren in tribute to this true servant of God for whom I have always had unbounded love and admiration. May his children, who have been so blessed and favored of the Lord in being born of such goodly parents, continue to enjoy the blessing pronounced upon the posterity of their martyred ancestor, Hyrum Smith, the Patriarch, is my prayer in the name of Jesus Christ. Amen."[15]

LDER JOSEPH W. MCMURRIN'S TRIBUTE

Joseph W. McMurrin of the First Council of Seventy, also speaking in the Assembly Hall, followed Rulon S. Wells. Elder McMurrin was born at the time young Joseph F. was defending Zion against military invasion by federal troops in 1858. Later, during the time that Joseph F. was serving as second counselor to President Wilford Woodruff, Joseph W. McMurrin was sustained as one of the Seven Presidents of Seventy in 1897. He told the congregation gathered in June 1919:

"We have but one theme, my brethren and sisters, to dwell upon this morning. We were instructed by President Heber J. Grant, when we were appointed to come to this meeting, to devote our time and the remarks that we made to the memory of President Joseph F. Smith. I don't know just how my fellow laborers feel in approaching a task of this character. I feel that it is impossible for me to say anything quite up to the standard of the man.

"Joseph F. Smith, in my feelings, is one of the greatest men, if not the greatest man, with whom I have ever been acquainted. I have never been in his presence without being impressed with the feeling that he was indeed a servant of the living God, and that he was a prophet of the Lord. Thirty-eight years ago, when I was laboring as a boy missionary afar off, a brother related to me the prophecy that has been referred to by Elder J. Golden Kimball, that was delivered in the Ogden tabernacle forty or fifty years ago. I do not know just how long ago. President Woodruff declared in that prophecy that the time would come when Joseph F. Smith would stand as the mouthpiece of God. In making the declaration he invited the fathers and mothers in the congregation to write down the prediction, that their children after the parents present were dead and gone, might read and know that God had spoken in relation to the future life of Joseph F. Smith. We are all witnesses to the fulfilment of the inspired prophecy. While listening to what has been said in this meeting, I have been impressed in much the same way as my brother, Elder Rulon S. Wells, has just stated. I have often felt, when listening to words spoken by President Joseph F. Smith, that the very word of God was being declared, and that the inspiration and power of the Holy Ghost was resting upon the mouthpiece of God in a most remarkable and unusual manner.

"I had the very great pleasure, just about two years ago, of being one of a party invited by President Joseph F. Smith to make a journey to St. George. The brethren and sisters forming the party visited one line of settlements in going to St. George, and another line of settlements in returning to Salt Lake City. President Joseph F. Smith spoke in all of the meetings that were held, both going and returning, and notwithstanding the fact that he was under bodily ailment at the time, the spirit of his great calling rested upon him most marvelously, and he expounded the doctrines of the everlasting gospel in very great clearness. The hearts of thousands of people were made glad through his inspired teachings and testimony.

"I always felt in his presence that I was indeed in the presence of God's anointed servant, and always rejoiced in knowing that he was a man filled with prophetic power; and, above all else, that he was a man who had consecrated to the very uttermost his time, and talents, to the upbuilding of the kingdom of God.

"I believe that President Joseph F. Smith was just as true to the work of God, just as true to the Prophet Joseph Smith, just as true to his brethren in the holy priesthood as any man who ever lived. I believe that President Joseph F. Smith accepted the wonderful mission of the Lord Jesus Christ, and understood that he was to be saved through the atoning blood of the Redeemer of the world by obedience to the doctrines of the gospel, just as fully and completely as any man that ever lived. President Joseph F. Smith, in my judgment, gave his time, and his thought, and his ability in the most unselfish manner for the benefit and blessing of the Latter-day Saints, and for the advancement of the work of God. I thank God that it was my privilege occasionally to be in his presence. I am grateful for the words of blessing that he has

PREACHER OF RIGHTEOUSNESS

spoken to me individually. I thank the Lord for the impressions that have been made upon me by his splendid life. I believe those impressions are of an indelible character, and that they will be beneficial to me, and be a blessing to me as long as I live in mortality.

"I also thank God for the splendid family of President Joseph F. Smith. I have been very happy in my association with some of his boys, and know them to be true men. I am not closely acquainted with all of his sons. I believe, from what I know of them that they are all true men; I have had close companionship with Hyrum M. Smith, with Joseph Fielding Smith, with David A. Smith, with E. Wesley Smith. I am proud of their acquaintance. There are no better men in my judgment to be found among the people of the Latter-day Saints.

"God bless the family of our late President, and may the truth of the gospel of Jesus Christ, that was always the greatest thing in the thought of President Smith, be the greatest thing in the affections of his sons and daughters, and their children, and their generations after them for ever and ever."[16]

A TRIBUTE TO PRESIDENT JOSEPH F. SMITH

Elder Charles H. Hart's Tribute

Charles H. Hart of the First Council of Seventy followed Elder McMurrin. Joseph F. married his first plural wife, Julina Lambson, and was ordained an apostle the same year that Elder Hart was born in southern Idaho in 1866. Charles H. Hart was set apart as one of the Seven Presidents of Seventy by President Joseph F. in 1906. Charles naturally felt a special bond toward the man who called him as a General Authority of the Church:

"I feel it a great honor to say a few words in commemoration of that great character, Joseph F. Smith, the greatest preacher of righteousness, in my opinion, of this dispensation. I have been with his son Hyrum very much, and I think it is appropriate, in view of his recent demise, to mention his name. I have heard him deliver more than fifty sermons in succession, and after each of which I could say 'that indeed is worthy of an apostle of our Lord and Savior.' And yet the training of his father was such that I always placed his father first as a great preacher of righteousness.

"I may be pardoned if I relate a personal incident which will illustrate the effect of his preaching and his spirit upon myself. Under peculiar circumstances, I came into a meeting at Logan at which he spoke and at which he presided. I had taken a long trip by team through the mountains and held many meetings. It had taken me through the mountains from Cache county to Rich county, from thence to Bear Lake county, and from thence to Wyoming and back to Gem Valley, as they call it now, and through Oneida county. We had held many meetings, and it was cold and there was much loss of sleep and much fatigue, so that when I came into that meeting I was thoroughly exhausted both in body and mind, and it was only by force of circumstances that I was induced to go into his company and the company of the Saints. But under the inspiration of his speaking as the Spirit of God seemed to flow from him to his audience and back again to him, the result upon me was such that at the close of the meeting I was as free from fatigue and weariness as I ever was in my life. I paid special attention to my condition, and could not detect the slightest weariness either in body or in mind. A veteran newspaper reporter who was in attendance to report the speaking, became so absorbed that he failed to take any notes of the inspired talk of President Smith.

"I think that the Prophet Joseph F. Smith, had more elements of greatness in him than any other man that it has been my privilege to know. He was great in a larger number of ways than any other man I ever knew. He was great in courage, and stern in righteousness, and yet there was a rare combination of kindness, meekness and gentleness. He was as kind and loving as a child. In fact it could be said of him that he had 'the heart of childhood taken up and matured in the power of manhood.' No man would have met death more willingly, in my judgment, for his convictions. He was a man great in his fidelity to his people and to the truth, and great in his testimony of the prophetic calling of the Prophet Joseph and of the divine mission of our Lord and Savior Jesus Christ. He had elements of strength so combined that he was indeed a truly great man; the favor of God was upon him. I think he exemplified more than any other man I ever knew the fulfilment of the scriptural injunction and promise to 'seek first the kingdom of God and His righteousness,' and all other things should be added thereto.

"Here are some lines that I think of, in connection with the life and character and ministry of our late lamented Prophet:

> 'He was one who never turned his back,
> But marched breast forward;
> Never doubted clouds would break;
> Never dreamed, though right were worsted,
> Wrong would triumph.
> He held, we fall to rise, are baffled.
> To fight better, sleep to wake.'

"He was such a man as Holland describes or asks for when he exclaims:

> 'God give us men. The time demands
> Strong minds, great hearts, true faith and willing hands;
> Men whom the lust of office does not kill;
> Men whom the spoils of office cannot buy;
> Men who possess opinions and a will;
> Men who have honor; men who will not lie,

LIBERTY IS OBEDIENCE TO JUST LAW

Men who can stand before a demagogue
And damn his treacherous flatteries without winking;
Tall men, sun crowned, who live above the fog
In public duty and private thinking!'

"I pray the Lord to bless the memory of President Joseph F. Smith and his posterity. His works will live after him. He has left an impression upon the Church that will be enduring. I had the deepest love and the greatest admiration for him during his life, and I regret that I did not let him know at least a fractional part of the love and admiration I had for him and his ministry and the things he accomplished. May the Lord bless his memory and bless us that we may follow the good example he set for us, I pray in the name of Jesus. Amen."[17]

Elder Levi Edgar Young's Tribute

Levi Edgar Young of the First Council of the Seventy spoke next. Joseph F. was a well-seasoned member of the Twelve and President of the European Mission the year Elder Young was born in Salt Lake City in 1874. Levi Edgar Young was called by President Joseph F. to be one of the Seven Presidents of Seventy in 1910. And while his association as a General Authority with President Smith had been for only eight years, Levi Edgar Young provided an insight to President Joseph F.'s humility:

"I bear you my testimony, my brethren and sisters, that all that has been said this day in reference to the character of President Joseph F. Smith is quite true.

"I look upon a man as great when he stands for great principles;

and that is the standard by which we should judge people. When people stand for principle, and know by their faith in God that the principle is true, it is always a mark of true greatness; and when a man links up his life with God, becomes one with God, and he and God are friends, you may depend upon it you have the truest standard of greatness that can be possibly created.

"The glorious thing to me in the life of President Joseph F. Smith was not only his wonderful strength of character, his true conception of life, his splendid idealism of religion and his great faith in God; but his living the divine injunction 'unless ye can become as a little child ye cannot enter the kingdom of heaven.' He was great in his power to understand life and to see God. His faith was one of the most sublime things I ever knew. He never compromised with wrong or with evil in any form. Man to him is free, but free to do right, not free to do wrong. I remember a statement that he once made concerning the meaning of liberty which I shall never forget. Said he: 'Liberty is obedience to just law.' That to me is one of the most wonderful ideas concerning liberty and Americanism that I have ever heard. Obedience to law is liberty. What kind of law? Law that is founded on truth. Law that is an expression of God's will to his people. Therefore, he was very democratic. He was very loving of his fellow man. How true it was that he showed his love for God because he loved his fellow men so much. He feared no man. He loved his God, and with his great linking of truth with God's truth, he lived a truly inspiring life. Standing upon the principle of right living, he truly entered the kingdom of heaven. 'Unless ye become as a little child, ye cannot know God.' To me he was very great, very courageous, very brave, very true, and above all, he was the child of God. He looked up, and with sublime faith made his life divine.

"May we see the beauty of his life, the truth of his words, the greatness of his soul, the magnanimity of his spirit, his great relationship to God. Amen."[18]

President Seymour B. Young's Tribute

Seymour B. Young, President of the First Council of the Seventy, was the concluding speaker at the overflow meeting held in the Assembly Hall. President Young was a year old when Joseph F. was born in 1838. Because they both grew up in Salt Lake City, they had been friends for decades when Seymour B. Young was sustained as one of the Seven Presidents of the Seventy in 1882. At the time, Joseph F. had already served two years as President John Taylor's second counselor in the First Presidency. This lifelong friend recalled:

"I also want to speak in regard to President Joseph F. Smith, as this day has been chosen. At the funeral of his son, Hyrum M. Smith, just as the family were taking leave of the remains in the Beehive house, I entered the house that morning, and while standing a little way from the bier of our beloved apostle, there came from another room President Joseph F. Smith, the father of the beloved deceased. He saw me and came directly to me, and putting his arms around me drew me to his bosom, and we kissed and embraced each other. And he said, 'Seymour, we have been boys together.' And when we thus embraced I found that we were both weeping. President Joseph F. Smith has been indeed a remarkable man. He has maintained the love of his people from the beginning of his ministry to the end of his life. I don't believe that he had an enemy in the world, or an enemy that could give any reason for his enmity; because all men saw in Joseph F. Smith, our recent president, a man who stood high in the estimation of humanity, and of God our eternal Father.

"President Heber J. Grant has now been sustained by the congregations of the Saints, and by the special quorums of the priesthood, and I beseech for him that love, reverence, and sustaining power that he so well deserves and has so well merited through his life of devotion and faithful labors all the days of his life. For I have known him since the days of Nauvoo, and I say that I have never known better and truer men, than President Joseph F. Smith and President Heber J. Grant. We are all glad today that so noble a man has been chosen by the people and sanctioned by the voice of our heavenly Father to be the President of the Church of Jesus Christ of Latter-day Saints. May the Lord add his blessings to you fathers and mothers, boys and girls, friends and strangers, who are here attending our general conference, I pray in the name of Jesus Christ. Amen."[19]

JOSEPH F. SMITH
EXEMPLARY IN ALL HIS WAYS

President Charles W. Penrose's Tribute

In the afternoon session of the conference, President Charles W. Penrose of the First Presidency addressed the Saints in the Tabernacle. Six years older than President Joseph F., President Penrose was ordained an apostle by him in 1904. Later, he was sustained as second counselor in the First Presidency in 1911, serving there with President Joseph F. until November 1918 when his beloved leader went to try the realities of eternity. Following a few comments on the succession of President Heber J. Grant, Charles W. Penrose turned his attention to paying President Joseph F. one last tribute:

"I had the pleasure of laboring under the direction of those great men who were talked about this morning, President Taylor, President Woodruff, President Lorenzo Snow, and President Joseph F. Smith. When we had finished our voting we sang the song: 'How firm a foundation, ye Saints of the Lord, is laid for your faith in his excellent word. What more can he say than to you He hath said?' I thought, when President Grant sat down, if I was called upon to speak, as he announced that his counselors would have something to say, and after Brother Lund had finished his excellent remarks, what more could I say than to you these have said. I felt very much as a witness did, when called into court to give testimony on a certain case, and had been preceded by a man who told what he knew and who said: 'Your Honor, I says as he says,' and that was all he could tell. I was very much in the same condition, but I know that would not suffice, so here this afternoon I take pride and pleasure in adding my testimony to the remarks made here this morning concerning each one of the presidents of the Church of Jesus Christ of Latter-day Saints, from the time of the

A Tribute to President Joseph F. Smith

AWAKE & ALIVE TO HIS DUTIES

Prophet Joseph down to the decease of our beloved Brother Joseph F. Smith. I loved him with all my heart, and I am always glad to know that he loved me.

"From the first time we met, we felt as though we were kindred spirits. The first time I met him was about 59 years ago, in Liverpool, and when we struck hands and were introduced to each other our hearts went with our hands, and we have always loved each other from that time to the time that he departed; my love remains and abides in my heart, and I am proud of having been associated with him in the ministry. It was through him, that I was called to the apostleship, and ordained under his hands, and also afterwards to be one of his counselors in the First Presidency. In this, I had opportunities of knowing the kind of a man be was and is. He was one of the grand men of the age. He was great in all things he undertook. He had failings, no doubt, like others had, but they were not very manifest. He was a great man in the ministry. He was, indeed, as was pronounced upon his head this morning, a preacher of righteousness and he was a lover of righteousness. He was exemplary in all his ways, in public and in private, and he had a kind heart as well as a strong mind. In all things that came [to] his notice and his direction he was strong and mighty, not only spiritually, but in what we call temporal things his judgment was splendid. He was accurate. He was awake and alive to his duties. He loved to perform them faithfully and he did so. I am sure that his labors were acceptable unto God, and when 'the books are opened and men are judged out of the things written in the books, according to their works,' he will stand in the front rank, and he will shine in the fulness of the celestial glory, with the sons of God who minister before the Most High.

"God bless his family, those whom he has left to follow in his footsteps. He had a splendid family, men and women that ought to be honored, and will be in Israel all their days and throughout all their generations. They will be prospered in all things; the Lord will be with them, and the influence of the great man who stands as a patriarch at their head will be upon them.

"I believe in the influence of those who hold the priesthood behind the veil. The testimony given concerning the falling of the mantle of Joseph the prophet upon Brigham Young, when he became the leader of the Church, has been repeated in these times, and quite recently, concerning our late president and the president who has been elected, appointed and sustained today, and I believe that the prophet Joseph will be near to Heber J. Grant when necessary—Joseph F. Smith, I mean. And so in regard to his family. I am satisfied in my own mind, and by my own experience, that the powers on high are with the powers on the earth. Men holding the Holy Priesthood, who have ministered in the flesh and have gone into the world of spirits, and are laboring there in the same great cause as that in which we are engaged in the flesh, help the brethren in their times of need, and are with them, and stand by them in times that try men's souls. I am assured of this, I say, in my own experience; and this is the power by which we shall prevail over the things of the world. The time will come when the priesthood behind the veil will minister personally in the temples of God to men holding the priesthood in the flesh, revealing matters that are needful to be known concerning the departed that the work being performed for the dead, as well as for the living may go on and be accomplished and perfected properly, and that we may grow up together in Jesus the Christ, who is our living head.

"Now, my brethren and sisters, there are two or three things that I think President Joseph F. Smith would talk about, if he were present with us today. One is that great truth concerning Jesus of Nazareth. During the later years of his life, President Smith took great pleasure and joy in bearing his testimony to his certainty of knowledge that Jesus is and was the Christ, that he died for mankind, that through him and by him the worlds were made, under the direction of the great Eternal Father, and that he came on the earth in the meridian of time, and laid down his life, voluntarily, for the sins of mankind, that through faith and repentance and baptism, and obedience to all the ordinances of the house of the Lord, men might be raised from the dead and saved and become perfected in the celestial glory, to inherit the fulness of the blessings pertaining to eternal lives; and that through him and by him all the dead, small and great, will come forth from their tombs and stand upon their feet and be judged according to their works, the good, bad or indifferent, of all races and countries and climes, for he is the Redeemer of the world; and 'as in Adam all die,' so in Christ shall all be raised from the dead. This was one of the themes on which he dwelt before he departed from us, and especially in later years.

"Another truth is that this Church, to which we belong, is the only Church of Christ on the earth. This is not saying anything against the views or opinions of our friends and neighbors, or people afar off, who differ from us in our views, not at all. We are quite willing that they shall go their way, particularly if they will allow us to go ours. Sometimes they have tried to prevent us, but they have not accomplished very much in their efforts, no matter what they have done, but this work has gone on in spite of opposition as it will go on until everything beneath the eternal heavens is subdued unto the Father, and the Son, and the Holy Ghost, and divinity shall reign on the earth instead of mortality and wickedness and corruption. This Church of Jesus Christ of Latter-day Saints has a special mission in the world and that mission has come from on high, not from the minds of men, not from the reading of books, not inherited from old creeds, but it is the gospel of Jesus Christ, restored to earth in its fulness, in its purity, in its power, in its authority and its unity with the heavens; and it will prevail. All the different sects and organizations in Christendom and the others that are in heathendom suit pretty well the people who adhere to them. All right. Let them stay by them, if they think they are good enough; but they are not good enough for Latter-day Saints. We want the truth as it is on high, and as it is revealed from on high to the servants of God on the earth; and this organization to which we belong is peculiar to itself.

"That introduces another point that I am sure President Joseph F. Smith, if he were here, would touch upon at this conference, and it is this: That when we are in this Church and members of it, we belong to the body of Christ, and there is no need for us to go outside of it for anything in the world, particularly of a religious character. We have no need to dabble in the things of the world; we have no need to join other organizations that are antagonistic to or out of harmony with this Church. Here is something for the Latter-day Saints to consider at this conference. There is nothing new in what I am saying, but it needs to be impressed upon the minds of our people in every part of the Church, and these men who hold the holy priesthood who have lifted up their hands today to sustain the authorities of this Church should carry with them, when they go home, this spirit and this determination as advice for our people. We will serve the Lord! Let the dying world go to its grave if it will. Let the wicked that are being bound in bundles go to the burning if they do not repent, but as for us, we, with all we are and with all we have, should be in this Church in body and in spirit, in every capacity, and there should be no need and no desire on our part to go outside of the strait and narrow way, the only way which leads to the presence of the Eternal Father and to the gift of eternal life.

"Now, this is not saying anything against people who desire to belong to other societies. If a man is satisfied with any of the Christian sects, if it suits him or suits his wife, that is his concern. Generally speaking it is the wife who does the religion in the outside world. I have conversed with a great many very prominent men, some of them

JOSEPH F. SMITH
HIS WORDS WERE GOLDEN

members of Congress, and this is what they say: 'Oh, I don't care about religion, my wife does all that and I go to Church with her.' Well, let people who like that kind of thing keep on liking it and if they do not choose to receive what we have—which is perfection in religion, which is Godlike and comes from God, and leads to God—if they do not like that, why they have the privilege of letting it alone. We would not do anything to compel them, if we had the power, to walk in our way; but that is not the point. If men like to believe in the doctrines and principles and sermons that are preached in the world, all right, but as for us, what should we do? What is the duty of the elders of Israel and of men holding the holy priesthood, and of the members of the Church who have been baptized into the Church? Their duty is to be with Christ, baptized into Christ, having put on Christ, coming unto him, belonging to him, to be part of the body of Christ, which is his Church, and to have no entangling alliances with anything outside. Not to do any injury to anybody else who does not see as we do, not at all; not to find fault with them for taking their own way, but our way should be the way of the Lord.

"We have no need of anything else. In the troubles that are

coming—for the world is menaced now with troubles and strife and division which will bring misery and sorrow and destruction to many souls—let our place be in the Church of Jesus Christ of Latter-day Saints, in the order of the holy priesthood, and we have no need to join other orders to take away part of our time, part of our influence, and part of our means and to hinder us from devoting ourselves entirely to the work of the Lord. Let me urge this upon the attention of my dear brethren and sisters who are here this afternoon. This is the Lord's work and it is marvelous in our eyes. Brother Lund alluded to the revelation of the Lord in the beginning, before there was any organized church of the Saints: 'A great and marvelous work is about to come forth unto the children of men. Therefore, thrust in your sickle and reap.' Yes, indeed, a marvelous work and a wonder, just as Isaiah predicted; and one of the signs of it was that the wisdom of the wise would perish and the understanding of the prudent would come to naught; but wisdom and inspiration and knowledge and certainty and power are in the gospel of Jesus Christ, revealed from him and by him and under his direction in the last days. Oh my brethren and sisters, why waste your time, your talents, your means, your influence in following something that will perish and pass away, when you could devote yourselves to a thing that will stand forever? For this Church and kingdom, to which you belong, will abide and continue in time, in eternity, while endless ages roll along, and you with it will become mightier and more powerful; while the things of this world will pass away and perish, and will not abide in nor after the resurrection, saith the Lord our God.

"So I say of our dear president, Brother Joseph F. Smith, to whose grandeur of character and faithfulness in the ministry and power and authority from God I add my humble testimony, if he were here I feel assured that he would touch on these questions in a far better way than I could attempt to do. He was a mighty preacher before the Lord. His words were golden. Many of them are treasured up; others have passed away and will be heard perhaps no more until many ages may come in the future. The time will come when all things will be made manifest and the veil of the covering be taken away and we shall see as we are seen, and know as we are known. Our true character will come up and we will be judged and valued for what we are, not for what men have thought about us. In that time all these great things that are hid shall be revealed, from the beginning to the end of time, down through the great dispensations of the past and brought forth in the greatest dispensation of all, the dispensation of the fullness of times.

"Now I add my testimony to the eulogies pronounced this morning so beautifully by our brethren upon the great men who have been with us and who have departed from us. The Lord has proved to us that great as they were, others can come forth to perform his work, when he is with them; that this work does not depend upon any single individual or any little coterie of individuals. It is the Lord's work, and is marvelous in our eyes. We will abide with it and give it our support, do what little we can while we live on the earth, and when we depart we fully expect, without any doubt in our souls, to go over to the great multitude of men and women behind the veil who are engaged in this same work, carrying it to those who sit in darkness in the spirit world, working for Christ and for the salvation of mankind under his direction, fighting under his banner the powers that are evil and preparing the great day when he shall come, and the Saints with him, and reign over all the earth in mighty power and glory. God help us to do this.

God help us to see things as they are, to withdraw our influence from those things that are not of God, center our affections, our thoughts, our means, our influence, our power, and especially the authority of the holy priesthood in this great Church that the Lord has set up, which shall win its widening way until all the generations of men that can be saved in this world and in the world behind the veil, shall be brought out of darkness into light and bow the knee to King Immanuel, and serve God our heavenly Father and acknowledge Jesus the Christ as King and Lord of all. Amen."[20]

Elder Rudger Clawson's Tribute

Rudger Clawson of the Council of the Twelve followed President Penrose and addressed those gathered in the Tabernacle. Elder Clawson was born during the year of Johnston's Army's march to Utah. He was ordained an apostle in 1898 at the time when Joseph F. was serving as President Lorenzo Snow's second counselor in the First Presidency. He said:

"The late President Joseph F. Smith—I loved sincerely and deeply. I loved him because of his integrity to the work of God. I loved him because of his good example before the Church and before the world. I loved him because of his kindly and thoughtful consideration for his brethren and associates in the ministry and for the Latter-day Saints generally, for he was a most genial and lovable man. I loved him because of the wise counsel and timely admonitions that constantly fell from his lips. He was indeed a powerful preacher of righteousness. The influence of his words will be felt by the coming generations. A righteous man may die and pass from the earth, but his words of truth and testimony can not die and will not pass away, but they will live in the hearts of the people and bear fruit to the honor and the glory of God.

"The following fervent exhortation was uttered by President Joseph F. Smith, at the April conference of 1902, which was shortly after he had been sustained as President of the Church. Brethren and sisters give ear to these words:

"'Let us sustain the cause of Zion. Let no man speak lightly of the ordinances of the house of God. Let no man hold in derision the priesthood that the Lord has restored to the earth. It is the authority that He has given unto men. Let no man look contemptuously upon the organization of the Church of Jesus Christ of Latter-day Saints as it has been established in the earth through the instrumentality of the Prophet Joseph Smith, whom the Lord raised up when he was but a child to lay the foundation of the same. Let no man treat these things lightly or doubtingly, but let every man seek to instill and understand the truth and teach his children to become familiar with those truths of heaven which have been restored to earth in the latter days. I believe with all my soul in God the Father and our Lord and Savior Jesus Christ. I believe with all my might, mind and strength in the Savior of the world and in the principles of redemption from death and sin. I believe in the divine mission of the Prophet Joseph Smith. I believe in all the truth that I know, and I believe that there are many principles of eternal truth that still lie hidden from man and from the understanding of men which will yet be revealed by the power of God unto his faithful servants. I believe that the Lord has revealed unto the children of men all that they know. I do not believe that any man has discovered any principle of science or art, in mechanism or mathematics or anything

No Duty Too Arduous

else that God did not know before man did. Man is indebted to the Source of all intelligence and truth for the knowledge that he possesses and all who will yield obedience to the promptings of the Spirit which lead to virtue, to honor, to the love of God and man, to the love of truth and that which is ennobling and enlarging to the soul will get a clearer and more expansive and more direct and conclusive knowledge of God's truths than any one else can obtain. I believe this because I know it is true. The Lord Almighty lives. He made the heavens and the earth and the fountains of water. We are his children, his offspring and we are not here by chance. The Lord designed our coming and the object of our being here. He designs that we shall accomplish our mission to become conformed to the likeness and image of Jesus Christ that like him we may be without sin unto salvation, and like him we may be filled with pure intelligence, and like him we may be exalted to the right hand of the Father to sit upon thrones and have dominions and power in the sphere in which we shall be called to act. I testify to this doctrine for the Lord has made me to know and feel the truth of it from the crown of my head to the souls of my feet. I love good honorable men, even men who may be mistaken, as far as their judgment is concerned, but who try to do right. I love them for the reason that they are my brethren and sons of my Father and I would that they might all see the truth as it is in Christ Jesus and accept it and receive all the benefits of it in time and throughout all eternity. If the Lord has revealed to the world a plan of salvation and redemption from sin by which men may be exalted again into his presence and partake of eternal life with him, I submit as a proposition that can not be controverted that no man can be exalted in the presence of God and attain to a fulness of glory and happiness in his kingdom and presence save and except he will obey the plan that God has devised and revealed.'

"Brethren and sisters, if we will take these few precious words to heart, treasure them up in our souls, and conform our lives to them, we will surely attain to a salvation and an exaltation in the celestial kingdom, which is God's greatest gift to man. May the Lord bless us and help us to do his will, and to follow in the steps of our file leaders, is my prayer in the name of Jesus. Amen."[21]

Elder George Albert Smith's Tribute

George Albert Smith of the Council of the Twelve followed Elder Clawson. The son of John Henry Smith and Joseph F.'s cousin and longtime associate among the General Authorities of the Church, Elder Smith was ordained an apostle by President Joseph F. in 1903. George Albert approached the congregation on this occasion and spoke:

"It is with peculiar feelings that I stand here today. At our last general conference I was stricken ill, and was only able to attend one meeting of the conference, being taken to the hospital from the first meeting in the morning. I am grateful that the remembrance I have of President Smith was his wonderful testimony borne on that occasion to us. I look back and feel that it was a privilege to be at that meeting, because it was the last assembly that he addressed in this great building. His work is done. The beautiful tributes that have been paid to him by loving brothers and sisters of this Church have no effect now other than to comfort those of us who remain, but his wonderful devotion to duty, his magnanimous feeling toward mankind, his tender love of the weak and the erring, will be sources of inspiration to all of us who knew him, as long as we live upon the earth.

"There was no duty too arduous for him to perform, if he felt it was the will of the Lord. He began his work in infancy almost, and I might say in passing that his life was preserved from being smothered to death by a mob when he was a little baby in his mother's arms. He was resuscitated and brought back to life after his little body had turned black as a result of suffocation. He came across the great plains with his mother, and while only a child was a man in determination, standing by the side of his mother and those who were with her, determined to do his duty and serve God and keep his commandments. When a mere youth he was called to the islands of the sea as referred to here this morning. He had to work his way across the ocean and was willing to do anything that he might be able to reach his field of labor; not going as some of us do today, in a palace car and in a palatial steamer, but he went in a humble manner. He wrought upon the hearts of the people of that land until today there are thousands in the islands of the sea who call his name blessed; and in that land to which I have been called to go, he ministered in his young manhood, devoted himself in faith and devotion to win mankind to repentance, to warn men of the judgments that were impending, calling them from the error of their ways, begging them to turn to the Lord, to receive the gospel, and to accept of the mercy of our Father to those who love him and keep his commandments.

"These are some of the memories that come to me upon my feet regarding this blessed man. Of course, most of you, many of you, know how near he was to me, almost like a father. I had the opportunity of traveling with him from ocean to ocean, and from the north land to the south, all over the United States. I had the pleasure of watching over him by day and guiding him by night. I have rejoiced in the testimony of the gospel that I have heard him bear in many places, and I have been made glad when I have seen the great strong men of the earth shake his hand and go away with the impression that he was indeed no ordinary man. I have known of people who, out of curiosity, called at the office here in Salt Lake City to see President Smith, and before they have left the ground upon which the building stands, I have heard them say, turning to each other: 'What a wonderful character!'

"Think of him as a little boy whose father was taken from him in his childhood—this little boy who was willing to go where the Lord wanted him to go. He had not the opportunities of college, of university training, but he was lifted up day by day, under the inspiration of almighty God, until he could stand among his fellows, honored and blessed, and loved, not only by all Israel, but by many of those who are alien to the gospel of Jesus Christ. What did it, my brethren and sisters? It was the gospel of our Lord. It was devotion to the Father of us all. It was a desire to bless mankind, and a knowledge that our Father lives; that Jesus is the Christ, and then a determination to live up to that knowledge in order that he might gain a place beside his beloved father and mother and the prophets who had gone before, to be worthy of their companionship throughout the ages of eternity.

"He was blessed as few men have been blessed in this world—indeed I might say as no other man I know of in this world—by a most remarkable family, to which reference has been made today, men and women who honor the Lord and keep his commandments, who revere their husband and father. We do well to remember, even at this remote period of time from his passing, the man who has been lifted from poverty to affluence, who was able to stand among his fellows unsurpassed by any child of our father who lived in his day. I am grateful that I have had the touch of his hand, I am thankful that I have had the press of his lips upon mine, I am pleased that he considers me one of his family, and today I mourn his departure and remember his passing as if it were but yesterday.

"I am grateful to be permitted to walk along the paths that he has walked, and as I go to that land referred to by President Grant, I desire, with all my soul, to be worthy of those who have preceded me—the great and good men of this Church who have presided there in honor and dignity, and among them our beloved brother and president, Joseph F. Smith. There are those sitting here upon this stand who have been there and have performed a wonderful labor. I would like to say to you, my brothers and sisters, that I esteem it an honor—nay, more than an honor, I esteem it a very great blessing—that the Lord has raised me from the feeble condition that I was in a short time ago, restoring me to such a condition of health that the brethren have felt that it will be possible for me to fill a mission in a foreign land. I would not undertake it if it were any other kind of a mission. I know that my

Redeemer lives; I know that Jesus Christ is the Son of God and is exalted at the right hand of his Father. I know that Joseph Smith was a prophet of the Lord. While he gave his temporal life in order that his testimony might be binding upon the children of men, I am sure as I stand here that today he is exalted in the presence of the Redeemer, rejoicing in the development that has come to the work of the Lord since the gospel of Jesus Christ was restored to the earth through his humble instrumentality. I am grateful for the testimony that burns in my bosom that this is our Father's work.

"Be diligent, ye men of Israel, who bear the Priesthood of our Lord. Do not think that you can gain the honor, the distinction and the eternal blessings that President Smith will gain if you do the works that are less than he has done. It is not necessary that a man should be a member of the Quorum of the Twelve, or the Presidency of the Church, in order to obtain the greatest blessings in the kingdom of our heavenly Father. . . .

"May the joy of the memory of that devoted man, President Joseph F. Smith, in whose honor, in part at least, we have met here today, remain with us. Let us try, so far as may be, to measure up to his splendid virtue and, by and by—it may not be long for any of us—when the Father of us all shall summon us home, that we may find awaiting us on the other shore these splendid men and women who have honored God and kept his commandments, who have earned celestial glory in our Father's kingdom. That we may rejoice with them and they with us throughout the ages of eternity, is my desire! O may the Lord bless us all; may he help us to appreciate the opportunity that is placed in our way and give us a burning desire to bless our kind. May we honor him and keep his commandments, and in the end obtain eternal life and celestial glory with our Father's children wherever they may be in the world, who are worthy, is my prayer in the name of Jesus Christ. Amen."[22]

Elder Orson F. Whitney's Tribute

Orson F. Whitney of the Council of the Twelve followed Elder Smith. Elder Whitney was the grandson of Heber C. Kimball and was born in Salt Lake City in 1855, at the time Joseph F. was serving his first mission in Hawaii. He was ordained an apostle by President Joseph F. in 1906. He highlighted President Joseph F.'s fatherly role in the kingdom:

"President Joseph F. Smith was not only a Prophet; he was also a Patriarch—a fatherly man in every sense of the term. Second only to his loyalty and devotion to the work of God, was his warm and tender love for his family—his wives and children. Their welfare and happiness in time and for all eternity were his constant care.

"And how rich was his recompense! In all that numerous flock of sons and daughters, not one 'black sheep' is to be found, not one wanderer from the fold of the Good Shepherd. This reflection must have been to him an unfailing source of comfort and consolation. The divinest work of Divinity, the most Godlike of all achievements, is in 'bringing to pass the immortality and eternal life of man.' Next to that, and indeed a very part thereof, is the rearing of a family as President Smith reared his. He fully realized that it represented the nucleus and foundation of his eternal glory.

"His paternal affection, though it began at home, did not end there. It went out far beyond the boundaries of his domestic domain. It

JOSEPH F. SMITH
SPIRITUAL GIANT

embraced God's people as a whole, rich and poor, high and low. All who served the Lord were sharers in his sympathy and esteem.

"Few things pleased the President more than to welcome to his hospitable home, or to public halls owned by the Church, his friends and fellow-laborers, for purposes of entertainment. A marked feature of his administration was an extended series of receptions, given at Conference time, in honor of the veterans who drove ox teams or pulled hand carts over the plains in pre-railroad days, or were occupying posts of hardship, if not of danger, in out of the way sections.

"His kind thoughtfulness for the aged, and his tender concern for little children, were among his most pronounced characteristics. He held that children as well as men and women have rights, and that these rights should always be respected. I was present on one occasion when he expressed himself indignantly over the conduct of a woman who, coming late into a public assembly, drew a child out of a seat that she wished to occupy. I have known him to leave his place on a railroad train to speak a word of comfort to a poor old lady, whose feelings had been hurt by an ill-mannered conductor. Once I saw him, when an excursion was about to start, walk the full length of the crowded train, with no apparent object but to satisfy himself that everyone else was comfortably seated; and not until every chick and child was provided for, did the President of the Church take his seat.

"'Safety first' was his business motto. He never plunged recklessly into an enterprise, however inviting, and always looked before he leaped. Like Longfellow's Blacksmith, he 'owed not any man,' and this was ever his counsel to the people. Nor would he allow the Church to become indebted for a single dollar that it could not pay on demand. As Trustee-in-Trust, he permitted no needless expenditure of the funds entrusted to his care, and he kept and rendered strict account of all monies or other properties that came into his hands as custodian. He was determined that the credit of the Church, which he had helped to make 'gilt-edged,' should so remain.

"A complete list of the public works connected with President Smith's career would form a lengthy catalogue. Never before in the history of the Latter-day Saints was there such a building administration. Those who criticized him for what they deemed a too active participation in commercial affairs, and thought that he should have been engrossed in spiritual things to the exclusion of the temporal, overlooked the fact that from the 'Mormon' point of view, the spiritual includes the temporal.

"Every one who truly knew Joseph F. Smith recognized in him a man of mighty faith and religious power—a spiritual giant. A wonderfully impressive public speaker, he was deliberate and slow of utterance until aroused, when his words came like a torrent, with the roar of the cataract or the thunder peal. In forceful and vehement oratory, or what might be termed emotional eloquence, he had no equal in the Church.

"President Smith's dominant traits were his unflinching courage and his unflagging devotion to duty. A man more diligent, more industrious, more zealous in the practice of the principles he professed, it would be impossible to find. Honest, fearless, and determined, he did not court martyrdom, but neither would he have shrunk from it, had the choice been between death and dishonor. He was an example of moral rectitude, of clean conduct, of right living. His noble qualities, his illustrious lineage, and his exalted station gave him a prestige all but unrivaled in the annals of the Church over which he presided. From his youth up, throughout his entire career, he stood a stalwart in the land, a man of unblemished integrity, a rock against which the billows of temptation beat and dashed in vain.

"What made Joseph F. Smith such a character? Two things: In the first place, he was a big man—big by nature, and developed by experience. In the next place, God was with him. The machinery is one thing, and the power that moves the machinery is another. The two combined constitute greatness."[23]

Patriarch Hyrum G. Smith's Tribute

During the second overflow meeting held in the Assembly Hall, Hyrum G. Smith, Presiding Patriarch of the Church, provided his remarks on President Joseph F. Smith. Patriarch Smith was part of the Smith clan over which Joseph F. presided following the death of George A. Smith in 1875. Hyrum G. Smith was born in 1879, just a year before Joseph F. became a counselor in the First Presidency with President

John Taylor. Patriarch Smith was ordained a high priest and Patriarch to the Church by President Joseph F. in 1912, filling the vacancy created by the death of his grandfather, John Smith (half brother to President Joseph F.). Patriarch Smith spoke to those assembled and said:

"As was announced this morning in our general conference, the program for this afternoon is to remember both in spirit and in word the life, mission and works of our late president, Joseph F. Smith, and I am very grateful for another privilege of raising my voice in testimony concerning his life and mission. . . .

"I also have a very distinct memory of the life of my dear uncle, President Joseph F. Smith, and I learned to love him, although we were separated about three generations. There are many people in the Church who, perhaps, due to their lack of acquaintance of the family history, have taken me to be a member of his family. But had I been an actual son of his, he could not have treated me better. His latest words to me were to the effect that I was not a real member of his family, but that he felt towards me as though I were a member of his immediate family; also in tenderness expressing his love for me. His kindness toward me was so manifest, I could not help but love him. I was always happy while in his presence, and I never had that feeling of timidity or desire to withdraw from him. There seemed to be power in his spirit that drew me toward him rather than repelled me from him. I love his memory, and look upon his testimony and his works as those of a prophet of the Lord, as those of one who was among the leading prophets and presidents of the Church in all the world.

"I have often contrasted the events of history, when he took the office of president and when he left it. Outsiders, as we speak of non-members, looked upon him, how they hated him. Many of them said violent words about him; and they not only said words but they drew hideous pictures about him, caricatured him, and maligned his name and family.

"Although I was not present upon either of the occasions to which I shall refer, I have heard that when Prest. Joseph F. Smith was taken as a witness before the United States Senate that people in the gallery, many of them influential persons and officers of the government with their friends, actually hissed at him when he was brought in before them as a witness; but before the close of that great case, these very persons, sought an opportunity to pay respect to him.

"Upon another occasion, the genealogists of Utah were gathered in a great meeting in California, where there were many friends gathered, many influential men and women gathered in an outdoor meeting. Many of them were wearing their hats, and when President Joseph F. Smith arose and declared that he wished to speak to them as a servant of the Lord Jesus Christ, those men took off their hats and paid him due reverence, not as just an ordinary man, but as a servant of the Lord who was to speak to them in the name of Jesus Christ. And they gave reverence to him, by uncovering their heads.

"Little by little these changes took place until, as you remember, the hour of his funeral, by the proclamation of the Governor of this State, every house of business, every piece of machinery, almost, that was run by the state was closed and stopped for one hour; and not only the places of business throughout the state, but all men who knew him, whether they once hated him or not, once slighted the work that he

I LOVE AND BLESS HIS MEMORY

did, or the cause which he represented, gave reverence to him and his name, and the work that he represented, the work of God. I am also told that in the distant and remote towns of this state the stores were closed. All business was closed. Street cars here in this busy city stopped for one hour, no matter where they were, at the given time. Other tokens of respect also were shown to him. This was a wonderful contrast to show that the people of the world, not only our friends, but our very enemies, have given honor to this man 'whom God hath chosen.'

"So I love and bless his memory. I join with my fellows in praying God to bless his memory, and those who shall live after him, that his teachings may live in our hearts, that we may honor them, and through them honor God, in the name of Jesus Christ. Amen."[24]

Elder Richard R. Lyman's Tribute

Richard R. Lyman of the Council of the Twelve followed Patriarch Smith's remarks. Elder Lyman was the son of Joseph F.'s associate in

the Twelve, Elder Francis M. Lyman. Richard R. Lyman was born not too many years after Joseph F. began laboring with Elder Lyman in the Twelve in 1870. Richard R. Lyman was the last apostle called and ordained by President Joseph F. before his death. Elder Lyman told the Saints gathered:

"My feelings were greatly touched, as no doubt yours were also, when, in the Tabernacle this morning, President Heber J. Grant took the place as presiding officer, which for some seventeen years had been occupied by President Joseph F. Smith.

Last Thursday at the regular weekly meeting of the First Presidency and the Council of the Twelve, President Grant explained that all but three of the members of the Council have come into their places during the administration of President Smith. 'Therefore,' he said, 'it will be very fitting for all of us to speak briefly in honor of this wise and now immortal man and prophet, President Joseph F. Smith, at the memorial services which will be held for him as a portion of the general conference next Sunday.'

"Not only are the members of the First Presidency and of the Council of the Twelve assembled here today to do honor to his memory, but the presidents of nearly all the stakes, and the bishops of nearly all the wards, and the counselors to all of these, are also present. . . .

"The heart of President Smith must be glad and gratified at this hour if he knows that all of these worthy officials are assembled, and so many other thousands of the members of the Church, that three great services are being held simultaneously in order to accommodate the multitude that is here for the purpose of paying respect to his dear memory.

"During the administration of President Smith great changes have come. The intense prejudice that existed in the beginning has disappeared. The Patriarch, in his remarks has just referred to conditions that existed at the time of the Smoot investigation. Well do I remember those conditions. I was a graduate student at Cornell University. The Ithaca papers printed glaring headlines drawing attention to the testimony and published grotesque cartoons of those who, as witnesses, were being examined. These were trying days for me. They must have been much more trying for those of our people who were in Washington. The public jeered at the president. They spoke to him and of him disrespectfully. His keen sensibilities were deeply cut when in derision they called him 'Prophet Smith.' But truth will prevail. Right is might. When right and righteousness really come to the attention, then are people convinced.

"It was but a few years after this investigation that President Smith went again to the city of Washington. Instead of being addressed as 'Prophet Smith,' he was greeted on every hand with 'Mr. President, I am delighted to see you.' The Vice-president of the United States said to him: 'Mr. President, may I have the pleasure of your company at the great foot-ball contest this afternoon?'

"Fairy tales hardly draw pictures more thrilling than that of the life of President Joseph F. Smith. When, as a boy at the age of nine, he drove an ox team into Salt Lake Valley, there was here, I have heard him say, but one green spot. If I remember correctly, he said there was in sight but one green tree and that tree grew on City Creek. This was then a prairie—a desert. During the seventy years since his coming, barrenness has been changed to beauty. This is today a veritable garden of roses. We are surrounded with every luxury and convenience of modern times.

"The story of the life of President Smith is not unlike the story of David, King of Israel. The Lord said unto the Prophet Samuel: 'How long wilt thou mourn for Saul, seeing I have rejected him from reigning over Israel? Fill thine horn with oil and go. I will send thee to Jesse, the Bethlehemite: for I have provided me a king among his sons.

"'Samuel did that which the Lord spake, and came to Bethlehem.'

"When Jesse brought before him one of his handsome sons, tall and erect, the Prophet Samuel said: 'Surely the Lord's anointed is before him.'

"'But the Lord said unto Samuel, look not on his countenance or on the height of his stature; because I have refused him; for the Lord seeth not as man seeth; for man looketh on the outward appearance, but the Lord looketh on the heart.' And Jesse brought another son, and another, and another, until seven had passed by.

"Then Samuel said unto Jesse: 'The Lord hath not chosen these. Are here all thy children?' Jesse said: 'There remaineth yet the youngest and behold he keepeth the sheep.'

"Who was [Joseph F. Smith]? The carpenter's son? Was he the widow's boy that drove the ox team across the prairie in 1848? Was it the little fellow who herded cows bare-footed in this great valley long years ago? 'Yes,' said Jesse, 'There remaineth yet the youngest and behold he keepeth the sheep.'

"And Samuel said unto Jesse: 'Send and fetch him: for we will not sit down till he come hither.'

EVERY FEATURE OF HIS LIFE IS AN INSPIRATION

"When the shepherd boy with the ruddy, handsome countenance appeared, the Lord said: 'Arise, anoint him, for this is he.'

"As it was with the shepherd David, so was it with the carpenter's son, and so was it with the widow's son who drove the ox team into the valley, in 1848. 'The Lord seeth not as man seeth; for man looketh on the outward appearance, but the Lord looketh on the heart.' All honor to the memory of President Joseph F. Smith, the widow's son. Under his leadership and the blessings of God, we find ourselves today a united, happy and prosperous people.

"The sterling strength and nature of Joseph F. Smith would permit him to make no compromise with sin. On one occasion, he was approached by an attractive young woman, a member of the Church, who said: 'My profession brings me on the stage where short sleeves and low necks are a positive necessity. Is it not possible in my case to have the regulations of the Church slightly modified? Are you going to require me to live in the same strict conformity with the technicalities of the gospel in this respect as you do others?'

"Some might ask the president: 'In my case, may I not take just a little tea?' Or another in poor health might say: 'May I not be permitted to take just a little coffee?' Still another might ask: 'In this one case, will you not permit me to take just a little liquor?' Still others: 'Is it necessary for me in my condition to remember the Lord every night and morning in my family and secret prayers?'

"To all such questions as these, President Joseph F. Smith would reply, as he did to the charming little lady: 'My dear little girl, if you do any of these things, you must do them on your own responsibility.'

"One of the great lecturers speaking before the Bonneville Club, at the Hotel Utah recently, said: 'After the names in your city directory or telephone book you frequently find such words as doctor, merchant, dentist, lawyer, engineer, etc., etc. These words do not indicate the main business of those whose names they follow. They only indicate their sidelines. The main business of every man and the main business of every woman is the rearing of a family.'

"There is no part of the excellent life and labor of President Joseph F. Smith that he did with more pronounced success than he performed this, the main business of his life, the rearing of his family. History, ancient or modern, does not record a more perfect example of man's first and highest duty well done than that of President Joseph F. Smith in the rearing of his large and worthy and wonderful posterity.

"For this good man and for his good life and wise leadership our hearts are full of gratitude. May we put forth successful efforts to follow his teachings and his worthy example. Every feature of his life is an inspiration."[25]

LDER STEPHEN L RICHARDS' TRIBUTE

Stephen L Richards of the Council of the Twelve spoke next. Elder Richards was born in 1879, a year before Joseph F. was called as second counselor to President John Taylor in the First Presidency. Stephen L. Richards was ordained an apostle by President Joseph F. in 1917. Elder Richards stated during this session of general conference:

. . . "I can hope, at best, to make but little contribution to the splendid eulogies that have been paid to our late President. I do not hesitate, however, to respond with some little feeling of satisfaction as well as trepidation to the call which gives me the opportunity of acknowledging, in some measure at least, my obligation to President

A Tribute to President Joseph F. Smith

A Friend
To Every Man

Joseph F. Smith, a debt of gratitude to him that I feel I cannot express, and I can scarcely ever hope to repay.

"I believe that every man and every woman requires an ideal. President Smith was my ideal in so many respects that I have a very large obligation to him for the leading of my life and for the inculcation of the principles which have controlled it. He was my ideal in nearly every respect. He so embodied in his life the great principles which I hold dear that he gave them a significance and a meaning and a tangibility that they could have had in no other way. I believe that he was the greatest living exponent of the gospel of the Lord Jesus Christ that we have known, at least in our day and generation. So perfectly, indeed, did he incorporate into his life the great principles to which he dedicated himself and his effort, that those principles were vitalized and made plain and sacred in his living, to an extent seldom achieved in the life of any man. When I think of the great principle of faith, I immediately think of the manner in which that principle was made plain and tangible in the life of President Joseph F. Smith. He was the very incarnation of faith. He made faith a plain, livable principle of the gospel of the Lord Jesus Christ. That great principle which is at the foundation of all religious life radiated from his very person. When you heard him bear testimony of the truth and give expression to the faith that was in his soul, you never doubted, not for a moment, the truth of that which he felt and that which he spoke. It seemed so perfectly plain to him that he in turn could make it plain to others.

"When you think of the other great principles of the gospel—repentance, the Word of Wisdom, and prayer, and other fundamental truths, you cannot dis-associate those principles from the life and attributes of Joseph F. Smith. He taught them in the one great way that all great principles of truth must be taught, in order to be effective in the lives of men, by living them. Great as were his words, potential as was the great message that he always had to bear to the people, his words and his message were never so forceful or so powerful as was the sermon of his life and his works. Above all other men that I have ever known he adhered to the very letter of the law of the gospel. With him there was no deviation from truth. As has been well said, he could never compromise with sin in the least degree, and yet he was possessed of that marvelous faculty of being kind and considerate and compassionate with the sinner, but uncompromising and intolerant with and of the sin. He would never deviate from the strict path of righteousness. And yet to those who had sinned, he held out more of hope and mercy, of encouragement in repentance, more of kindness, more of sympathy and true love than most any other man I have ever known.

"President Smith possessed that rare combination of upholding all the laws and standards of the Church and of the gospel, and at the same time extending the hand of helpfulness to those who needed help. Such were his remarkable traits of character that he was indeed a friend to every man, and a truer, a juster, a kinder man, and more considerate friend, has never graced this earth than our late President. His friendship was of that fine quality that always led his friends up, and never under any circumstances encouraged them to do that which was not in accordance with the truth and the law of the Church and the gospel. Every man who really knew him, loved him. Those who did not know him came to love him as they became more intimate with his real motives, and as they understood better the high principles for which he constantly stood. I believe that God so mixed up the elements in him that he was able to stand all of the temptations, all of the distresses, all of the sorrows and joys of life in a manner that has no parallel among our generation.

"Bishop [Charles W.] Nibley, I think it was, standing at his grave, said he was the greatest man in the world. I believe that he was. I believe that from every standpoint he came more nearly measuring up to the stature of a man made in the image of God than any other man on God's footstool. It means a great deal to us. I recognize the fact that in our admiration and love we are apt to be extravagant in our praise and in our tribute, but I think that it is only the truth to say that there are no greater men than our late beloved President Joseph F. Smith.

"I care not from what angle you view his life. If you will consider his life and his public career, as a public teacher of the people, as a servant in the cause of humanity, there are but few who could equal the record of service that he has made. Indeed, so devotedly did he work for the welfare of the state, for the welfare and the uplift of his people that during the greater portion of his life he gave his whole effort to the good of the common cause.

"I think it was President Grant who said the other day that not until long after he had been made the President of the Church did he ever occupy any business positions that brought personal emolument to him. All that he had and all that he was he gave to the people. He believed in service. He believed in that devoted service which gives one's whole life to the people and so he gave his life. He was the greatest of all public servants in this, that he served the souls of men. He sought to raise the standard of living. He sought to impress the glorious principles of the gospel of truth on the lives of men and women, to raise their standards of life and to enable them to conform their lives with the principles of the gospel; and all that he could do for this cause he did do. No man could do more.

"As a father and a husband, as Brother Lyman has just remarked, he had but few if any equals in the history of all time. I have had the opportunity of being somewhat intimate in his homes, and know something of the love which he had for his wives and his children. I have seen the expression of that love in his homes, and have seen the

JOSEPH F. SMITH

ADVOCATE OF TRUTH

love that he gave reciprocated in the hearts and the actions of those who loved him. Indeed, I never knew a man who had a stronger love for his home than did the President, and I never knew a man whose family loved him more than did his wives and his children. I have seen him go about among his homes, and he had a large family as you know, when at the close of a day his powers were well nigh exhausted, when he had worked from early morning until late at night, go from home to home to plant the loving kiss of a father upon his children and his wives in recognition of the great love that he bore them. And this love was the bond that bound them to him and to each other; and I think it may well be said in truth and with propriety that there are no finer families in all the land than the large, splendid family of Joseph F. Smith.

"He was a home builder. In this respect as in other respects he has set a glorious example to the world. He has taught that good homes are at the foundation of all that is best in life; that the nation itself can never hope to accomplish and achieve its great destiny unless the homes of the people are right; that the home is the foundation of society; and he set the example by making a home from which good citizens came, from which Latter-day Saints came, where could be found always the spirit of the gospel, and wherein are taught the things of God, and wherein are practiced deeds of righteousness. So that in his public life and in his private life he was the great exemplar of the truth of the principles of the gospel of Jesus Christ. He vitalized those principles by living them. He made it plain for men and for women, that they can live the principles of the gospel individually. He taught them that the beauties and the glories of the kingdom of God are to be had by those who will conform their lives to the commandments.

"As an advocate of truth, it has been well said President Joseph F. Smith was well nigh without an equal. As a preacher of righteousness he held first place among us. His burning words have entered the hearts of those who have sat under his voice and have stimulated them to higher deeds and to better lives. Why, I have heard his voice ring out under the inspiration of God, in those majestic tones of his, in such a manner as to fairly raise the audience from their seats. You could well imagine men and women rising to their feet as he expounded the glories of the kingdom and cry, 'Glory to God' for the way in which he expounded the principles of the gospel of Jesus Christ.

"He was not a learned man in the ordinary acceptation of that term. He had not attended schools and colleges and universities, but he was learned in the great school of experience. He was truly educated. All the latent faculties that God had given to him had been developed and had been augmented until they had reached the very full measure of their power, and that is real education. That is real training. He was truly cultured, truly refined, a gentleman of the highest type and order. All his thoughts and his speech and his life were clean and wholesome and uplifting.

"I think perhaps one of the predominant traits of his life was his absolute cleanliness. He was clean in body, he was clean in mind, and he was clean and pure in his soul. The strength of being clean was his. He yielded obedience to the laws of the gospel which require men to be clean and pure. He never took into his body anything that would pollute it, anything that would desecrate it. He was the most forceful of all the teachers of the Word of Wisdom, because he lived the law all his life to the very letter, and his family lived it. He taught it. He

HIGH STANDARDS

abhored things that were impure and obnoxious to the body. He believed that the tabernacles which God has given us in which to house these God-given spirits of ours were sacred in the sight of God, and he would no more have desecrated his body than he would have desecrated the temple of the Most High. Such was his faith, and such his belief in this divinely given body of ours. I remember how he abhorred the filthy habits of drinking and of smoking, or any of the habits which did not conform to the laws of the gospel. I remember how he inveighed against them, and yet he loved men and women. And while at times he may have seemed harsh in the condemnation of these practices and in the condemnation of those, too, who persisted in the practice of these things, he loved men and women with his whole soul. He would strive for them. He would pray for them. He would recall them from their sins and their troubles if he could. I know of no man who would have gone farther than he to have reclaimed one who had fallen. Such were his remarkable characteristics that he seemed a friend to everybody at all times. I know that throughout his whole life he was pure and immaculate from sin, and just as freely yielded obedience to all the laws of the gospel, just so freely did God give to him power. Just so did God magnify him and make him great and mighty, giving him a power that has scarcely been known among our own people as among any other people, to draw men to him and to impress them with the greatness of the principles and doctrines of the gospel which he so perfectly lived.

"I want to say, my brethren and sisters, that I am indebted to

President Joseph F. Smith for the best ideals in my life. I am indebted to him in large measure for my genuine love of the truth. I have taken the best course, that is, the best course that I have taken, in large measure because of the splendid example that he set. Never did he meet me and shake my hand without thrilling me with his own goodness and with the desire to try to emulate, in small measure at least, the splendid example that he set. Never have I seen his venerable face without being encouraged in the work of God. Never have I heard him announce the great truths of the gospel without being built up in my most holy faith. I don't know how I can hope to pay the debt that I owe to him, unless it be, perchance, to try to do the work that he loved so well and to which he gave his life and his all. I don't know how I can ever in any measure repay him for the influence which he has had upon my life, unless it be by doing the things that he called me to do, and by attempting to serve in my weak way in the same manner in which he served in his most efficient way.

"I loved him as a son loves a father. I was present at his home the day that he died, or at least the night before. I remember shaking hands with him, and saying what I felt must be my last goodbye to him. As I shook his hand he drew me to him, and he planted upon my lips a kiss that I can never forget. I shall try as long as the memory of that embrace remains with me to live true to the great principles which he so loved, and while I cannot do one single thing to help him, while I cannot do one single thing to add to his greatness or to the love which you bore for him, all that I can do is to dedicate and consecrate my life, my service, whatever talent God has given me, to the great cause which he loved and for which he gave his noble life.

"If he has helped you, my brethren and sisters, as he has helped me, will you not join with me in the very high resolve to dedicate our lives and our services to the gospel of Jesus Christ, to uphold the high standards that he upheld, and to the very close of our days to love God as he loved God, to be parents such as was he, and to love humanity with that same tender devotion and love that he exhibited toward all men? To this end, my brethren and sisters, may we devote ourselves, lending all our might, our strength and the best that is within us, I humbly pray God, in the name of Jesus Christ. Amen."[26]

LDER JAMES E. TALMAGE'S TRIBUTE

James E. Talmage of the Council of the Twelve spoke next. Elder Talmage was born in 1862 in England during the time Joseph F. was serving his first mission in the British Isles. They associated with each other in Utah, as Joseph F. played a role in the expanding Church educational system at the time when James E. Talmage was one of Utah's most important young educators. Later, he was ordained an apostle by President Joseph F. in 1911, augmenting a long-term association with each other. Elder Talmage provided a scriptural insight about President Joseph F. before providing some personal observations about the recently deceased leader:

"'Now the Lord had shown unto me, Abraham, the intelligences that were organized before the world was, and among all these there were many of the noble and great ones. And God saw these souls, that they were good; and he stood in the midst of them, and he said, These I will make my rulers. For he stood among those that were spirits, and he saw that they were good; and he said unto me, Abraham, thou art one of them, thou wast chosen before thou wast born.'

JOSEPH F. SMITH
PROPHET OF GOD

"If you will substitute the name of our modern prophet for the ancient patriarch, you will have a conception of my firm belief as to the primeval state and the ante-mortal existence of President Joseph F. Smith. There was no chance in his call. The barefoot boy, the 15 year old missionary on the islands of the sea, the more experienced and mature proclaimer of the gospel in this and in distant lands, each was the prophet in the making, the leader in school, the ruler in preparation.

"We do but honor ourselves in thus assembling to pay tribute to his memory. Do you think that our feeble words can alter his status? Do you think that this memorial service is held for him? I pray you consider. He could withstand such inexcusable forgetfulness on our part as would have been manifest in letting the occasion pass unmarked; but we cannot do it, for our own self-respect; nor could we quell the desire in our heart, springing from the well of living water and genuine love for our dear departed brother and leader, to permit the time to pass without some expression from us as to the lessons he has taught. He was a man such as the prophets foresaw and whom they foretold.

"In the inspired writing of the Scripture of these days, days of fulness, days of relative finality, the days immediately preceding the coming of Christ the Lord, tell of the spirit of hatred that would be abroad. They tell of the confusion that would be rife: they tell of the blessings that God would give unto the world; and chief among these was the blessing of real men. Don't you remember His promise. 'Behold I will make a man more precious than fine gold, even a man than the golden wedge of Ophir.' Such gift found a realization in the person and ministry of President Joseph F. Smith. No man can ever take his place. There is a uniqueness about the real prophet, the prophet of God. He has no successor, and by the same rule he had no predecessor. True, other men may have filled the office that this one filled, as other men shall fill the place after he departs; but there is a distinctiveness about each of God's leaders that makes his place sacred. And yet shall there be other prophets in Zion as there have been mighty ones in the past; but no one has filled the place of the other. Without the special ministry of President Joseph F. Smith, the Church of Jesus Christ of Latter-day Saints could not be, and therefore would not be, what it is today. He was foreappointed and foreordained for the particular work of his epoch, of the work and ministry.

"I shall not repeat the many things in the way of personal experiences with President Joseph F. Smith that make me sure he was the great man we have had portrayed before us; but I do bear witness to you that Joseph F. Smith was one of the real apostles of the Lord Jesus Christ. I have listened to his ringing words of testimony and warning before the assemblies of thousands, and I have sat with him, on very rare occasions, alone; and on occasions less rare, but still not common, with my brethren and associates, I have heard him preach in conversation, and I have never seen his face so enlightened nor his frame so thrilled with power as when he was bearing testimony of the Christ. He seemed to me to know Jesus Christ as a man knows his friend.

"President Joseph F. Smith has been referred to on many an occasion as one of the last links connecting the present generation with that of the early days of the Church. But though that speaks of the long ago when measured in terms of years, did you ever think of the marvellous fact that President Joseph F. Smith was always fully abreast of the times? He was never behind, but always up to date, and down to date, in everything that was good. There was no clinging to old fashioned methods when better means had been evolved and proved practical with him. Scores of times before he passed away I said, as now I shall venture to say again, he was the living embodiment of the truth that schools and colleges do not make the scholar. To me he was one of the best read men with whom I have had to do and deal. Did you ever hear him use faulty language, poor English? He was no orator, and I am glad of it, for to him oratory and all associated with the name bore the tinge of bombast and verbal display, and he did not know how to talk in painted color pictures; but he possessed that gift which is as far above oratory as prophecy is above necromancy, the gift of eloquence. He did not speak to the ears, but right straight to the hearts of men.

"Well, where is he now? He was permitted shortly before his passing to have a glimpse into the hereafter, and to learn where he would soon be at work. He was a preacher of righteousness on earth, he is a preacher of righteousness today. He was a missionary from his boyhood up, and he is a missionary today amongst those who have not yet heard the gospel, though they have passed from mortality into the spirit world. I cannot conceive of him as otherwise than busily engaged in the work of the Master. And had any one tried, or should any one now try to distract his attention and lead him into other paths, he could answer without sacrilege in the very words of the Master: Wist ye not that I must be about my Father's business, who is in heaven.

"The Lord enable us to be in a measure like unto him, fit to take his hand and deserving of a smile from his countenance when we shall meet him again, I pray, in the name of the Lord, Jesus Christ. Amen."[27]

Elder Joseph Fielding Smith's Feelings

Joseph Fielding Smith of the Council of the Twelve, the son of President Joseph F., expressed briefly his thoughts on this occasion—obviously moved by the occasion. He was named after his venerable father and ordained an apostle by him in 1910, serving together in the leading councils of the Church for nearly twenty years. Elder Smith said:

"My *brethren and sisters*, it is not my purpose to detain you. Matters this afternoon come home to me with such force that I feel that I would not dare to undertake to express myself, nor could I do it, I think, if I should try. All that I desire to say is, amen to that which has been spoken by the brethren who have occupied the time."[28]

Bishop Charles W. Nibley's Tribute

Charles W. Nibley, Presiding Bishop of the Church, addressed a group of Saints in an outdoor meeting held at the Bureau of

Information Building on Temple Square during the afternoon session of conference. Bishop Nibley was a longtime friend of Joseph F. Bishop Nibley first met Joseph F. when President Brigham Young was on a visit to Mormon settlements in the north and brought the recently called apostle to Cache Valley in 1867. Later, Charles W. Nibley and Joseph F. both served in the British Mission in 1877, and it was during this time that a real bond of trust blossomed between them. President Joseph F. ordained him a high priest in 1901 and later called him to be the Presiding Bishop of the Church in 1907. He and President Joseph F. were traveling companions and close friends during this period. He told the Saints:

"I am asked to perform what to me is a rather difficult task, at this memorial service for the late President Joseph F. Smith. I knew him very intimately. Forty-two years ago, when I was a young man, he called me to go with him to Liverpool, England, there to take charge under his direction, of the business affairs of the European mission. From that day until the day of his death, I knew him well. I know his history, I know his family, I have lived in his home—been, indeed, as a member of his family; and so I can speak of him as I know him.

"Joseph F. Smith was one man picked out of millions of men. There was none like him. In his particular sphere, in his life and his life's work, I think that as an exemplar he has never been equalled. I know that is high praise, and I do not wish to make any comparisons with others, but to me he was the most God-like, the most God-fearing, and the least man-fearing of any man I ever knew in all my days.

"He had a perfect knowledge of the truth of this great Latter-day work. He had endured much for it, he had sacrificed much—losing his father when he was not yet six years of age, losing his mother when he was twelve or thirteen years of age, going alone, so to speak, in the world, with only friends who knew his father and mother to look after him. President Young took him under his care, or at least had a watchful eye over him; and in early days, as you know, sent him on a mission to the Sandwich Islands, when the boy was but fifteen years of age.

"I have heard him tell how, journeying down through the southern country to Los Angeles, they were followed by a band of hungry Indians—this little missionary party, among whom were John T. Caine, who used to represent us in Congress, William W. Cluff, and some fifteen others. They were down on the desert, this side of Los Vegas, and these Indians became a little troublesome. Joseph F. Smith and one other of the party—I forget who, were a little slow in getting their horses saddled, and the others of the company rode off or drove off, leaving these two behind. The Indians became more bold when the larger part of the company went on, and as President Smith was saddling his horse, pulling up the strap, he looked into the barrel of his own gun. An Indian had grabbed his gun from the saddle and pointed it at him. The boy, who was strong and an athlete, smiled merely; but quickly getting under his horse's neck, he grabbed that Indian, who pretended at first to play, and in the tussle, wrenched the rifle from his hands.

"I mention this to show the fearlessness of the youth. I never knew as brave a man. No number of men could daunt him or discourage him or put him down. If he knew he was right he stood before the whole world and sustained and manfully contended for the right as he understood it.

"On this mission to the Sandwich Islands, he encountered severe hardships. I remember on our first trip over to the Islands, and I was

JOSEPH F. SMITH
MAN OF GOD

over there on four trips with him, that sailing among the different small islands, he would point out to me such and such a place: 'There is where I lived so long in a little straw hut'—which burned down or which was destroyed by flood. Here was another place where he had lain sick and where the good Hawaiian people had ministered to him. This experience, and the other, he would tell as we journeyed along, all of which, if I had time to relate, are faith-promoting and inspiring, and would point out to you the manliness of the young boy—for he was then, as I told you, fifteen or sixteen years of age.

"He remained there on the Islands until he was nineteen years of age, when he returned home at the call of President Brigham Young, at the time of the move south and when Johnston's army was marching here for the avowed purpose of disturbing the Latter-day Saints.

"On a later occasion, when we arrived at the harbor of Honolulu, we were met by the Royal Hawaiian Band. This band was instructed to come up to the 'Mormon' meeting house—a quite prominent place in the city of Honolulu, and play for the people in honor of President Smith and his company. In the midst of the proceedings, after we were gathered in the meeting house and President Smith was conversing in the native tongue with this one and the other one, and shaking hands with all, there was led into the room an old Hawaiian lady, tottering, blind—led because she could not see. The moment he saw her he turned from everyone else and rushed to this dear old native lady. She was calling 'Iosepa, Iosepa'—Joseph, Joseph, her Joseph. He rushed to her and gathered her in his arms, and with tears streaming down his cheeks, said: 'My mamma, my mamma, my dear old mamma.' And he turned to me, wiping his cheeks, and said, 'Charlie, she tended me while I was sick, more than fifty years ago, and here she is now; should I not bless her and love her?'

"From courage to tenderness—for the bravest are the tenderest always—what nobleness and grandeur of character may we not expect between these two angels. In the maintaining and rearing of a large family you all know what manner of a man he was. A man is known by the work he performs, by the labor he does. Give him the opportunity and we will see what he can do with it. If he does his best, well and good. Joseph F. Smith always did his best. He was just in his family. He was the kindest man I ever knew, and the tenderest, most loving and compassionate to little children. I have seen him when one of his little babies was sick, walk the floor at night for hours together with that babe in his arms, tenderly caring for it and nursing it—caring for it better, I think, than I ever saw any mother care for her child, so tender was he, so loving, so pitiful, so compassionate.

"He was a man, take him for all in all. I do not know where you will ever see his like again. You can imagine, from the association I was privileged to have with President Joseph F. Smith, especially during the later years of his life—and indeed for more than forty years of his life—what the loss of him means to me. I feel at times alone.

"As President Grant said this morning in the Tabernacle, no two preachers of righteousness like him and his son, Hyrum M., has this Church ever produced. I endorse that sentiment.

"He was a manly man, a man of God, a man whom it was an honor to know and a pleasure to be with, a man whose example has meant much to me—and indeed, had it not been for him, I know that I could not have accomplished what little I may have done in this world. In a way he was my guiding star. I did not worship him—I worship only God, and that I try to do faithfully—but he was more like unto God, the most godlike man that I ever knew in all my life.

"Such is my testimony concerning Joseph F. Smith. I love his memory. I revere his name. There is not anything I would not do for him or his, that I possibly could do. And loving him and his, so likewise I try to love my brethren and sisters, with the same spirit that he loved the brethren and sisters of this Church, and the people of the world as well—for he was not narrow.

"Some people have thought Joseph F. Smith was a narrow-minded man. His comprehension and vision were the broadest, most extended, most glorious, of any man's I have ever known. He could grasp and comprehend futurity. He knew what was in store for those who served God and kept his commandments. He knew the principles of the gospel. They were so thoroughly imbued and indoctrinated in him that they were a part of his very being. It was natural for him to be a Latter-day Saint, and he was willing to sacrifice for the work, and he did sacrifice. Without father, without mother, alone, he sacrificed as much as the Lord required of him.

"Let me beseech you, my brethren and sisters, that we get some of the spirit of sacrifice in our hearts, that we, too, may be willing, and may say before God: 'I'll go where you want me to go, dear Lord; I'll work where you want me to work; I'll try to be what you want me to be.'

"If we have this in our hearts, we will grow in some humble way, at least, in small degree, to be like this the noblest of men whom I have ever known, Joseph F. Smith."[29]

Elder David A. Smith's Tribute

Elder Melvin J. Ballard, who was conducting the outside overflow meeting, introduced the next speaker: "Although we have lost our beloved leader, we rejoice that he has left with us an illustrious posterity. We feel grateful that the children of President Smith are following in his footsteps, and I take pleasure in introducing one of his worthy sons, Bishop David A. Smith, of the Presiding Bishopric, who will now address us."

David A. Smith was President Joseph F.'s son, born in 1879, just before Joseph F. was called into the First Presidency. Elder Smith was sustained as the second counselor in the Presiding Bishopric in 1907 and as first counselor in 1918, allowing him the opportunity to work closely with his father in the ministry. Elder Smith said:

"*My brethren and sisters.*—When I look over this assembly and think of the thousands of Latter-day Saints who are meeting in the Assembly Hall and in the Tabernacle, my heart is filled with joy; yet I cannot approach this task at this time without a feeling of sadness. All my life, I have known President Joseph F. Smith. As a little fellow, I only saw him occasionally, and knew him best through the letters he wrote to me, as it was his custom to write personal letters to his children when absent from home. And during my early childhood he was away from home on missions most of the time. But when at home, no father ever took more pleasure or greater delight in his children than he did.

"I remember when Bishop Nibley, as he has said, made it a custom to call at our home occasionally. He was almost as much a father to us as our own father, and we learned to call him Uncle Charlie. I did not know for many years that Charles W. Nibley was not my own uncle.

"For over eleven years it has been my privilege to be nearer, closer to President Joseph F. Smith, I believe, than any other man. Morning, noon, and night, I have been with him. Having been honored by him, having been trusted with many of his private affairs, being urged on by Bishop Nibley, who loved him and knew what work he was doing, I was finally given much of his private work to do. And when, today, in coming to this conference, I recall the fact that never before for over eleven years had he attended a general conference on this block that it was not my privilege to accompany him here and home again, you can, therefore, imagine to a small degree at least, the reason for that feeling of sorrow which comes to me at this time, for I loved him and miss him greatly.

"It is not because he loved me more than he did other of his boys that I was with him perhaps more than they, for President Smith had no favorites. It could not honestly be said of him that he loved one boy more than he loved another, or that he loved one of his girls more than he loved another, or that he loved one of his wives more than he loved another. As Bishop Nibley has said, President Smith was a just man, and he loved his wives and he loved his children, and tried to treat them as wives should be treated and as children should be treated—no favorites among them, and they loved him and tried to honor him. I was greatly honored, and more so than some of the others, because of

JOSEPH F. SMITH
SOUND IN JUDGEMENT

the position I had been blessed with, which gave to me a greater degree of freedom, which permitted me to associate with him more and to assume part of his responsibilities, which would gladly have been assumed by any one of his children had any one of the others been placed in the same position and given the same opportunity.

"I rejoice, my brethren and sisters, today, in the fact that I had such a father. And O, I pray God that I shall prove worthy of such parentage. Think of the honor that has come to me: honored by you, my brethren and my sisters; honored of God, having been permitted to come through this lineage which has been so blessed of him. . . .

". . . I pray sincerely that I may have an interest in your prayers, in your faith, the sustaining influence of which will enable me to do that which is required of me, that I may better uphold and emulate the noble example which has been set me by my beloved father."[30]

ELDER JOHN WELLS' TRIBUTE

John Wells, of the Presiding Bishopric of the Church, followed Elder Smith. Elder Wells was born in England just months before

Joseph F. returned from his second mission to Hawaii in 1864. Later, he was employed in the Presiding Bishop's office, giving him an opportunity to associate with President Joseph F. to a degree. He was eventually sustained as second counselor to Presiding Bishop Charles W. Nibley in 1918, allowing him a short time to serve as a General Authority under President Joseph F.'s leadership. Elder Wells said on this occasion:

"It has been my pleasure and privilege, as an officer and an employee of the Church, to become personally acquainted with the late President Joseph F. Smith. I remember him well, from the year 1893, when I was an employee in the Presiding Bishop's Office. I called upon him for counsel, many of the leading brethren being away, and some of the duties of the Presiding Bishop's Office had at that time devolved upon me. I waited upon President Smith and asked his counsel and advice concerning what to me was a very intricate problem, and my first impression of President Smith was that he was sound in judgment, and had a wonderful comprehension of human nature. It was my first interview with him, and we sat side by side talking on the problem I presented to him. I had looked upon him previous to this as a great man because of his exalted position as one of the First Presidency, but when I had concluded that interview, I had a more profound impression of his greatness than ever before.

"At one time I was coming across the continent. I met President Smith and some of his family at Omaha. We traveled westward in the same car. I was sick with something akin to sea-sickness, caused through traveling several days on the train. I appreciated his kindly sympathy. He blessed me, and that blessing I will never forget, because it came from the Prophet of the Lord and his blessing gave me peace and rest for most of the night. That same night, as the train was moving across the plains of Wyoming, President Smith stood at the back of the car taking a rest from a long, tedious day's journey. Any of you who have traveled day after day in a railway train know what relief it is to stand up or move around for awhile. I tell you this incident to show you how President Smith was susceptible to the Still Small Voice. While standing at the back of the train he heard a voice telling him to go into the car, and he did so. Later he was walking up and down the corridor and was told by the same Voice to sit down. He did so. A few moments later the engine ran off the track and tilted the train on an angle which scared us all. Had President Smith been in the back of the train or walking in the corridor he might have been very seriously injured, but the Lord had regard for him and he was prompted by a Voice which he understood so well, and he acted accordingly. President Smith has always been susceptible to the influence of the Spirit of the Lord. He knew its promptings, and what they meant. As he heard the Still Small Voice directing him and inspiring him, he knew that Voice and knew it well.

"President Smith was a kind man, kind to employees as well as to his friends and family. He frequently gathered the employees of the Bishop's Office at the Beehive House and other places, and mingled with them in social gatherings, showing that even with the dignity of his position and calling he was always the same unaffected and kindly-disposed man.

"I revere his memory. I revere him for many things. I will never forget as long as I live the blessing he gave to me when he ordained me a bishop. I never want to forget those sweet, kindly words, the admonition and counsel that he gave to me before I assumed my duties as a counselor to Bishop Charles W. Nibley."³¹

Elder Melvin J. Ballard's Tribute

In concluding the outdoor overflow meeting during the afternoon session of conference, Melvin J. Ballard of the Council of the Twelve spoke to those assembled. Elder Ballard was ordained an apostle in January 1919, filling the vacancy created by the death of President Joseph F. [Smith]. Elder Ballard previously served as the president of the Northwestern States Mission for ten years, beginning in 1909. And while he had not served as a General Authority during President Joseph F.'s ministry, he had a close association and grew to love him as a father. He told the Saints at the close of the overflow meeting:

"There is no task that I have been asked to perform which gives me greater pleasure and more real happiness than on this memorial day to speak of our late beloved prophet-leader, President Joseph F. Smith, whom, like my brethren who have preceded me, I love with that same love and affection I had for my own father—for he was a father to me and to every man and woman who became acquainted with him who loved the Lord and sought to keep his commandments. I bear witness that President Smith was a lover of such men and women.

"The selection of President Smith to preside over this Church, as in the case of his predecessors, is one of the remarkable evidences of the truthfulness of the work called 'Mormonism,' that God is in it, that his hand has been over this work and guiding the destinies of this Church, and he is indeed the source from which light and truth and knowledge have come to the men who have directed the affairs of this Church....

"... The men whom God raised up [after Brigham Young], each in his turn the man for the hour, and the Lord was with him, and the Lord has been with our late President Joseph F. Smith—we are all witnesses to that.

"I recall my early recollections of President Smith with a good deal of pleasure—because I admired him, he was to me my ideal, I tried in my life, as I became acquainted with him, to be as he was. I knew as a child, for the Lord revealed it unto me, that President Smith would some day preside over this Church; and in connection with that I saw many things that President Smith would do; and when, last October, he stood before the congregations of the Saints, feeble and weak as he was, my soul was filled with great sorrow, because I knew that all that the Lord had for President Smith to do had been done. That which I saw as a child was fulfilled, finished, completed. And yet there was a feeling of great regret that we should soon have to part with him and let him go on to the work which the Father has prepared him to do in that realm where he is now.

"It was my privilege, I presume, to deliver the last public address that President Smith ever listened to, being the last speaker of the last Conference of the Church. And I recall, as I had concluded, he grasped my hand and pressed it and gave me a blessing that I shall not forget, for my whole soul was thrilled with his blessing and with his love.

COURAGE

"I bear witness that he was a man who loved the souls of the children of men in the world—not only those who belong to the Church; for no man has done more, than he, looking toward the establishment of the work of the Lord among the nations of the earth. He has built more meeting houses in the mission field, and mission headquarters, than in the rest of the years of the Church put together. His heart was in the preaching of the gospel, and so he lent himself to uphold and sustain those who were engaged in this work.

"His coming into the world was at a time when his own father and his own uncle the Prophet, were incarcerated in a foul dungeon, with chains forged upon them by a blacksmith, condemned to be shot, confined in this condition for the gospel's sake, held as hostages for the Church, a ransom for the balance of the people that they would leave the state of Missouri; the father, Hyrum, was separated from his beloved companion, the mother of Joseph F. Smith; and under these conditions, Joseph F. Smith was born into the world, without a father's love and protection for the mother of the child; there was one occasion when the enemy ransacked, as they were accustomed to do, the homes of the Latter-day Saints, and invaded the home of Mary Fielding Smith, the mother of President Joseph F. Smith; and in their anxiety to find treasure, tumbled bedclothes over and finally succeeded in almost exterminating the life of President Smith—for he was buried under bedclothing when rescued by his mother after the invader had left their home. The boy was so black that life was almost extinguished, but the hand of the Lord was over him: from that moment the Spirit of the Lord attended him in the midst of trials, in the midst of vicissitudes, and has preserved his life marvelously to complete that which the Lord had in store for him to do.

"And I thought of him as a child. How few boys would have shown the courage, the manhood, that he did, while scarcely eight years of age, driving a yoke of oxen part way across the plains, and then when a little over nine years of age, in 1848, driving two yoke of oxen the entire distance from the Missouri river to these valleys of the mountains, taking a man's part. But as I have thought of it, I know what was in President Smith's heart. He did not take the credit unto himself. A very large part of that credit shall forever belong to his illustrious mother, Mary Fielding Smith. He often said it, and I know if he were here today he would be delighted to have these words of praise spoken of that good woman who was his inspiration in his childhood. . . .

"When the President was taken away, in the imaginations of my own mind by the enlightenment of the Spirit of God that came to me, I saw President Joseph F. Smith received on the other side. Tongue cannot tell the joy that was in Hyrum Smith's heart when he received his beloved son, Joseph F. Smith. Joy beyond expression was in the heart of Hyrum Smith when his true, tried, noble, and God-fearing wife, the inspiration, the protection of her son Joseph Fielding—came to him. . . .

"All honor to Mary Fielding Smith, the mother of the boy Joseph F., who, in his tender years turned him right, led him into the paths of truth, started him on the way. And then all honor and credit to the sterling character of that noble man of God who did follow the footsteps of his father and his mother and wavered not.

"He was not privileged to obtain an education like others, nevertheless he was a student, and I do not think that a man ever preached the gospel of the Church of Jesus Christ of Latter-day Saints more eloquently, used better language, more perfect and choice and finished, than President Joseph F. Smith. I remember, following an address he delivered in Portland at the dedication of our church several years ago, a prominent lawyer in Portland, himself an orator, said, 'I have never heard a finer utterance from a man than President Smith delivered.' 'Why,' said he, 'you must be a lawyer, for you arranged your argument—everything was done in such a logical way, most convincing.' He was an all-round educated man. As a citizen in this city, he has left his mark, that will never be effaced. I am told that it was through his influence more than any other man's that Liberty Park belongs to this city. When he fought for that blessing to the people, he stood almost alone, but won out.

"There was a time, as President Grant remarked this morning, when men doubted the financial ability of President Smith, schooled in poverty, knowing the burden of debt. Yet the Lord had prepared him to come into the Presidency of the Church during its most prosperous financial period, to take charge of the affairs when it would require men of great financial ability, looking at it from a human point of view, to succeed. But he had it—God-given financial ability came to the prophet; he had the inherent qualities and the willing spirit, listened to the voice that prompted and directed him, so that he had to do with the finances of the Church during its most prosperous period, and handled, I presume, more funds of this Church than all the other presidents put together; and the Lord at the same time blessed him, as has been remarked, to be the greatest preacher of righteousness of this dispensation. It does seem marvelous what the Lord has done. President Smith's wisdom in financial affairs excelled all his companions, for he was guided by the light of the Lord.

"Now, my brethren and sisters, I have no doubt but that President

Smith is busy and active. How I want to live to go where he is! I do not care whether the streets are paved with gold, whether there are diamonds and jasper in the walls. I do not care what kind of place it is. If I can go where President Smith has gone and be with him and men like him, it will be heaven to me, I want to be there.

"I realize that I cannot come there by wishing, but that I must follow the example of men like President Smith if I shall ever come to be associated with them; and so his life is like an anchor sent out from that world to which he has gone, to my soul, and I hope it shall be to all the Latter-day Saints, pulling us, beckoning us, calling us unto that realm to which he has gone, where he will be honored, as are those with whom he is associated.

"I want to say to you that this generation, who did not receive the Prophet Joseph Smith, who have not listened to the testimony of President Joseph F. Smith and the elders of this Church, shall yet hear them and honor their names and receive from them the message of the everlasting gospel in the spirit world, or they shall never be saved. God said in the beginning, that this generation should hear the message of this gospel through the men to whom he revealed himself. Men and women who die shall not see Peter, they shall not look upon the face of the Redeemer of the world, they shall not have Paul to come and visit them; but they shall have the elders of this Church, whom the Lord sent to them in the earth; and they shall receive this gospel from none other, for the Lord will vindicate them, and he will have them honored. He will not discredit them. And when they go to the other side, we shall find standing in places of honor, representing the Lord Jesus Christ, men like President Joseph F. Smith, who will be given greater authority and greater power than they ever had upon the earth.

He is not shorn of anything because he is gone from this world. The place and position which belongs to him is one of greater presidency, greater influence and power and authority than he has ever had in the earth; for over there are countless billions of our Father's children who are receiving this gospel and they shall come under the administration of the elders of the Church who have been faithful; and presidency and power and authority shall belong to President Smith forever and ever, among the redeemed and the sanctified in the eternal world."³²

Summary Comments

The June 1919 conference was one of those rare and significant events in Church history when a new President of the Church was sustained by the Saints according to the law of common consent. Additionally, the June 1919 conference was also a public tribute to the sixth President of the Church who, because of health concerns in the nation at the time, was deprived of a public funeral. And while President Heber J. Grant may have followed the same course in outlining specifically the contents of the addresses to memorialize President Joseph F. even if there had been a public funeral, this conference was President Grant's effort to pay public tribute to someone who meant so much to him and so much to the Church.

In fact, the June 1919 conference may have been the first time since the April 1844 general Church conference in Nauvoo, where the Prophet Joseph Smith delivered the funeral oration for King Follett, that the Saints held a conference and funeral service all in one.

The addresses by those who knew President Joseph F. Smith intimately provided an opportunity for all the Saints to hear what was in their hearts and minds, providing a window to the life and ministry of President Joseph F. Smith—the sixth President of The Church of Jesus Christ of Latter-day Saints.

NOTES

1. James E. Talmage Diary, 1 June 1919, BYU.
2. In CR, June 1919, 3.
3. Ibid.
4. Ibid., 10.
5. Talmage Journal, 1 June 1919.
6. In CR, June 1919, 10–11.
7. "Providence Is Over All"

When dark and drear the skies appear,
    And doubt and dread would thee enthrall,
Look up, nor fear, the day is near,
    And Providence is over all.
From heaven above, His light and love,
    God giveth freely when we call.
Our utmost need is oft decreed,
    And Providence is over all.
With jealous zeal God guards our weal,
    And lifts our wayward thoughts above;
When storms assail life's bark so frail,
    We seek the haven of His love.
And when our eyes transcend the skies
    His gracious purpose is complete,
No more the night distracts our sight—
    The clouds are all beneath our feet.

The direst woe that mortals know
    Can ne'er the honest heart appall
Who holds the trust—that God is just,
    And Providence is over all.
Should foes increase to mar our peace,

Frustrated all their plans shall fall.
Our utmost need is oft decreed,
    And Providence is over all.
—Emily Hill Woodmansee.

8. "Uphold the Right"

Uphold the right, though fierce the fight,
    And powerful the foe,
And freedom's friend, her cause defend,
    Nor fear nor favor show.
No coward can be called a man,
    No friend will friends betray;
Who will be free, alert must be;
    Indifference will not pay.

Note how they toil whose aim is spoil,
    Who plundering plots devise;
Yet time will teach that fools o'erreach
    The mark and lose the prize.
Can justice deign to wrong maintain,
    Whoever wills it so?
Can honor mate with treacherous hate?
    Can figs on thistles grow?

Dare to be true, and hopeful, too;
    Be watchful, brave and shrewd.
Weigh every act; be wise, in fact,
    To serve the general good.
Nor basely yield, nor quit the field—
    Important is the fray;
Scorn to recede, there is no need
    To give our rights away.

Left-handed fraud let those applaud
    Who would by fraud prevail:
In freedom's name, contest their claim,

> Use no such word as fail;
> Honor we must each sacred trust,
>   And rightful zeal display;
> Our part fulfill, then come what will,
>   High heaven will clear the way.
> —Emily Hill Woodmansee

9. From "Their Yesterdays." "If the men of a race will perfect the manhood strength of the race; if they will exalt their manhood power; if they will fulfill the mission of life by perfecting and producing ever more perfect lives; if they will endeavor to contribute to the ages to come stronger, better, men than themselves; why, the work of the world will be done even as the plant produces its flowers and fruit, the work of the world will be done. In the exaltation of Life is the remedy for the evils that threaten the race. The reformations that men are always attempting in the social, religious, political, and industrial world are but attempts to change the flavor or quality of the fruit when it is ripening on the tree. The true remedy lies in the life of the tree; in the soil from which it springs; in the source from which the fruit derives its quality and flavor. In the appreciation of Life, in the passion of Life, in the production of Life, in the perfection of Life, in the exaltation of Life, is the salvation of human kind. For this, and this alone, man has right to live—has right to his place and part in Life."

—Harold Bell Wright.

10. "A Real Man"

> Men are of two kinds, and he
> Was of the kind I'd like to be.
> Some preach their virtues, and a few
> Express their lives by what they do.
> That sort was he. No flowery phrase
> Or glibly spoken words of praise
> Won friends for him. He wasn't cheap
> Or shallow, but his course ran deep,
> And it was pure. You know the kind.
> Not many in a life you find,
> Whose deeds outrun their words so far
> That more than what they seem they are.

There are two kinds of lies as well:
The kind you live, the ones you tell.
Back through his years from age to youth
He never acted one untruth.
Out in the open light he fought
And didn't care what others thought
Nor what they said about his fight
If he believed that he was right.
The only deeds he ever hid
Were acts of kindness that he did.

What speech he had was plain and blunt.
His was an unembellished front.
Yet children loved him; babe and boy
Played with the strength he could employ,
Without one fear, and they are fleet
To sense injustice and deceit.
No back door gossip linked his name
With any shady tale of shame.
He did not have to compromise
With evil-doers, shrewd and wise,
And let them ply their vicious trade
Because of some past escapade.
Men are of two kinds, and he
Was of the kind I'd like to be.
No door at which he ever knocked
Against his manly form was locked;
If ever man on earth was free
And independent, it was he.
No broken pledge lost him respect,
He met all men with head erect;
And when he passed I think there went
A soul to yonder firmament
So white, so splendid and so fine
It came complete to God's design.
—Edgar A. Guest.

11. In CR, June 1919, 11–14.
12. Ibid., 17–19.
13. Ibid., 21–22.
14. Ibid., 23–24.
15. Ibid., 24–25.
16. Ibid., 25–27.
17. Ibid., 27–29.
18. Ibid., 29.
19. Ibid., 30.
20. Ibid., 33–38.
21. Ibid., 39–40.
22. Ibid., 40–43, 45.
23. Ibid., 45–47.
24. Ibid., 49–51.
25. Ibid., 51–54.
26. Ibid., 54–58.
27. Ibid., 58–60.
28. Ibid., 60.
29. Ibid., 61–63.
30. Ibid., 63–65.
31. Ibid., 65–66.
32. Ibid., 67–72.

INDEX OF PHOTOGRAPHS AND ILLUSTRATIONS

Added Upon, Joseph F. inscription in, 212
Alaska, Church leaders in, 92, 93
Alberta Temple site dedication, Joseph F. and party at, 190
Americana magazine, 173
Anderson, Oluf, and Joseph F., 178
Autograph album, L. C. Snow, 96
Automobile, Joseph F. and party in, 143

Beach, Joseph F. at, 184
Beehive House, 137
Beneficial Life Convention, Joseph F. at, 187
Bennett, Emma, 89
Bennett, Joseph Temple, 89
Bible: page from Julina Lambson Smith's, 51; Joseph F. inscription in, 181; of Joseph F., 260, 261
Bond certificate, 159
Book of Mormon, Joseph F. inscription in, 205
Brigham Young Academy, Joseph F. at, 113, 171
Brigham Young University Training School, Joseph F. at, 167
British Mission home, Joseph F. and party at, 162

Cardston, Alberta Stake Tabernacle, Joseph F. speaking in, 189
Cartoons, political. *See* Political cartoons
Certificates: Missionary, 140; Joseph F. as Director and President of SaltAir Beach Company, 157; Trustee-in-Trust bond, 159; Joseph F. Death Certificate, 233
Chicago Journal political cartoons, 145
Church Administration Office, 137
Church Chronology, Joseph F. inscription in, 109
Church Headquarters, Liverpool, England, 58
Church Historian's Office, 33
Cove Fort, Joseph F. and party at, 217
Death Certificate, of Joseph F., 233

"Editor's Table," 126, 127
Endowment House, 35
European missionaries, Joseph F. and, 60

First Presidency: ca. 1880, 63; 6 April 1893, 86; 10 October 1898, 100; ca. 1902, 140; ca. 1910, 176; ca. 1911–12, 182; ca. 1916, 213
First Presidency and Council of the Twelve: 9 October 1869, 46; ca. 1898, 99
First Presidency and General Authorities, 221
Funeral, of Joseph F., 234

General Conference, 157
Golden wedding anniversary, Joseph F. and Julina Lambson Smith, 209, 210
Grand Canyon, Joseph F. and party at, 162

Groves Latter-day Saint Hospital, 150

Hawaii: Joseph F. and party in, 169, 202; Joseph F. and party en route to, 201

Homes. *See* Smith, Joseph F., family homes

Homestead, Joseph F. and family at, 174

Hotel Utah, 180

Hyrum Smith Monument dedication, Joseph F. and family at, 223

Inscriptions: in Andrew Jenson's *Church Chronology,* 109; in Joseph Fielding Smith's *The Origins of the Reorganized Church and the Question of Succession,* 170; in *Bible,* 181; in *Book of Mormon,* 205; in *Added Upon,* 212; 7 October 1917, 219

Interment, of Joseph F., 236

International Congress of Genealogy, Joseph F. and party at, 203

Invitation, Joseph Smith Monument dedication, 153

Jenson, Andrew, and Joseph F., 178

Joseph Smith Monument dedication: invitation, 153; Joseph F. and party at, 153

Karl G. Maeser Building cornerstone ceremony, Joseph F. at, 171

Kimball, Alice Ann. *See* Smith, Alice Ann Kimball

Kimball family reunion, Joseph F. at, 214

King, J. B., and Joseph F., 161

Laie, Church plantation at, 72

Lambson, Edna. *See* Smith, Edna Lambson

Lambson, Julina. *See* Smith, Julina Lambson

Letters: to Joseph Fielding Smith, 68, 69; to John W. Woolley, 74, 75; to Orson F. Whitney, 80, 81; to Emma Mosheer, 198, 199

LIFE magazine political cartoons, 145

Lobbyists, Utah, and Joseph F., 76

Manti, Utah, Joseph F. and party at, 218

Manti Temple, Joseph F. and party at steps of, 219

Memorial service, for Joseph F., 237

MIA Superintendency, Joseph F. and, 206, 207

Missionary Certificate, 140

Montefiore Jewish Congregation, 140

Mosheer, Emma, letter to, 198, 199

Ocean Park, California, Joseph F. and family at, 183

Origins of the Reorganized Church and the Question of Succession, The, Joseph F. inscription in, 170

Plantation, at Laie, 72

Political cartoons: *Salt Lake Tribune,* 4, 5; *Chicago Journal,* 145; *LIFE*

magazine, 145; *Saturday Globe*, 145; source unknown, 145
Postcard, 200
President's home, 137
President's office, 137

Rail Pass, 186
Richards, Sarah Ellen. *See* Smith, Sarah Ellen Richards

Sacred Grove, Joseph F. at, 155
SaltAir Beach Company certificate, 157
Salt Lake 20th Ward, Joseph F. attending, 139
Salt Lake Tribune political cartoons, 4, 5
San Diego, California chapel dedication, Joseph F. and party at, 211
Santa Monica, California, Joseph F. and family on porch of Church home in, 187
Saturday Globe political cartoons, 145
Schwartz, Mary Taylor. *See* Smith, Mary Taylor Schwartz
Senate Record, Joseph F. testimony in, 146
Smith, Alice Ann Kimball, 66
Smith, Edna Lambson, 37, 197
Smith, George A., 22
Smith, Hyrum, 12
Smith, John, and Joseph F., 90
Smith, Joseph F.: personal belongings, x; and wives Julina, Sarah, and Edna, 37; family members, 43; and European missionaries, 60; and Utah lobbyists, 76; family members at home, 82; and John Smith, 90; and Church leaders in Alaska, 92, 93; at Brigham Young Academy, 113, 171; attending Salt Lake 20th Ward, 139; and party in automobile, 143; at picnic, 152; and party at Joseph Smith Monument dedication, 154; at Sacred Grove, 155; and J. B. King, 161; and party at British Mission home, 162; at Brigham Young University Training School, 167; and party in Hawaii, 169, 202; at Karl G. Maeser Building cornerstone ceremony, 171; and family at the Smith homestead, 174; and party at Grand Canyon, 175; and party changing tire, 175; with Andrew Jenson and Oluf Anderson, 178; and family at Ocean Park, California, 183; at the beach, 184; and party on train, 186; at Beneficial Life Convention, 187; and family on porch of Church home in Santa Monica, California, 187; speaking in Cardston, Alberta Stake Tabernacle, 189; and party at Alberta Temple site dedication, 190; and party, 28 July 1913, 191; and Mary Taylor Schwartz Smith, 195; and Joseph Fielding Smith, 196; and Edna Lambson

Smith, 197; and party en route to Hawaii, 201; and party at International Congress of Genealogy, 203; and MIA Superintendency, 206, 207; golden wedding anniversary, 209, 210; and Julina Lambson Smith, 209; and party at San Diego, California chapel dedication, 211; and party, ca. 1917, 213; at Kimball family reunion, 214; and party at Cove Fort, 217; and party at Manti, Utah, 218; and party at steps of Manti Temple, 219; and family at Hyrum Smith Monument dedication, 223; Death Certificate, 233; funeral of, 234; interment of, 236; memorial service for, 237; writings, 256

Smith, Joseph F., family homes: Alice Ann Kimball Smith, 134; Mary Taylor Schwartz Smith, 134; Edna Lambson Smith, 135; Sarah Ellen Richards Smith, 135

Smith, Joseph F., family portraits: with Mary Taylor Schwartz Smith, 94; with Edna Lambson Smith, 95; with sons, 95; with Sarah Ellen Richards Smith, 100; 13 November 1898, 101; three generations, 112; 13 November 1904, 148; with Alice Ann Kimball Smith, 166; with Julina Lambson Smith, 210

Smith, Joseph F., portraits of: ca. 1889–90, ii, 77, 78, 79; undated, iii; ca. 1858, 28; ca. 1860, 30; ca. 1861, 31; ca. 1867–68, 45; ca. 1869, 55; ca. 1874, 57; ca. May 1874, 58; 25 September 1874, 59; ca. 1880, 65, 66; ca. 1885, 71; ca. 1893, 84, 85; ca. 1901, 124; 26 May 1903, 144; ca. 1905, 151; 13 November 1913, 193; 1915, 204; ca. 1915, 208; 1916, 212

Smith, Joseph F., wives: Edna Lambson Smith, 37, 197; Julina Lambson Smith, 37, 209; Sarah Ellen Richards Smith, 37, 48; Alice Ann Kimball Smith, 66; Mary Taylor Schwartz Smith, 67, 195

Smith, Joseph Fielding: letter to, 68, 69; ca. 1900, 109; and Joseph F., 196

Smith, Julina Lambson, 37, 209

Smith, Mary Fielding, 19

Smith, Mary Taylor Schwartz, 67, 195

Smith, Mercy Josephine, 48

Smith, Sarah Ellen Richards, 37, 48

Tire, Joseph F. and party changing, 175

Train, Joseph F. and party on, 186

Whitney, Orson F., letter to, 80, 81

Wives. See Smith, Joseph F., wives

Woolley, John W., letter to, 74, 75

Writings, of Joseph F., 256

SUBJECT INDEX

"Address, An. The Church of Jesus Christ of Latter-day Saints to the World," 163–65
Alaska, trip to, 91–93
Alberta Temple, 188–92
Allen, James B., 6
Americana magazine, 172–74
Anderson, Edward H., 226–27
Arrington, Leonard J., 14
"Authoritative Declaration, An," 220–22

Ballard, Melvin J., 350–56
Barratt Hall, 136
Beehive House, 133, 136, 230–31
Bennett, Benjamin, 91
Bennett, Emma, 88–89, 91
Bennett, Joseph Temple, 88–89, 91
Bishops' Building, 136
Bitton, Davis, 5–6
Boggs, Lilburn W., 11
Bowen, Albert E., 255
Brigham Young Academy, 114, 171–72
Brigham Young Memorial Building, 136
Bunker, Gary L., 5–6
Bureau of Information, 136

Cartoons, political, 5–6
Church Administration Building, 136
Church Historian's Office, 33–34, 136
Clawson, Rudger, 121, 307–10
Committee on Privileges and Elections of the United States Senate, 143, 146–47
Comprehensive History of the Church, 172
Congregation Montefiore Synagogue, 141
Contention, avoiding, 97–98
Cook, Amanda P. Savage, 88–89, 91
Cosmopolitan magazine, 6
Cowdery, Oliver, 222–25

Davis, Albert J., 72
Dean, Joseph H., 54
Debt, Church, 158–59
Deseret Gymnasium, 136
Deseret News Building, 136
Deseret News Office, 136
Deseret (southern California home), 185
Deseret Sunday School Union, 136
Doniphan, Alexander W., 11

Endowment House, 35
England. *See* Great Britain
European missions, tours of, 162–63, 177–79
Evolution, 251–52
Extermination order, 11

"Father and The Son, The: A Doctrinal Exposition by The First Presidency and The Twelve," 252
First Presidency Office, 136
Free agency, 106–7

Gates, Susa Young, 94, 96, 203

Genealogical Society of Utah, 136
Gibson, Walter M., 32
Gospel Doctrine: Selections from the Sermons and Writings of Joseph F. Smith, Sixth President of The Church of Jesus Christ of Latter-day Saints: as a Melchizedek Priesthood quorum course of study, 253; original contents of, 253; as part of "Classics in Mormon Literature" series, 254; sources of writings, 254; original preface to, 254–55; original introduction to, 255–57; paperback edition, 262
Grant, Heber J.: and persecution, 2; reaction to Alberta Temple announcement, 188; on Joseph F.'s doctrinal legacy, 263; tribute to Joseph F., 268–77
Great Britain: Joseph F.'s first mission to, 29–32; additional missions to, 56
Grosebeck, William, 142–43
Groves Latter-day Saint Hospital, 150–51

Harris, F. S., 255
Harrison, Benjamin, 132
Hart, Charles H., 291–94
Hawaii: Joseph F.'s first mission to, 21, 23–26; Joseph F.'s second mission to, 32; Joseph F.'s third mission to, 72–73; vacation trip to, 168–70
Hawaii Temple, 32, 201–2

Hinkle, George, 11
Hospitals, 150–51
Hotel Utah, 136

International Congress of Genealogy, 203
"In the Presence of the Divine," 246–48
Ivins, Anthony W., 125

Jenson, Andrew, 177–79
John, David, 123, 129–30
Joseph F. Smith Memorial Building, 136
Joseph Smith Memorial, 153–54, 156

Kimball, Alice Ann. *See* Smith, Alice Ann Kimball
Kimball, J. Golden, 284–85
Kimball family reunion, 214

Lambson, Edna. *See* Smith, Edna Lambson
Lambson, Julina. *See* Smith, Julina Lambson
LDS College, 136
Lee, Harold B., 238, 249
Lehai, Kawa, 160
Leonard, Glen M., 6
Lewis, Alfred Henry, 6
Loyalty, 2–4
Lund, Anthon H., 122, 179, 229–30, 248–49, 277–81
Lyman, Amasa, 11, 13
Lyman, Richard R., 125, 321–26

Mack, Jason, 75–76, 80

Subject Index

Mahuhii, Ma, 23–24
Manifestos (plural marriage), 81, 147–49
Martyrdom, 14
McConkie, Amelia Smith, 230
McKay, David O., 125
McLellin, William E., 61–62
McMurrin, Joseph W., 287–90
Missionary work, purpose of, 98
Moyle, Henry D., 177

Nibley, Charles W., 23–24, 56, 142, 185, 339–45
Nuttall, L. John, 123

Origin of Man, The: By the First Presidency, 251–52

Partridge, Edward, 103
Paxman, James W., 4–5
Penrose, Charles W., 125, 180, 229–30, 298–307
Peterson, Parley, Jr., 102–3
Plural marriage, 67–82, 147–49
Political cartoons, 5–6
Political offices, Joseph F.'s, 36
Pratt, Orson, 61–62
Pratt, Parley P., 11, 13
Prayer, 15
Presiding Bishop's Office, 136

Quinney, Joseph, 255

Richards, George F., 125
Richards, Sarah Ellen. *See* Smith, Sarah Ellen Richards
Richards, Stephen L, 125, 326–35

Rigdon, Sidney, 11, 13
Roberts, B. H., 172–74, 281–84
Robinson, George W., 11, 13
Royal Hawaiian Band, 160–61, 168

Salt Lake City Council, 36
Salt Lake Temple Bonds, 158–59
Salt Lake Temple dedication, 83, 87–89, 91
Salt Lake Tribune: vilification of Joseph F., 5–6; tribute to Joseph F., 6–8
Sandwich Islands. *See* Hawaii
Schwartz, Mary Taylor. *See* Smith, Mary Taylor Schwartz
Second Manifesto, 147–49
Smith, Alice Ann Kimball: children of, 64; marries Joseph F., 64
Smith, Bathsheba Wilson, 152
Smith, David A., 142, 345–47
Smith, E. Wesley, 142
Smith, Edna Lambson: children of, 56; marries Joseph F., 56; leaves home to avoid subpoena, 73
Smith, Emily Jane, 183
Smith, George A., 21
Smith, George Albert, 2, 125, 170, 236, 237, 310–15
Smith, Hyrum: taken under shackle to Independence, Missouri, 11, 13; tried for treason, 11; martyrdom of, 14; moves family to Nauvoo, 14; monument honoring, 222–25
Smith, Hyrum G., 318–21
Smith, Hyrum M., 220

Smith, John, 122
Smith, John Henry, 121–23, 180
Smith, Joseph, Jr.: persecution of, 1–2; Joseph F.'s loyalty to, 3–4, 44, 47; taken under shackle to Independence, Missouri, 11, 13
Smith, Joseph F.: origin of name, 1; name known for good and evil, 1–2, 9; persecution of, 1–2, 4–6; loyalty of, 2–4; loyalty to name, 3–4, 8–9; vilification of, in press, 4–6; cartoons of, 5–6
Smith, Joseph F. (Birth to Apostleship, 1838–1867): events surrounding birth, 11, 13; nearly smothered as infant, 13; recollections of father's martyrdom, 14; childhood in Illinois, 14–15; exodus to Winter Quarters, 15; learns efficacy of prayer, 15; travels to Salt Lake Valley, 16–17; recollections of oxen team, 17–18; recollections of tithing clerk incident, 18; baptized in City Creek, 19; reflections on baptism, 19–20; confrontation with school teacher, 20; death of mother, 20; first mission to Hawaii, 21, 23–26; travels to California, 21, 23; arrives in Hawaii, 23; nursed back to health by Ma Mahuhii, 23; reunited with Ma Mahuhii, 23–24; talks with Joseph Smith in dream, 24–25; difficulties of mission life, 24–26; grows in spirituality, 25; loses possessions in fire, 25–26; shares suit with companion, 26; returns to Utah, 26–27; boldly confronts mob, 27; called as high councilor, 29; hired as sergeant-at-arms of Territorial Legislature, 29; joins territorial militia, 29; marries Levira Smith, 29; ordained a high priest, 29; ordained a seventy, 29; first mission to Great Britain, 29–32; deals with apostate Walter M. Gibson, 32; second mission to Hawaii, 32; works as clerk in Church Historian's Office, 33–34; labors in Endowment House, 34–36; begins service in Territorial Legislature, 36; marries Julina Lambson, 36, 38; participates in prayer circles of leading brethren, 36; children by Julina Lambson, 38; ordained an apostle, 38–39; service as counselor to Church Presidents, 39; set apart as counselor to First Presidency, 39; Levira Smith obtains divorce, 39–40
Smith, Joseph F. (Doctrinal Legacy): "Address, An. The Church of Jesus Christ of Latter-day Saints to the World," 163–65; "An Authoritative Declaration," 220–22; Wilford Woodruff on Joseph F.'s power as a preacher of righteousness, 245; Emmeline B.

Wells on Joseph F.'s power as a preacher of righteousness, 245–46; "In the Presence of the Divine," 246–48; Anthon H. Lund on Joseph F.'s power as a preacher of righteousness, 248–49; Harold B. Lee on the clarity of Joseph F.'s writings, 249; first published discourse, 249–50; *The Origin of Man: By the First Presidency*, 251–52; "The Father and The Son; A Doctrinal Exposition by The First Presidency and The Twelve," 252; *Gospel Doctrine: Selections from the Sermons and Writings of Joseph F. Smith, Sixth President of The Church of Jesus Christ of Latter-day Saints*, 253–57; Vision of the Redemption of the Dead, 257–62; *Teachings of Presidents of the Church: Joseph F. Smith*, 263; Heber J. Grant on Joseph F.'s doctrinal legacy, 263

Smith, Joseph F. (President of the Church, 1901–1918): set apart as sixth President of the Church, 121–23, 125; physical appearance of, 123, 125; apostles called by, 125; sustained as President in local stake conferences, 128–30; sustained as President in special general conference, 130; on the power and authority of presidency, 130–32; disperses families to separate homes, 132–33; Beehive House becomes personal residence, 133; constructs administrative buildings, 136; on the joy of missionary service, 138; issues 1901 First Presidency Christmas message, 138–39; speaks at synagogue cornerstone ceremony, 141; first Church President to own automobile, 142; warns of dangers of automobile travel, 142–43; testifies before U. S. Senate committee, 143, 146–47; issues Second Manifesto, 147–49; responds to accusations of former Church members, 149; dedicates Groves Latter-day Saint Hospital, 150–51; honors Bathsheba Wilson Smith, 152; dedicates Joseph Smith Monument, 153–54, 156; retires Church's debt, 158–59; honored by members of Royal Hawaiian Band, 160–61; tours European missions, 162–63; issues declaration following Reed Smoot hearings, 163–65; visits Hawaii to rest, 168–70; encourages George Albert Smith on health, 170; presides at Karl G. Maeser Building cornerstone ceremony, 171–72; supports publication of Church history installments in *Americana* magazine, 172–74; makes second tour of European missions, 177–79; visits Scandinavia, 177–79; calls Anthon H. Lund as first counselor in the First Presidency, 179; calls Charles W. Penrose as second counselor in the First Presidency, 180; calls John Henry Smith as second counselor in the First Presidency, 180; calls James E. Talmage as apostle, 181; travels extensively by train, 183; finds refuge at southern California home, Deseret, 184–85; as a golfer, 185; announces temple in Alberta, Canada, 188; dedicates site for Alberta Temple, 188–92; celebrates 75th birthday, 192, 194; dedicates site for Hawaii Temple, 201–2; attends International Congress of Genealogy, 203; celebrates 50th anniversary of marriage to Julina Lambson, 209–10; dedicates new meetinghouse in San Diego, 211; attends Kimball family reunion, 214; visits Saints in central and southern Utah, 215–17; mourns death of son Hyrum M., 220; issues declaration of divine authority, 220–22; speaks at dedication of monument honoring Hyrum Smith, 222–25; delivers final general conference addresses, 225–27; makes final address to family members, 228; death of, 228–30;

lays in state in Beehive House, 230–31; funeral services and procession, 231–33, 235; graveside service, 235–37; state of the Church at time of death, 237; testimony of, 238

Smith, Joseph F. (Quorum of the Twelve and First Presidency, 1867–1901): sent "underground" by John Taylor, 35–36, 67–82; children by Sarah Ellen Richards, 44; devotion to sister and aunt, 44; loyalty to Joseph Smith and Brigham Young, 44, 47; marries Sarah Ellen Richards, 44; serves as counselor to First Presidency, 44; set apart as member of Quorum of the Twelve, 44; deaths of children and wives, 47; death of Mercy Josephine, 47–53; devotion to his children, 53–54, 73; compassion for others, 54; children by Edna Lambson, 56; marries Edna Lambson, 56; presides over European Mission, 56; called home upon death of Brigham Young, 61; interviews William E. McLellin and David Whitmer, 61–62; mission to gather Church history records, 61–62; called by John Taylor as second counselor in First Presidency, 62; children by Alice Ann Kimball, 64; marries Alice Ann Kimball, 64; Wilford Woodruff prophesies Joseph F.'s future calling, 64; children by

Mary Taylor Schwartz, 67; marries Mary Taylor Schwartz, 67; travels among Saints in western states, 68–70; blesses family members on departure, 69–70; raids on houses, 72–73; third mission to Hawaii, 72–73; First Presidency reunited, 73; recollections of period of exile, 74; sent to Washington, D. C. by Wilford Woodruff, 75; reflections on avoiding capture, 75–76; uses pseudo-name Jason Mack, 75–76, 80; called by Wilford Woodruff as second counselor in First Presidency, 80; returns from "underground," 81–82; speaks at Salt Lake Temple dedication sessions, 83, 87–88; reads Salt Lake Temple dedicatory prayer, 88; blesses baby born during temple dedication, 88–89, 91; travels to Alaska with First Presidency, 91–93; letter to Susa Young Gates, 94, 96; desire to become a Saint, 96–97; advises missionary son on avoiding contention, 97–98; advises missionary son on purpose of missionary work, 98; letters to wives and daughters, 98–99; called by Lorenzo Snow as second counselor in First Presidency, 101; responds to missionary calls and recommendations, 102–5; encourages son Joseph Richards in missionary labors, 105–7; encourages son Joseph Fielding in missionary labors, 107–8; counsels son Joseph Fielding on dealing with anti-Mormon activity, 110; counsels son Joseph Fielding on talking with ministers, 110–11; informs son of death of "Alibo," 111–13; speaks at Brigham Young Academy Founders' Day, 114–15; called by Lorenzo Snow as first counselor in First Presidency, 115

Smith, Joseph Fielding, 125, 203, 228, 260–61, 339

Smith, Joseph Fielding, Jr., 69–70

Smith, Julina Lambson: marries Joseph F., 36, 38; children of, 38; concern for Levira after divorce, 40; on Joseph F.'s love for Mercy Josephine, 53; remains in original Smith home, 133; celebrates 50th wedding anniversary, 209–10

Smith, Levira: marries Joseph F., 29; divorces Joseph F., 39–40; death of, 40, 47

Smith, Martha Ann, 14, 20

Smith, Mary Fielding: illness at birth of Joseph F., 13; martyrdom of husband, 14; moves family to Winter Quarters, 15; beats pioneer company into Salt Lake Valley, 16–17; pays tithing over objections of clerk, 18; death of, 20

Smith, Mary Taylor Schwartz: children of, 67; marries Joseph F., 67; situated in separate home, 133
Smith, Melissa L., 72
Smith, Mercy Josephine, 47–53
Smith, Rachel, 158–59
Smith, Sarah Ellen Richards: children of, 44; death of, 44, 47; marries Joseph F., 44; leaves home to avoid subpoena, 73
Smoot, Reed, 143, 147, 163, 202, 228–30
Snow, Lorenzo: persecution of, 2; calls Joseph F. as second counselor in First Presidency, 101; calls Joseph F. as first counselor in First Presidency, 115; death of, 115, 121; first Church President to ride in automobile, 142; initiates steps to retire Church's debt, 158
Steward, John J., 69–70
Stohl, Lorenzo N., 255

Talmage, James E.: called as apostle, 125, 181; on Joseph F.'s last days and death, 225, 227, 229, 231; on acceptance of the Vision of the Redemption of the Dead, 261–62; tribute to Joseph F., 335–39
Taylor, John: persecution of, 2; sends Joseph F. "underground," 35–36, 67–82; calls Joseph F. as second counselor in First Presidency, 62; death of, 73

Teachings of Presidents of the Church: Joseph F. Smith, 262
Templeton Building, 136
Territorial Legislature, 29, 36
Tithing Office, incident at, 18
Tributes to Joseph F. Smith: *Salt Lake Tribune*, 7–9; June 1919 general conference devoted to, 267–68, 356–57; Heber J. Grant, 268–79; Anthon H. Lund, 277–81; B. H. Roberts, 281–84; J. Golden Kimball, 284–85; Rulon S. Wells, 285–87; Joseph W. McMurrin, 287–90; Charles H. Hart, 291–94; Levi Edgar Young, 294–96; Seymour B. Young, 296–97; Charles W. Penrose, 298–307; Rudger Clawson, 307–10; George Albert Smith, 310–15; Orson F. Whitney, 315–18; Hyrum G. Smith, 318–21; Richard R. Lyman, 321–26; Stephen L Richards, 326–35; James E. Talmage, 335–39; Joseph Fielding Smith, 339; Charles W. Nibley, 339–45; David A. Smith, 345–47; John Wells, 347–50; Melvin J. Ballard, 350–56

United States Senate committee, testimony before, 143, 146–47

"Viper on the Hearth, The," 6
Vision of the Redemption of the

Dead: circumstances surrounding receipt of, 220, 258–59; as Joseph F.'s greatest doctrinal legacy, 257–58; acceptance by First Presidency and Quorum of the Twelve, 260–62

Wells, Emmeline B.: on Joseph F.'s abilities as a speaker, 123, 149, 152, 245–46; on special conference to sustain Joseph F. as President, 130; on Joseph F.'s last days and death, 225, 229, 236–37
Wells, John, 347–50
Wells, Junius F., 222, 223
Wells, Rulon S., 285–87
Whitmer, David, 61–62
Whitmer, Jacob, 61
Whitney, Orson F., 125, 315–18
Widtsoe, John A., 255
Widtsoe, Osborne J. P., 255
Wight, Lyman, 11, 13
Willard, Rev. E. P., 47
Winder, John R., 83, 122, 179
Winter Quarters, 15
Wood, Edward J., 188, 189

Woodruff, Abraham O., 122
Woodruff, Wilford: persecution of, 2; prophesies Joseph F.'s future calling, 64; sends Joseph F. to Washington, D. C., 75; calls Joseph F. as second counselor in First Presidency, 80; issues Manifesto ending new plural marriages, 81; travels to Alaska, 91–93; struggles with health, 93; death of, 101; on Joseph F.'s power as a preacher of righteousness, 245
Worthington, A. S., 147

Young, Brigham: persecution of, 1–2; calls Joseph F. to Apostleship and as counselor to First Presidency, 38–39; Joseph F.'s loyalty to, 44, 47; sets Joseph F. apart as member of Quorum of the Twelve, 44; death of, 61
Young, Brigham, [Jr.?], 121–22
Young, Don Carlos, 83
Young, Levi Edgar, 294–96
Young, Seymour B., 296–97